What Leading World Scientists and Other Readers are Saying About Darwin's Lost Theory of Love

"David Loye's rediscovery of the 'real' Darwin rehabilitates one of the most cited yet also most misunderstood scientists of all times: Darwin the visionary, the moral thinker, not the mechanistic random-evolutionist, as his followers have it. For this rediscovery not only biologists, and not only all natural and social scientists, but everyone concerned with our understanding of evolution on this planet owes Loye a deep debt of gratitude."

> **Ervin Laszlo, founder of the General Evolution Research Group and the Club of Budapest**, Editor of *World Futures: The Journal of General Evolution*, former Director of Research for the United Nations Research and Development Program, author of *Evolution: The General Theory, The Interconnected Universe*, and over 30 other books on evolution and systems science.

*　　*　　*

"The idea that Charles Darwin himself believed that the final climb to human civilization required the enactment of a principle of moral conduct far above the "selfish gene" concept so prevalent in today's popular accounts comes as a surprise. But the fact that he argued at length and with passion for the recognition of this principle, along the way anticipating scientific concepts from far beyond his time, and further that this work has been utterly disregarded by the official keepers of evolutionary theory ever since, boggles the mind.

"Here, prominent social and evolutionary theorist David Loye treats us to a scientific mystery story of the first order. Taking us back to the final years of Darwin's life, in his home at Down and during the summer of 1868 at his Freshwater cottage on the Isle of Wight, where he struggled to find expression for the thoughts that would form the core of *The Descent of Man*, Loye leads us with sure steps through Darwin's emerging work, and through the Great Invisible Book that lies within, unfolding its vast implications and leaving no doubt that Darwin's long ignored plea for a larger vision of human nature is still relevant in the modern world and more desperately needed than ever.

"This is an immensely important book with an engaging and easy style that will recommend it to readers of all backgrounds and interests."

> **Allan Combs, psychologist and evolution theorist**, author of *The Radiance of Being* and *The Enchanted Loom*, psychology department, University of North Carolina in Asheville, and Saybrook Institute.

*　　*　　*

"This is the most exciting, most revealing book on Darwin that I have ever read. More than any other, it has restored the full grandeur to Darwin's thesis as it evolved, as living beings evolved, from the survival of the fittest, through altruistic acts in social communities to the final affirmation of a desire for good, more compelling even, than our desire for self-preservation."

> **Mae Wan Ho, biophysicist and evolution theorist**, author of *The Worm and the Rainbow, Genetic Engineering*, and editor, *Beyond Neo-Darwinism: The New Evolutionary Paradigm*, biology department, The Open University, London

*   *   *

"Once in a decade or more a special book comes along, of urgent importance to the intellectual discourse of the time: Darwin, Freud, Jantsch, Lovelock. David Loye's *Darwin's Lost Theory of Love* is this special. It represents the culmination of the Chaos Revolution, and the critical application of General Evolution Theory. It corrects an oversight in the history of science which has swerved the modern world off its track. It provides the key to the reintegration of the sciences: physical, biological, and social. It can be the spark to jumpstart the social sciences to a new golden age of relevance to popular culture, by clearly showing how evolution theory bears on the survival of our species and our biosphere. In this work Loye has brought his unique erudition to an enormous and critical task, and carried it off with genius. We urgently need this book, and we need it now."

> **Ralph Abraham, mathematician and chaos theorist**, author of *Chaos, Gaia, and Eros: A Chaos Pioneer Uncovers the Three Great Streams of History, Dynamics: The Geometry of Behavior*, and *The WEB Empowerment Book*, Professor Emeritus, University of California at Santa Cruz.

*   *   *

"One of the central difficulties in modern biology is how to account for the origin of those human features we are inclined to consider superior, traits such as morality, ethics, rationality, self-consciousness, and spiritual experiences. The difficulty is that they must have arisen in evolution from a manner of living that did not contain them. *Darwin's Lost Theory of Love* shows that Darwin saw this, and that his vision of a detailed answer to the question in terms of human emotional and cognitive development beyond the basic operation of natural selection has not been acknowledged. It is important that this part of Darwin's writing be recovered, as Loye does very clearly and in a compelling manner in this book. *Darwin's Lost Theory of Love* also provides important insights into the cognitive processes of Darwin himself and the history of biological thinking."

> **Humberto R. Maturana, professor, Department of Biology**, The University of Chile, developer of the concept and theory of autopoiesis, author (with Francisco Varela) of *Autopoiesis and Cognition* and *The Tree of Knowledge*, and (with G.Verden-Zoller) of *Amore e Gioco* and other books in Italian, German, and Spanish.

*   *   *

"In his book on Darwin's 'lost theory,' Loye grips the reader's imagination somewhat as if glued to watching him put together a giant jig-saw puzzle showing the whole sweep of evolution in the light of both former and recent thinking. I have been particularly fascinated by Loye's discovery of the connection between Darwin's projection of the evolutionary development of the moral sense and my own brain research. In the notebook of 1838 Darwin asked himself, 'May not moral sense arise from...our strong sexual, parental, and social instincts?' This is point for point what I found 100 years later in my own extensive exploration of the primate brain in regard to primal sex-related functions. I had summed up these findings by saying that 'in the complex organization of the evolutionarily old and new structures under consideration, we presumably have a neural ladder, a visionary ladder, for ascending from the most primitive sexual feeling to the highest level of altruistic sentiments.' I am very impressed with how Loye shows that Darwin expanded this core insight into the full theory so long overlooked in *The Descent of Man*."

Paul D.MacLean, M.D., Senior Research Scientist, National Institute of Mental Health, evolutionary brain theorist, author of *The Triune Brain in Evolution*.

*　　*　　*

"At the end of ten years studying the application of chaos and other new theories to human evolution and researching the moral studies of the founding fathers of social science, David Loye unearthed a major scientific treasure: Darwin's 'hidden' theory of moral choice. Carefully piecing together fragments scattered in *The Descent of Man* and in Darwin's other writings, Loye reconstructs the 'hidden' theory and shows that Darwin believed that love, rather than the "selfish gene", is the prime mover in human evolution. Loye's book offers an unparalleled portrait of Darwin the social scientist, both in the range and originality of Darwin's thinking in what later became the fields of psychology, sociology, anthropology, and systems science. Loye's book will cause a revolution in social theory as diverse fields such as human ecology, urban studies, population dynamics, collective organization, and the study of culture and moral order are rethought and recast in the light of Darwin's moral theory. *Darwin's Lost Theory of Love* is absolutely essential reading for every social scientist."

Raymond Trevor Bradley, sociologist, Director, Institute for Whole Social Science, Carmel, CA, Associate Research Professor, BRAINS Center, Radford University, Radford, VA, author *Charisma and Social Structure: A Study of Love and Power, Wholeness and Transformation.*

*　　*　　*

"Since selfish gene theories are often linked to Charles Darwin, it is exciting to see a psychological theorist of Loye's quality and productivity argue that Darwin's own viewpoint was not that of the selfish gene theorists. Loye gets us into the heart of Darwin's works and shows that when it came to human evolution at least, love and connectedness were regarded not as anomalies but as intricately related to the entire evolutionary process. Altruism has for too long been explained away as just a devious form of selfishness, if not of one's own body then of one's genes. So have other common activities that make us human, such as the arts, religion, and creativity. Sexuality has been assumed to be motivated solely by reproductive needs, and its pleasurable and bonding aspects discounted, whereas Loye shows that Darwin saw sexual evolution as the primary basis of bonding and love in many animal species including our own.

"Loye's book will stimulate a dialogue that has hitherto been lacking, particularly in academia. Discussion of love, partnership, and concerns for the larger society has been largely absent from professional discussion of behavioral biology. This would be the first widely read book for a general educated audience that lays out the claims for a partnership-based approach to evolutionary and behavioral biology and ties such an approach to the originator of natural selection himself!

"*Darwin's Lost Theory of Love* will fill an important gap. It will be a widely read and controversial book by an experienced and thoughtful author with style and flair. I expect it will become one of the major books of the early Twenty-First Century."

Daniel S. Levine, theoretical psychologist and neural network theorist, author of *Introduction to Neural and Cognitive Modeling* and (forthcoming) *Common Sense and Common Nonsense*, psychology department, University of Texas at Arlington.

* * *

"David Loye has passionately called our attention to a part of Darwin's work that not only significantly modifies his construction of natural selection, but does so more prominently in *The Descent of Man* than many other modifications scattered throughout his vast writings. Even a number of neoDarwinians are now getting ready to accept some version of what Loye identifies as Darwin's discovery of 'organic choice,' usually under the label of 'self-organizing processes.' I think Loye's work comes along at a propitious time."

Stanley Salthe, biologist and evolution theorist, author of *Development and Evolution* and *Evolving Hierarchical Systems*, Professor Emeritus, biology department, Brooklyn College of the City University of New York.

* * *

"This book is a block-buster and an old paradigm smasher! I read it with a deep sense of its importance in balancing the biological reductionist myopia about our possible future and the evolution of our moral sentiments. Congratulations!"

Hazel Henderson, **economics theorist and futurist**, author of *Building a Win-Win World, The Politics of the Solar Age, Paradigms for Progress*, and *Creating Alternative Futures*.

* * *

"Loye's thesis is nothing less than revolutionary. In a carefully researched and beautifully written work, he dramatically changes our understanding of Darwin and of evolution itself."

Alfonso Montuori, Chair of Graduate Studies, School for Consciousness and Transformation, California Institute of Integral Studies, Associate Editor, *World Futures: The Journal of General Evolution*, and author of *Evolutionary Competence*.

DARWIN'S
LOST THEORY OF LOVE

DARWIN'S
LOST THEORY OF LOVE

A Healing Vision for the 21st Century

David Loye

toExcel

San Jose New York Lincoln Shanghai

Darwin's Lost Theory of Love

Published by toExcel
an imprint of iUniverse.com, Inc.

For information address:
iUniverse.com, Inc.
620 North 48th Street
Suite 201
Lincoln, NE 68504-3467
www.iuniverse.com

ISBN: 0-595-00131-9

Printed in the United States of America

To Riane, eternal partner in the evolution of love

CONTENTS

PART II: The Theory

Chapter Seven:
Emergence of the Golden Rule ***87***

Chapter Eight:
Our Animal Heritage ***98***

Chapter Nine:
Closing the Gap ***115***

PART III: The Vision

ACKNOWLEDGEMENTS

For encouragement over the long pull to complete and publish this book, among General Evolution Research Group members, I am above all indebted to Riane Eisler, for basic intellectual and emotional support; to Ervin Laszlo, for much of the same when the chips were down; and to Ralph Abraham, Eric Chaisson, Allan Combs, Alfonso Montuori, Stanley Salthe, Karl Pribram, Sally Goerner, Vilmos Csanyi, Mauro Ceruti, Gyorgy Kampis, and Pennti Malaska.

Among scientists whose research is pivotal to what is presented here and others, I am also very grateful for encouragement by Paul MacLean, Humberto Maturana, Mae-Wan Ho, Hazel Henderson, Howard Gruber, Ray Bradley, Daniel Levine, and Brian Swimme.

Appendix A, which takes a brief look at some of the people, organizations, and creativity involved in the surge of advanced evolution studies as we move into the 21st century, also indicates many others to whom I am grateful for what I have learned from them and for having been able to share this great experience with them.

I am also indebted to Donald Weinshank for the copies of pages dealing with morality from the invaluable Darwinian concordances he built with the late Paul Barrett and for pointing me to the invaluable Darwinian CD-ROM produced by Pete Goldie and Lightbinders of San Francisco. My thanks also to James Moore and the late Ashley Montagu for useful suggestions regarding Darwinian books.

I trust that those with critiques will be gratified to see that I heeded their good advice. And where I did not, I hope they may feel that it was perhaps best after all that I persisted despite warnings.

I am especially indebted to my long time good friend and agent, the remarkable Bill Gladstone. I cannot express adequately how enjoyable and meaningful our association has been in going up against the paradigm on behalf of this book and all that Charles Darwin really wanted to get across to a needy world. I know he joins me in thanking Kenzi Sugihara, Dana Isaacson, and Julie Breese in making it possible for this book to be published on the internet worldwide along with release to book stores throughout the U.S.

I am grateful to Bela Banathy, then president of the International Society for the Systems Sciences, and to Fred Abraham and Bob Porter, then president of the Society for Chaos Theory in Psychology and the Life Sciences, for quickly recognizing the importance of this lost side to Darwin's theory, for specially honoring me in the case of Fred and Bob, and for inviting me to give the addresses to their memberships that initiated what has become the ongoing Evolution Project.

I must also thank all those who so quickly responded from ISSS, SCT-PLS, and the General Evolution Research Group and others to this idea that we simply go ahead and launch a pilot project to flesh out the greater theory of evolution that Darwin dreamed of. Our first attempt with The Evolution Project fell short and ended prematurely. But it helped set the stage for what I am now certain will gradually lead to the building of the full spectrum, action-oriented theory and story of evolution that I feel is the single most urgent task for the 21st century.

INTRODUCTION

A LOST THEORY?

A "lost theory" of Charles Darwin's? How could this be? Don't we by now know Darwin from A to Z?

Certainly few other figures have been so comprehensively covered by biographies. And surely the story is one of which we must by now know every detail. The amiable, indifferent student, cowed by a domineering father. The fervent collector of beetles. The year of trying out medicine at Edinburgh. The three years of tentative commitment to the ministry at Cambridge. How he then went off to sea in the Beagle. And how transformed by this journey of journeys—which was also to transform the lives of every one of us living today—he became Darwin the ruminating, troubled, but ever steadily ascendant man of science.

We know seemingly everything about the long years of his immersion in the development of his theory of evolution—only to be nearly upstaged by Alfred Wallace. If we happen to be interested in the family life of the great figures of the past, we know of the sunny and quirky charm of the Down household and what at times seem to have been dozens of children and pets. If we are interested in medical details, we also know that he was mysteriously sick for much of his working life.

If we are interested in science, we also know of the incredible range of his experiments with pigeons, barnacles, wild ducks, and lizard and snakes' eggs. Also: cabbage, lettuce and celery seeds, orchids, passion flowers, purple loosestrifes, wild cucumbers, Venus fly traps, and on and on. We may even have chuckled over the story of how he sought evidence of the roots of intelligence in earthworms, once even assembling a family orchestra—his wife Emma on the piano, son Francis on the bassoon, grandson Bernard with a whistle—to play to a dish of earthworms to see how they might respond to this form of cultural advancement.

Thereafter, it is true, to all but the most devout of Darwinians, the story fades away into the pleasant mush of a few more books after the pivotal *Origin of Species*, then death and a ceremonious burial in Westminster Abbey. But where in all this well-plowed ground could anything like a lost theory have been hidden?

Theories do not leap into being overnight. Indeed, the story of Darwin's development of what we know today as his theory of evolution has become the favorite story of how long theories take time to build—at least eighteen years, in this case. It just does not seem possible to tuck away in all those years a lost theory that amounts to anything.

And yet there was such a theory, and for over 100 years it was ignored—a theory that might have changed the course of the 20th century in countless ways for the better. Could we have gone to war so often, or tolerated being globally inundated with television violence, had we believed we were not incurably selfish and vicious by nature? This, we were told, Darwin's theory proved.

Or could this theory—the core of modern science—have been attacked so successfully by right-wing religious forces as to endanger not only the teaching of science itself but also our hard-won heritage of free inquiry in a democracy?

It goes in and out of the news so fast as to hardly register, but the theory of evolution has been on trial again not only in Tennessee but elsewhere in the U.S. The decision in 1999 of the Kansas State Board of Education to drop the requirement that evolution be taught in schools sent out a shock wave that circled the educated world.1 A few months later Oklahoma followed suit with a requirement that all new textbooks carry a disclaimer saying that evolution is a "controversial theory." This after more than 100 years of science to establish evolution theory as the floor under modern mind. Could this have happened had Darwin's theory been seen after all this time not merely as the "godless" plaything of "pointy head" scientists, but rather as something of practical value that could provide the growing child, as well as the rest of us, with some sense of dignity, purpose, direction, and meaning to life?

The fact is that, buried for 100 years within the lost theory, has been the proof that the beliefs of *both* regressive religion and reductionist science are gross distortions of what Darwin really believed.

Most meaningful today, as we emerge—still shellshocked—from the 20th century, this lost theory is astoundingly attuned to both our deepest yearnings socially and our most advanced scientific probing. It is a theory, moreover, that in a time of increasing doubt and fear of the future offers a new burst of hope for the 21st century.

The Old Theory and the New Theory

How can I most quickly convey the nature of this "new" theory, or the startling story that lies ahead? Perhaps the best way is to briefly characterize Darwin's theory as it is known to us today and then go to the largest chunk of his writing, long ignored, in which he so radically departed from what we have been told.

One of the great difficulties holding back both advances in evolution theory and, I believe, the advance of humanity globally is the immense gulf between the social "footprint" and the scientific "head trip" of Darwinism. In other words, most scientists interested in evolution theory today are aware of many refinements, shadings, and qualifications of the prevailing Darwinian story line.2 But what gets "out there" to us—or what we are generally told—has the raw psychological impact of the footprint of a King Kong. Everywhere the story is that science tells us that evolution is basically a matter of the great predatory force of Natural Selection that feeds on the wild output of Random Variation in order to pick out only the very best of organisms or efforts and discards the rest. This "footprint" theory is dressed up in much biology and paleontology, but at the core it seems to work very much like a giant motorized threshing machine moving through a wheat field. Through the front end it swallows up sheaf after hapless sheaf of wheat, and out the rear end it spews out mountainous piles of the rejected straw and a thin stream of the precious grain.

In classrooms throughout our world, in an unending stream of beautifully packaged books, and routinely over television, we are shown what is further pursued here in Chapter 2—how this combination of forces has not just shaped every living thing prior to the emergence of the human, but also ourselves: our species, we humans, and everything about us. This theory is dressed up in ways to make it more palatable, and summaries such as this are always attacked as exaggerations. But basically we are told that this is why by necessity we are so aggressive and violent, or why by necessity we are driven by selfish genes, or why by necessity we must be ruthlessly competitive and exploitive. We are told that only in this way can our species evolve according to the sacred Darwinian principle of survival of the fittest.

We are also told that, with a few modern improvements, this was and is Darwin's one and only theory. But what happens if, with an open mind, we move from *The Origin of Species*, where he first articulated this theory, to *The Descent of Man*, or to the early notebooks he filled out just after getting back from the famous voyage of the Beagle?

What became for me many years of exploration can be condensed into a simple bit of research toward the end of this process that I believe reveals it all in one fell swoop, as they say. In *The Descent of Man* Darwin moves on from the world of the "lower organisms" supposedly to show how the great threshing machine operates among us, at the human level. Now for over 100 years the index at the back of the book—dutifully put to use by scholars as a guide to what is of importance in *Descent*—has shown but a single listing for "love." This of course is not unusual. Until quite recently, this simple word, which not only fills our songs but also our minds much of the time, was considered not only suspect but wholly outside the realm of science. "Love" was just not what science was all about. Yet through the use of a modern computerized search of the whole book I discovered that in *Descent* Darwin is actually exploring the usage and evolutionary meaning for "love" ninety-five times![3]

What is going on here, one wonders? What could account for such a massive contradiction? And why should the discrepancy involve a concept that in a world everywhere now torn apart by hate has become of increasing scientific as well as popular interest?

I then tried searches for what we should, with more certainty, expect to find in *Descent*. According to what we have been told is Darwin's binding theory for us at the human level, we would, for example, expect to find much about the survival of the fittest. The computer found only two entries. And in one of the two he tells us he exaggerated its importance in *Origin of Species!* Or what about competition? Nine entries. From all we have been told, we would certainly not expect to find anything about cooperation. Yet for the nearest equivalent to this word for Darwin's time, mutuality—as in *mutual aid*, which Darwin coined as a phrase—there were twenty-four entries.

And if what primarily operates at our level is only the impersonal grinding of the great machine of Natural Selection and Random Variation, why do we find Darwin talking so often not of the power of the great machine. Why, instead, is he so often talking about the powers of the supposedly hapless organism at the heart of this process—that is of ourselves, of you and me. Why does he speak so often of the powers of our minds to perceive, and puzzle over what is going on, and decide what to do, and thereby make our way so effectively in this world? Why does he speak so often, for example, of our power of reasoning—twenty-four entries. Or of imagination, twenty-four entries. Or of sympathy for one another—which jumps to *sixty-one* entries.

And why do we find ninety-five entries for *habit*, a concept explored by psychologists, as against ninety-five entries for *instinct*, which used to be the biological equivalent for habit but was more often probed by psychologists than by biologists?

And why, if science has nothing to do with values, and what happens to us is up to the random action of a fate in which we supposedly have little voice, do we find the entries for Darwin's use of the word *moral*—or how we decide what is right and what is wrong for us to do—skyrocketing to a number just short of that for love, *ninety* in all?

Why, in short, do we find this overwhelming interest on Darwin's part in what in actuality most interests and concerns every one of us about ourselves at our level—not that of barnacle, finch, or amoeba? In contrast to what we have been told, why does he seem to find love, sympathy, reason, and morality of overriding importance for evolution at *our* level? Why do we find so much about the mind and the future for our species in this book that for over 100 years has been written off by evolution theorists as of little interest other than for its passages on sexual selection?

The Challenge for 21st Century Science

The answers I found to these and many other questions can be put quickly and bluntly. Although present evolution theory represents a considerable and I believe an enduring achievement, because of a purblind immersion in a theory overwhelmingly fixated at the biological level we have overlooked something huge and meaningful for over 100 years. Through the research over a number of years reported in this book, I discovered there were actually two halves to Darwin's theory. There is the first half, or foundation, of a biological base for his theory, with which we are somewhat familiar. *But then Darwin went on to complete his theory with the superstructure of a psychological, systems scientific, humanistic, and morally-grounded "higher" half—of which today we know almost nothing.*

Moreover, the understanding of the lost Darwinian superstructure casts a wholly new and more hopeful light on the biological foundation. The biological picture, to put it quickly, looks more like a slate upon which each organism writes its own brief message than like the heedless rolling among us of first-half Darwinism's beloved threshing machine.

What this discovery can mean for science is a jolt of the earthquake proportion that is needed to speed up the all too slow-moving rearrangement of thinking and priorities for all scientific fields as we enter the 21st century. Within the comfortable, snail's pace world of academia as it is— and often plans to here, now, and ever after be—this matter of a so-called "lost theory" of Darwin may not seem to be of earthshaking importance. But what it can mean for every one of us—scientist, layman and lay woman alike; that is, for every one of us with children and grandchildren or larger hopes for humanity—is something of exceptional urgency and meaning. In a world increasingly desperate for guidance out of science, it can mean that at last there may emerge an adequate theory of who we really are, and how to get from here to the better world we want to build.

It can mean that out of the science that gave us atomic bombs and pesticides and acid rain there might at last emerge a unified theory not of atoms, quarks, and strong and weak fields but of what accounts for what is *best* in us, rather than of excuses for what is *worst* in us. It can mean that out of science can emerge a theory that soars beyond so much that is secondary, trivial, and wasteful to show us how to achieve what is of first rate importance and our highest aspirations. Of increasing importance in a world everywhere involved both in massive breakdown and the drive for the hopeful breakthrough, it can show us how to build the radically better world that we human beings have sought for thousands of years.

We hear much of chaos, complexity, or the abiding mystery of the cell these days, but in reality there are far more pressing challenges for science. As an evolutionary scientist myself, I express the conviction of increasing numbers of us about the one most urgent task today for all scientists. This is to find and advance whatever their field can do to better serve the needs of humanity as we enter a century in which, in terms of evolution, it seems evident we face a threat to the survival of our species.

What other conclusion can we come to? It does not take a scientist to read the handwriting on the wall. Who but the most blind among us can fail to see the warning in the widening global gap between rich and poor, the proliferation of nuclear and all other forms of superbomb, the polluting of sky, land, and water already beginning to silence the voices of the birds and frogs.

Yet at the same time—if we can find the vision and the courage of leadership—there opens before us a great new opportunity for long-term improvement of the human condition. It is here that the most unexpected thing of all rises out of the past here recovered—for in the pages that lie ahead we are to encounter not only the revolutionary implications of Darwin's lost theory, but also the grandeur, majesty, and humanity of Darwin's lost vision of the real nature and destiny for our species.

How urgent is the need for an updating of Darwin's theory of evolution can be seen from the cry for something better out of the very fields of biology and physics to which the task of building a modern theory of evolution was mainly relegated.

Those who are aroused—for example, the thousands of us responsive to the purpose of the Union of Concerned Scientists and similar professional bodies—write and speak out of a jolting recognition of the incredible danger our species faces at this juncture. Of the many questions that press upon us, one I believe is of overriding and inescapable meaning. After nearly 150 years since Darwin set the whole thing going, shouldn't we by now have a theory of evolution good for something more than scholarly squabbles and dubious mass entertainment? Shouldn't we by now have a theory of evolution that might provide us with *a source of guidance through these difficult years?*

A theory that can find a place for love as well as violence in our development? A theory offering hope rather than despair at the end of the line?

But instead we have this great, slick, gleaming and entrancing package of a one-sided story of the past and the prehuman. We have the half-truth of this story out of which, pumped up by a global orgy of media feeding on fear, we are given the vision of killer apes, selfish genes, blind watchmakers, and an incurably violent species that continues to drive us toward destruction.

The main news of this book is the surprising new voice that has been added to the ignored voices of those who have been trying to reach their scientific peers and everybody else with a larger and more hopeful vision of human evolution—the voice of none other than Darwin himself.

In page after page out of his own long ignored writings, he returns here to disavow much of what has been attributed to him by what is today known as the Darwinian tradition. He reaffirms the basic theory of his *Origin of Species*, of the centrality of natural selection and variation. But to this he now adds two startling departures.

One is his leap beyond biology and natural science into the psychology and the social and systems science that is the main focus for this book. We find ourselves able at last to marvel at the wonder of his lost leap to identify something far more important than natural selection and random variation at the human level. It is the power of moral sensitivity, he tells us—of love, mutuality, reasoning, imagination, habit, and education.

The other departure is even more surprising from the scientific standpoint. For I have brushed away the cobwebs from how Darwin discovered what is only today beginning to be explored as the possibility for a *new* major principle for evolution. As we enter the 21st century, in addition to natural selection and random variation, the focus is on *self-organizing* processes as a third candidate for being a prime shaper of our lives. This idea animates the new evolutionary theories of thermodynamacist Ilya Prigogine, biologists Stuart Kauffman and Humberto Maturana, and many others. And Darwin was already there more than a hundred years ago!

And what emerges in his vision of the completed theory? Very much what progressive science—as well as progressive spirituality—has long dreamed of. It is very much what humanistic psychologists as well as humanistic biologists, systems theorists, chaos theorists, general evolution theorists—and moral and spiritual theorists, mothers, fathers, grandmothers, grandfathers, uncles, aunts, and everybody else concerned with how our species is to get better before it wipes itself out—have wished that his theory *could* have been.

The story, ramifications, and explanation of how all this was buried for over 100 years is covered in Part I: The Story. Part II: The Theory provides the reconstruction of his lost theory made possible by an editing that frees Darwin's own extremely readable and engaging writings from the murk of their long time burial. Part III: The Vision then briefly explores the implications of what the story and theory have uncovered for the betterment of our lives during the 21st century.

A brief appendix takes the reader behind the scenes into the exciting new world of the advanced exploration of evolution theory for a glimpse at some of many new groups involved in this vital venture. In particular, I focus on the one I am best acquainted with. Drawn together by systems philosopher Ervin Laszlo, this is the General Evolution Research Group, of which I was a co-founder. This is a group composed of biologists, physicists, astrophysicists, mathematicians, systems, brain, social and computer scientists, psychologists, historians, philosophers, and chaos, feminist, and management theorists. Working toward the development of an evolution theory that might better fit the needs of our time, these heirs and heiresses of the new Darwin live in or are from Germany, Italy, England, France, Sweden, Belgium, Chile, China, Finland, Hungary, Russia, Sri Lanka, Switzerland, and the United States.

This book is an independent work, representing my own research and my own conclusions. But I owe the inspiration, the perspective, and key aspects of the data out of which I write to some of the members of the General Evolution Research Group, as well as to others among the much larger group of scientists trying to build a better and more useful evolution theory.

Increasing numbers of us in these groups look to this new century as not only one of the very greatest of challenges but also of the greatest of opportunities—as something really special for our species. As I sketch in the last chapter, beyond its inevitable horrors, we look to the 21st century for the opening of windows and doors into springtime after a long winter.

In this regard, however fierce the howls or the drubbing of the brick-bats this book may raise in certain quarters now, I feel confident that over time it will be met with increasing appreciation—and much relief.

PART I
The Story

CHAPTER ONE

A WINTER'S TALE

At some point during a six-week stretch spanning much of July and August of 1868, Charles Darwin ducked out of the family scene at the Freshwater cottage to shuffle through his notes and take a stab at writing a bit more of what was to become *The Descent of Man*.

It was not an ideal situation for the kind of intellectual heavy lifting he both hungered for and dreaded in getting underway. He had arrived at the Isle of Wight vacation spot, one of the family's favorites, with his wife Emma, his daughter Henrietta, his brother Erasmus, and his "huge horse" Tommy (who the following spring was to stumble and roll over on him, badly bruising him).[4] Whatever quiet he might find was further interrupted within their six weeks there by the brief visits of old cronies and the poets Tennyson and Longfellow. But still, given how difficult it was to get anything done at home with the experiments with orchids, earthworms, wild cucumbers, and such to tend, and each week's avalanche of letters, requiring an answer, it made sense to try for a little progress on the book here.

There was, too, the advantage of the lift of hope here, the touch of the memory of old adventure. This was not the Beagle, not *the* island, not Galapagos—a tame, family frolic substitute, after all. But yet on the ferry there had been the touch of sea again, the warm lift to the air to stir within his old bones the feeling of being at least half-alive again. It was here, too, just 10 years earlier, spurred by the horror of the letter from Alfred Wallace announcing *his* discovery of natural selection, that Darwin had begun the "abstract" of the earlier chunk of theory that became *Origin of Species*.

It had seemed then that all was lost—that after eighteen years of labor he was to be upstaged historically, that to Wallace they would build statues and he was to go down in science as Darwin the nice but rather plodding "also ran." Yet it was here on this sometimes magical isle of Wight that he began what became the book that established both his priority to the discovery of natural selection and what by now had become worldwide fame and an unquestionable place in history.

In any case, Wight proved to be much better than the grim months that lay ahead during the dreadfully cold winter of 1868-69 when, imprisoned within the cocoon of the home place at Down, he was to force himself to pick up what he had begun the year before, had given up until Wight, and now at last would actually dig in to try to write the damn thing through from beginning to end.

And so, exalted by anticipation, at times lifted to a height of thought that he found sublime (citing, as he wrote, the great moral philosopher Immanuel Kant in this regard), but more often so sick with dread he could barely get out of bed for days at a time, he wrote the book that was to suffer perhaps the strangest—and most revealing—fate in the history of science.

He wrote the familiar lines that once in a while over the next 100 years were to be dutifully noted. "I have been led to put together my notes, so as to see how far the general conclusions arrived at in my former works were applicable to man."[5]

Thereafter, he proceeded to lay out the second half to his theory of evolution, long lost to us, that both anticipates and is corroborated by the work of some of the most important scientists and other thinker s of the 20th century.

Astounding as it may seem, over 100 years ago in the long ignored results of his often interrupted and reluctant labor throughout 1868 and 1869, not only did Darwin anticipate the formative work of scientists destined to become familiar names well into the 20th century. Sigmund Freud, William James, Kurt Lewin, Jean Piaget, and Abraham Maslow, for example, are all foreshadowed in Darwin's glimpse ahead for the field of psychology. One can detect ideas later to engage George Herbert Mead and Pitirim Sorokin in sociology, even Ludwig von Bertalanffy and Norbert Wiener in systems science. But there was more yet. For he was also to anticipate—and to have his theory in part corroborated by— scientists whose names are only becoming familiar to a reasonably wide readership as we move into the 21st century: Humberto Maturana, Lynn Margulis, Richard Lewontin, Stanley Salthe, Francisco Varela, and Mae-Wan Ho in biology, for example; Paul MacLean and Karl Pribram in brain science; Ilya Prigogine and Ralph Abraham in chaos theory; Stuart Kauffman, Vilmos Csanyi, and Ervin Laszlo in evolution theory; and Franz de Waal in primate studies.[6]

But for Darwin back then there was no comfort possible in even daring to guess that what he wrote during that long winter would some day come to resonate with, and eventually enrich, the work of these late 20th century scientific heirs and heiresses.

And so with publication of *Descent* came what played itself out according to his worst fears. For even the most malevolent of those in his time who considered themselves his enemies could not have stage managed what happened to what he clearly intended to be the final distillate of his wisdom about and for *our* species—that is, the human, rather than the orchid or the barnacle or the earthworm.

As though cursed by the most powerful of wizards in some old fable, what mattered most to him about this difficult book was to be either ignored, skipped over, or grossly distorted by most of his successors in science, as well as by most of his biographers.[7]

The Trampling of the Dream

The case of the rediscovery of the long lost and ignored wonder of the music of Johann Sebastian Bach by Felix Mendelssohn, of Franz Schubert by Robert Schumann, of the relation of Darwin's friend Charles Babbage to the modern computer, or of the lost genetic code of Gregor Mendel that was to complete neo-Darwinian theory itself shows us how even the greatest of works can be buried or ignored for many years.[8] But in these cases both the work and the man were shoved out of history until the time came for rediscovery. With Darwin we have the strangest case of all, for the man became known as the greatest scientist of his age. But, as if with Bach and Schubert all the pages for the violins and flutes—and indeed for the human voice itself—had been ripped from the scores, his theory was slashed in two and only half used.

The first major distortion of Darwin's original theory and vision came with the rise of "Social Darwinism" in the late 19th century.[9] Serving chiefly to justify British and other European colonialism and the Robber Baron mystique of unregulated capitalism, this doctrine was formulated to assert the racial and/or class superiority that its adherents found to be the logical and rightful outcome for the now scientifically sanctified principle of the "survival of the fittest."

Since then, updates for Social Darwinism—ranging from the books of psychologist Arthur Jensen and the Nobel prize-winning physicist William Shockley during the late 1960s to the much deplored *The Bell Curve* more recently[10]—have emerged like clockwork during every period of conservative backlash to provide a "scientific" justification for racism in America and elsewhere.

But wasn't Darwin himself also racist—for this we sometimes hear today from certain quarters. What he actually wrote was that "only an artificial barrier" prevents our "sympathies extending to the men of all nations and races."[11] In *Descent* he also writes of "the idea of humanity" that it is "one of the noblest" virtues, which "seems to arise incidentally from our sympathies becoming more tender and more widely diffused, until they are extended to all sentient beings."[12]

As for unregulated capitalism—which concerned observers today fear may, through a resurgence for the doctrine of "survival of the fittest," drive the world toward fresh disaster[13]—the picture Darwin provides throughout *Descent* is of human advancement far more through "sympathy," "love," and "mutual aid."[14]

Following Social Darwinism, during the opening quarter of the 20th century, came an immeasurably more respectable development. This was the wedding of Mendelian genetics with the key Darwinian principle of natural selection that fixed in place what has become universally known as Darwin's theory of evolution. Identified today as either "neo-Darwinism" or as "the synthetic theory," this is the doctrine firmed up by the 1930s, which since then has become entrenched throughout American and global education. Resisting fresh input at every level from high school through graduate school, via neo-Darwinism two staunch tenets about evolution are implanted in the willy-nilly mind.

One tenet—as we glimpsed in the introduction—is that everything that can properly be called evolution is determined by the impersonal and generally brutal force of natural selection, which picks out of the variability of organisms what is to be obliterated and what is to survive. The other tenet is that the variability upon which natural selection preys is generated randomly—indeed some theorists (for example, the prestigious Jacques Monod)[15] insist that the whole process from beginning to end is ruled by chance.

At this point I must pause to recognize the discomfort some readers may understandably be experiencing. For isn't this beginning to sound like William Jennings Bryan and the Scopes trial all over again? Isn't this the standard Creationist critique? Are we off to join up with certain Kansans in the Land of Oz?

By no means, but the point is immensely important because this is the difficulty that both the lost Darwin and his modern heirs and heiresses face. This is why so little of the new science bearing on the advance of our understanding of evolution makes it out beyond the confines of scholarly symposia into the books and television programs that can reach minds of parents, social policymakers—and even scientists themselves. For another of the endless ironies that riddle this story is this. Unless they are themselves intimately involved in evolution studies, most scientists simply go along with the standard paradigm they learned long ago in college. So we have this incredible situation where the minute most people detect that standard-version Darwinism is coming under attack—for otherwise our minds cannot be opened to any other alternative—the warning bell rings and the mind shuts down. Who wants to join up with the moralizing Creationists in the new Oz? And so, having shut the door on the chance to learn that this is wholly against their best interests, they join up with all else that has pushed the real Darwin back into the grave for 100 years.

Back then to the problem with the Darwinism that most of us have been taught. Here is what we can see now with eyes and minds opened to the exciting new alternative laid out by Darwin himself in this book. The main problem is that what we have been taught is the Darwinian gospel is based primarily on observations by biologists of *pre*human evolution—that is, of the rise and nature of organisms *prior* to the emergence of our species.

It does seem incredible when at last one realizes that this is actually the case—that year after year, throughout the entire long span of the 20th century, this doctrine of *pre*humanity was applied wholesale to our species. Yet in trying to get across the vital difference between the theory of *Origin* and the theory of *Descent*, what Darwin actually wrote looms today in startling contradiction.

In what was at first Chapter 4 of *Descent*—shifted by Darwin to become Chapter 2 in a later edition—he tells us that in *Origin* he "perhaps attributed too much to the action of natural selection or survival of the fittest."[16]

He specifically tells us that at the level of the human other forces become more important—in particular "the moral qualities," which are "advanced, either directly or indirectly, much more through the effects of habit, by our reasoning powers, by instruction, by religion, etc., than through natural selection."[17]

Could this be?

We see the quote marks and the little number indicating an endnote that certifies this is something Darwin really said—but still the mind balks! Could the Darwin so long damned and consigned to hell by the old time religion actually have had a good word for religion? Not for the intolerance, ignorance, and violence that has so long characterized what we think of as the old time religion. He is pretty clear on that. But for what today we would call progressive spirituality, what he has to say—or at least, imply—is an unexpected and different story.

As for the "Darwinian" idea that we are wholly at the mercy of "chance," what he actually wrote is one of the most impassioned passages in *Descent*: "The birth both of the species and of the individual are equally parts of that grand sequence of events that our minds refuse to accept as the result of blind chance," he tells us. "The understanding revolts at such a conclusion."[18]

So much for Social Darwinism and the strange picture that emerges when we compare the gospel of neo-Darwinism with what Darwin actually said. Time now for the "killer ape."

Out of the 1950s and 1960s came a wave of "Darwinian" books designed to convince us that this most vicious of possible ancestors accounts for who we really are beneath a veneer of "playing nice." Via Darwinian evolution, we were told, the "killer ape" as our archetypal ancestor led inexorably over some hundreds of thousands of years to the modern ascendancy of "man the natural killer." That is, our species—man, woman, and child—is supposedly driven by "innate aggression" as well as by the overriding, implacable, indeed sacred force of "survival of the fittest." These books included Raymond Dart's *Adventures with the Missing Link*, Robert Ardrey's *The Territorial Imperative*, Desmond Morris's *The Naked Ape*, and novels such as William Golding's *Lord of the Flies*.[19]

As anthropologist Ashley Montagu noted,[20] books such as these in turn encouraged production of movies such as *A Clockwork Orange* and Sam

Peckinpah's *The Wild Bunch* and *Straw Dogs*—which became the pioneering trend setters for the all-out violence that worldwide has escalated ever since on television and in theaters.[21]

In *Descent* are many pages with a bloody accounting of the "savagery" of which our species is capable, as well as in *Voyage of the Beagle* earlier. But Darwin's purpose was to register the horror and the disgust he felt toward evolution's failures and throwbacks—as, for example, the "savage who delights to torture his enemies, offers up bloody sacrifices, practices infanticide without remorse, treats his wives like slaves, knows no decency, and is haunted by the grossest superstitions."[22]

What did the real Darwin actually think was our single most powerful motivator? In the one most important and indeed pivotal departure from the portrait we have been given of the man who ostensibly reveled in blood and guts, both obsessed with and blessing violence, Darwin actually found that at the evolutionary level for our species *the single most powerful motivator is the systems requirement of "the moral sense."*

And what tunes up and advances this moral sense among us? He found it to be advanced by love, habit, reason, education, and—the surprise that jolts the stereotype—by religion more than by natural selection.[23]

"Important as the struggle for existence has been and even still is, yet as far as the highest part of man's nature is concerned there are other agencies more important," he tells us in prefacing the case he makes for the "higher and highest" capacities in our evolutionary rise.[24]

The Rough Riders Arrive

But now came the most ingenious and effective assault on the dream—and all in Darwin's name. For in the 1970s up the hill charged sociobiology, and in the 1980s its offshoot evolutionary psychology. Of this new school for Darwinian evolution theory, biologist Richard Dawkins captured the imagination and book market with two striking new images.

According to Dawkins, everything in our lives is, through chance, put together through the operation of natural selection acting like a "blind watchmaker."[25] As for variability, Dawkins asserted that both the prime motivator and shaper of who we are is the drive of the "selfish gene."[26]

Darwin himself, as we have seen, found the notion of blind chance "abhorrent"—but who bothered to read *him* any more! He had become much more useful as a free-floating icon who could be used to legitimize one's own ideas or to intimidate the doubters.

"Don't come to me with this bosh about love," one can hear the voice of hundreds of faculty advisors admonishing by now countless thousands of naive students. Hat or books in hand, a hopeful smile masking the fear constricting one's throat and stomach all in knots, the student has come to submit the idea upon which the treasured degree may depend. It is to be an experiment or dissertation in biology or—under the influence of first-half Darwinism—even in psychology.

"Come back when you've got something suitably grounded in Dawkins," they are told—the indulgent smile also telling them they may have just stumbled badly if not fatally en route to any kind of career in science. "Something, for example, that looks at behavioral aspects of the selfish gene, or something similarly grounded not in Cloud Cuckoo Land but in the rigor of mathematics or respectably hard science."

And so, keying to the mystique of the gene, selfishness now swiftly became the identifying leitmotif, if not indeed the battle cry, for this new expansion of the "Darwinian" paradigm. With a pyrotechnical display of mathematics, biologist William D. Hamilton proved that altruism depends on "kinship selection"—or the degree to which the person requiring help is a blood relative who may be involved in perpetuating your own "gene pool."[27]

In other words, you may jump in to save a child or uncle or aunt from drowning, but forget it if it's just the passing stranger. Biologist Robert Trivers then came up with an explanation for why even the passing stranger is sometimes rescued. According to his widely influential concept of "reciprocal altruism," everything else that seems to be altruism—or doing good for others—is actually again driven solely by selfishness, or what we hope to gain from them.[28]

Synthesizing the mystique of selfishness and acting as the flagship for what was now becoming a scientific battle fleet, in *Sociobiology* entomologist and biologist Edward O. Wilson published the book that—combining the appeal of coffee table size and color plates with advanced textbook stature—both named and most prestigiously launched the new field.[29]

Wilson, however, came up with a surprise. For into first-half Darwinism he injected an idea that led to sociobiology's most solid and helpful strain of research. Re-attuned without knowing it to what had been Darwin's central concern, Wilson pointed to the gaping hole in science as well as evolutionary theory that was becoming a mounting social concern—most effectively, one must note, being articulated by conservatives.

The origin and nature of *morality*, Wilson said, was the key question not only for evolutionary theory, but for science as a whole and for something even larger that all too often science seemed to forget. For it did seem high time to make the point that a new scientific understanding of morality was an urgent priority for a society that seemed hell bent for environmental as well as social disaster.

Wilson elsewhere articulated the goal of morality in science in ways surprisingly in keeping with Darwin's original vision.[30] The sociobiological initiative has also been of considerable importance in generating research into the origins and nature of morality after long neglect by science.[31] But what has centrally characterized it—and has been used to bolster conservative cynicism and social policy for everything from dumping the mentally ill out on the streets to jacking up billions upon billions for the military—is the idea that the doctrine of selfishness provides the answers to all possible questions of our higher motivation and human advancement.

"True selfishness...is the key to a more nearly perfect social contract," Wilson wrote to set the tone and philosophy for the new field.[32] "Human behavior...is the circuitous technique by which human genetic material has been and will be kept intact. Morality has no other demonstrable ultimate function."[33]

And what behind the scenes was the actual position of the Darwin of reality, rather than the Darwin of their useful fiction?

Selfishness to Darwin was a "base principle." Indeed, at times it is anathema on a par with the abhorrent notion of "blind chance." Selfishness does have an important place in Darwin's theory, as we will see. But man and boy, one might say, the idea of selfishness as the prime generator of both altruism and morality was to Darwin not only a misguided notion for philosophy and theology—as we are to see, his knowledge of this heritage for the idea was immense. The idea was, further, both misleading and an astonishing truncation of the evolutionary evidence.

Few things are as firmly and consistently entrenched in Darwin as his position on selfishness. From the young Darwin of the private notebooks of 1837-1838 to the old Darwin of *Descent*—that is, over a thirty-year span—he specifically disavowed the idea of "laying the foundation of the noblest part of our nature in the base principle of selfishness."[34]

Instead, Darwin actually said we are driven by two kinds and levels of moral motivation. The higher—and at our level of development, evolutionarily the most important—he developed at great length in *Descent*. In both Darwinian science and Darwinian biography, this perception of a higher motivating structure has been almost wholly ignored.

The other, lower level is that on which sociobiology and conservative social policy—as well as Freudianism earlier[35]—over a century was fixated. Is it any wonder that, looking back today, all too often the 20th can be seen as the century of me-firstism, grab all for oneself while the grabbing is good, as well as the century blackened by the dark "morality" of Hitler and Deutschland über alles.

So far it is a tale compounded, one might say, of three parts Shakespearean tragedy, two parts of the comic insanity of Lewis Carroll or the Marx Brothers, and all too much Frankenstein for comfort. But, thank goodness, there is more to it.

CHAPTER TWO

THE LOST THEORY AND THE INVISIBLE STORY

This is not an easy book to write. To do so I must alienate a number of my fellow scientists, many powerfully placed in universities and on the committees that review the funding of research by foundations and governmental agencies. Many also control the output of university presses through the long time camaraderie and mutual back-scratching of faculty review boards. Others have only to frown, and the acquiring editors for the mainstream trade presses that account for most of what is read throughout America will quickly scuttle a book before it can reach a single reader.

To compound the problem I must bump up against this hornet's nest while mainly seeking something seemingly impossible—a reconciliation in the end. In other words, the worst possible outcome for this book would be for it to encourage the choosing up of sides, first half Darwinians versus second half Darwinians. For at stake here is something that must transcend the squabbling and the open warfare that characterized so much of 20th century science.

What is at stake requires a dissolving of old boundaries and an alliance in a new joining of one half to the other, for the task at hand is not an easy one and we must make up for lost time. The task is to build as quickly as possible a better theory of evolution in keeping with Darwin's larger vision. We must do this to give our species the best possible chance to outrun what has done in so many thousands of species before us—that is, the threat of extinction.

The goal is to join the two halves of Darwinian science. But for us to be able to see clearly both why we must do this, and how to go about it, I must continue to uncover what has long been hidden or is uncomfortable to look at. We have seen how Darwin's theory has been mangled as well as manhandled by science. We have seen him spun around and turned inside out by the relentless pressure of a racist and industrial dog-eat-dog Social Darwinism, by the subtle play upon us of the killer ape imagery, by neo-Darwinism and the synthetic theory of the implacable, overriding power of natural selection and random variation. We have also glimpsed the consequences of the enormous 20th century popularity of the sociobiology of the blind watchmaker, the selfish gene, and the scientific celebration of selfishness as not only the prime but sole principle of prosocial human motivation—or what we do to make ourselves look good when we really aren't.

If science were carried out in a vacuum tube, none of this would matter. But it isn't. In thousands of ways science is linked to every aspect of our lives. This means that what is theory today becomes the reality that can liberate or imprison us tomorrow. This is particularly true of evolution theory because here such a thin line separates theory from story. And as we have heard many times, it is stories that we live by.

The Story We Live By

The impact of first-half Darwinian science on the shaping of 20th century mind was not just through the books that the scholars argued about, decade after decade. The books were read by, at most, a few hundred thousand of the world's billions. But beyond the books is the periphery of social meaning globally generated by the technological leapfrogging and electronic acceleration of the multimedia revolution—the significance of which, other than among the extremely concerned ranks of media researchers, was and still is almost universally ignored by scientists.[36]

"Why all the fuss," generation after generation of well-intentioned scientists have, in effect, asked. "We are only scientists doing what we are trained to do on the behalf of humanity. You may not like it, but this is what Darwinism reveals."

So decade after decade, with an exponential expansion of the power to seize and hold and shape our minds, the media are pressured to narrow everything to formulas that guide the crafting of stories according to what first-half Darwinism tells us people are and what they want. Thus year after year, we are given a brutal and brutalizing diet of "Darwinian" plots, characters, and settings for movies, television, novels, plays, and computer games.

Around the clock, twenty-four hours a day, seven days a week, year in, year out, we are shown the dog-eat-dog world of people driven to be and do no more than what we have been taught to expect of them and of ourselves. It is this, or we are given the banal world of people provided with no sense of meaning, direction or purpose to their lives—and this by a science that actually takes pride in insisting that, according to Darwin, this is just the way the world is.

Moreover, this scientifically legitimized and now electronically enhanced Darwinian *Weltanschauung* not only shapes the shoot-em-ups, the sit-coms, and the computer games to which we are exposed. It even dictates the selection of what is and is not considered news. (It is really a very simple formula. Killing, rape, fraud, scandal, the pile-up of whatever is novel but meaningless is news; all that is otherwise is not news).

The impact of this collection of "Darwinian" horror stories not only works on us and our children through the ever-present television set and the sprawl of computer games over the living room floor. Beyond all this lies the widening impact of the standard Darwinian paradigm that, as seeded and spread from mind to mind with the email speed almost of light, became the guide for social, political, economic, educational, religious, technological, and military policy throughout the 20th century.

How much of the worldwide arms escalation over the 20th century may be attributed to this source, one wonders. How much of the one trillion dollars annually pumped into the military came from the fact that in every dispute both sides were able to point to the pent-up aggression, the perfidious selfishness, and the general untrustworthiness of "the other"—which Darwin supposedly certified—as justification for more and more and ever bigger and better bombs?

Moreover, looking to the future, one wonders about this grim prospect for the media. Many of us are still caught up in Marshall McLuhan's idea that the medium is the message. But isn't the critical question what message will the media carry?

Lest I seem to be somewhat "unscientifically" carried away by this theme, I should note a fact of background and professional experience. Before I became a systems scientist and evolution theorist I was, in my youth, a journalist, one of the earliest television news men in fact, and then for the better part of a decade, the director of research for a half million-dollar study of the impact of movies and television on adults, conducted under the auspices of the UCLA School of Medicine.[37] I also recently completed a twenty-year study of the factors in the money-making and creative ends of the entertainment industry that shape the stories that in turn shape our minds.[38]

It is from this perspective that I must ask: how long can our species afford to go on "shooting up" and pumping itself full of first-half Darwinism?

Love, the Magician

Fortunately, we don't have to. There is an alternative to this potentially most dangerous of all our addictions. But if the alternative is to prevail in our lives we must go up against the weight of exclusively first-half Darwinian theory still entrenched in science and in our schools. And we must go up against the weight of the exclusively first-half Darwinian story that each year becomes ever more securely entrenched in the multi-trillion-dollar sales of books, movies, television programs, records, and computer games that drive the global entertainment industry.

It has truly become a vicious cycle-the two interacting as a system, theory-feeding story, and story feeding theory. Together they comprise the highly profitable entity for both the businessmen and businesswomen and the scientists involved that may rightly be called the Darwin Industry.

In contrast to this Darwinian fiction that activates both our dreams and nightmares as we enter the 21st century is the real Darwin who re-emerges here to show us the better future. And what are some of the components of this alternative?

Love is perhaps the most striking "new" Darwinian difference. As the reader will find ahead, contrary to the trumpeting of selfishness and aggression that we have been told is bedrock Darwinism, as well as counter to the portraits of the gloomy old man in all the books, it might be said that love is the single most characterizing trait for the real Darwin. In fact, in research for this book, I found so much of this supposedly unDarwinian commodity that I wrote another book to better contain it. Considering the breathless beauty of its handling of young love and the success of the award-winning movie "Shakespeare In Love," the title for mine became inescapable. It had to be *Darwin in Love*. As I tell there in more detail, wholly contrary to expectation, in contrast to only two entries for "survival of the fittest," a computer word search revealed that in *The Descent of Man* Darwin was writing of love 95 times![39]

Writing there on the Isle of Wight and at home in Down over 100 years ago, what he foreshadowed was the uphill re-emergence of this theme among his late 20th-early 21st century heirs and heiresses in science. Here is biophysicist Mae-Wan Ho, better known among scientists for her pioneering work in the liquid crystalline structure for all organisms. She writes of love as "a desire for wholeness...for resonance, for intimacy, a longing to embrace and complete a larger whole...which motivates our social and creative acts."

The "true love of self is also inextricably the love of humanity and of all nature," she observes. "That is why we feel obliged to serve, to help, to alleviate suffering and pain just as if they were our own."[40]

For Chilean biologist Humberto Maturana, internationally known for his development of the concept of autopoesis, "the biology of love" is also becoming a central theme. In almost precisely the same sequence of stages that Darwin outlined over 100 years ago in his lost theory, Maturana notes how over the past four million years the interaction of sex, parental care, family life, tenderness, trust, pleasure, joy, "the networks of conversation," and the "braiding of languaging and emotioning," have been the cluster for the thrust of love within evolution.

"Only love expands intelligence because love is the domain of those behaviors through which the other arises as a legitimate other in coexistence with oneself," Maturana and co-author Gerda Verden-Zoller write.[41]

Given a choice, would you rather your child or grandchild learn of life from this tenet of the theory and story of the second half, or from the frenetic packaging of first-half Darwinism?

Another surprise we have never before heard a word of also coincides with the work of Darwin's 21st century heirs and heiresses. As we will see in Chapters 7 through 11, beginning with observations at the prehuman level and then escalating as he considers the evidence of the growth of human mind and society over a period of many thousands of years, *eleven times* Darwin identifies this "invisible discovery" within the "invisible story" as pivotal in evolution-but without naming it.

In Chapter 8 I will offer a theory as to why he didn't name what he clearly recognized was a major insight. Of more importance, however, for building both the theory and the story of the second half is the uncovering of the lost history of the perception by others of various aspects of Darwin's discovery-or better stated, rediscovery. Most startling are how his observations mirror those of Marx and Engels. They were contemporaries, Darwin dying in 1882 and Marx the following year, in 1883. It is startling today to realize that, although they never met, they lived only sixteen miles apart-Darwin the affluent country gentleman and scientist

eventually idolized, even worshiped worldwide. And Marx, the poor grub-
ber in the ghettos of Soho, whom half the world demonized while the
other half raised statues to.

This, however, is only the beginning for the surprises. For what Darwin
uncovered can be found back as far as the evolutionary theory of ancient
China that we know today as I *Ching*, the Book of Changes. Age by age it
re-emerges all the way to its latest reincarnation in modern cognitive psychology and cybernetic, chaos, and complexity theory. At the heart of this
process, which we will look at in Chapter 11, lies the fascination that animates the work of biologists and systems scientists today probing the
dimensions of "self-organizing" processes. Rejecting the neo-Darwinian
and sociobiological truncation of the evidence, their work, as with
Darwin's heresy, has all too often been assigned to Never Never Land. But
at the core of self-organizing processes lies the fundamental aspect of
choice by the organism of its destiny.

And why does this finding matter? Because it tells us that this is *our*
power, that this is *our* ticket to the better future.

In contrast to a destiny determined solely by natural selection and random process, Darwin's "invisible discovery" tells us that within reasonable
limits the choice of the future is ours not merely as a matter of hopeful
rhetoric, or "feel good" pop New Age philosophy, but as something
backed up by an ancient kind of science we are at last beginning to understand and highly value.

Again, given the choice, which version would you pick for the stories
your child or grandchild is to hear-or the theory to provide guidance for
our species during the 21st century? A theory and story of evolution that
is open-ended and ascending, in which we each have a part to play? Or a
one-way street to nowhere?

The Evolution Project

There is much more to tell of what was hidden, but that now re-emerging is in tune with the most advanced evolution studies of our time. But of all the wonderments of the second half, one of the most mystifying directly bears on the great task for 21st century science. This will be, must be, a project to join the two halves of Darwin's theory together to build the greater theory reflecting the full span and grandeur of his vision.

Once one has the facts, the way his theory of morality was written off or ignored is easy to understand, as we will see. But you would think that the idea that Darwin had written out a second half to complete his theory of evolution surely would have been the big news of the time for science at some point during the 120 years that have passed since his death. Yet this too is hidden within *Descent* in what remains the Great Invisible Book within a book.

It was not a matter of two theories, as at first it appears to be. It was not a matter of a theory of evolution involving the brutality of natural selection and "survival of the fittest" and then another theory that wholly contradicts the first theory with the development of a more noble and gentle theory of the evolution of "the moral sense." If we step through the fog of time to take a close look at what Darwin actually wrote at the time about his intentions for *Descent*, we begin to see the interrupted task it is the responsibility of 21st century science to take up and finish. It is evident that, after long delay occasioned by many fears, it was Darwin's original intention to go beyond *Origin* in *Descent* to put the contradictory halves together in order to *complete* his theory of evolution.

"I have been led to put together my notes, so as to see how far the general conclusions arrived at in my former works were applicable to man," we find him writing-but now we can see that he means precisely what he is saying.[42] He is going on to *complete* his theory.

Some pages later he writes that in *Origin* he has "perhaps attributed too much to the action of natural selection or survival of the fittest."[43] Then pointing to what is to become his central concern with the moral sense, he writes of how he intends to look into the evolution of "mental faculties...chiefly, or even exclusively gained for the benefit of the community."[44]

He will delve into "the higher mental qualities, such as sympathy and the love of his fellow creatures."[45] He will explore the "social qualities which lead him to give aid to his fellow men and to receive it in turn."[46]

After some brilliant passages to provide a fascinating point for point comparison of the bodies and the minds of ourselves and the prehumans, he concludes of the difference that nearly a century of both natural and social science has either downplayed or ignored, "*the moral sense or conscience is by far the most important.*"[47]

As with much else in Darwin's ruminations, one has to jump about a bit to piece this track of thought together. But most significantly, at the conclusion of some 800 tightly packed pages, where he is summarizing the thrust of his thought for *Descent* as a whole, he has this to say. Clearly differentiating between the first half and the second intended to complete his theory, he tells us that the "moral sense" and our "conscience" are advanced "either directly or indirectly, much more through the effects of habit, by our reasoning powers, by instruction, by religion, etc., than through natural selection."[48]

In *Origin* he has developed the first half of his theory. Now moving beyond the realm of the prehuman and natural science-focusing on the moral sense as the chief driver and source of process and principle, but also on everything else of a new importance at the human level in which he was to pioneer in social, systems, and cognitive science-he will attempt not only to develop the second half of his theory but also to put the halves together in some comprehensible way.

And as day after day his pen scratches upon the paper-as he interrupts to pace up and down his study; or as he lays down the pen to go for his daily walk; or as puttering about the greenhouse to check on the humidity for his orchids, he touches a petal with love for its beauty; or as he leans on his cane to peer groundward to check on the movements of his beloved earthworms; but always relentlessly returns again and again to the desk and the pen-his thoughts as to the destination as well as the origin of our species are destined for burial for over 100 years.

CHAPTER THREE
WHY WAS DARWIN'S LOST THEORY BURIED FOR OVER 100 YEARS?

The story of how and why this pivotal contribution could be buried in plain sight, accessible to anyone who cared, must rank among the strangest in the annals of science.

Darwin is not only generally recognized as one of the most important scientists of all time but his life and works probably have been pored over by more authorities than any other figure of modern times. And with the exceptions identified in Chapter 5 and in the notes, you may search the bulk of these commentaries and biographies from end to end and seldom find anything bearing on Darwin's theory of the moral sense, or the idea of a completion for his theory, as it emerges here!

This for me was a discovery so astounding and revealing that I will go into it in detail in a later book.[49] Here, for the benefit of those who find it impossible to believe that so much of Darwin could be buried for over a century, is a brief sketch of what I found.

The Great Invisibility

Howard Gruber, to whom I will return in Chapter 5, was the award-winning psychologist who first began to uncover the surprising extent to which Darwin was a pioneering social as well as natural scientist.

"This could become a classic," Howard wrote after reading an early version of this book in manuscript, "but you had better be absolutely sure of your facts."

He didn't have to spell it out. I would be crucified five times over by the Darwinian establishment if it could be discovered that I was, in even the slightest detail, exaggerating the massive oversight I report in this book. So to be absolutely sure of the precise extent to which Darwin on morality and the completion of theory had been ignored, thus in effect lost for over a century, I carefully sampled more than 100 Darwin biographies and books on evolution theory spanning practically the whole of the 20th century. Beyond this, from prior reading or scanning, was my personal knowledge of several hundred other books and articles on evolution theory.

Underlining the incredible power of the standard Darwinian as well as the larger, overriding paradigm to exclude everything that contradicts or threatens it, out of all these books I could find only a dozen or so offhand or cautious mentions of Darwin's theory of the moral sense. Moreover, in only eight instances—identified here in Chapter 5—did I find clear evidence of scholars who had gone beyond the mention to actually read something of the *verboten* moral parts of *Descent* and the private notebooks and write of it.

For example, I could find practically no evidence among the sociobiologists who have claimed both Darwin and the problem of morality for their own—for example, Robert Trivers, W.D. Hamilton, and E.O. Wilson—that they had ever bothered to look at what Darwin here lays out at length regarding morality.[50] Ironically, what he says in part supports them, but the part more relevant to what Darwin actually believed is our basic nature wholly contradicts them. This survey also revealed the same lack of awareness of Darwin's pioneering exploration of the evolution of morality or completion of theory was true of the earlier Social Darwinists, the neo-Darwinists, the synthetic theorists, and the killer-ape theorists. It was further true of their critics, such as Stephen Jay Gould and Richard Lewontin. It further appears true of practically all other kinds of evolution theorists throughout the 20th century!

But this was only the beginning for the spread of the Great Invisibility—or, perhaps more accurately, the great "invisibilizing." Added to this was my knowledge of several hundred more books and articles dealing with the lives and works of the scientific moral theorists throughout the 19th and 20th centuries. As we will see in Part II, Darwin's probe of moral theory as well as the completion for his theory of evolution fills ten chapters in this book. And yet it was wholly unknown to the founders of sociology and psychology who were influenced by Darwin's work, and were also significant moral theorists themselves: Marx and Engels, Emile Durkheim, Sigmund Freud, Jean Piaget, along with, more recently, Erich Fromm, Lawrence Kohlberg, and Carol Gilligan.[51]

It was further true of the leading moral philosophers, such as John Rawls, and theologians such as Reinhold Neibuhr.[52]

It was further true of Darwin's biographers, for in only one recent work—as noted here in Chapter 5—did I find anything indicating that *Descent* might be of abiding significance in the above regards.

Yet, as we are to see, what Darwin re-engaged on the Isle of Wight and finished during the following year or so back home at Down,[53] was not only the greatest and most comprehensive of all scientific theories of morality. It also transcended science to link up with the central story line for the history of our species on this planet. For the completion for his theory is aligned to the visions and stories of our evolution that, among gentle people, gentle cultures, and gentle islands of culture within the surrounding barbarity, have sustained humanity over many thousands of years.

The Return of the Invisible Man

Although the perception of a second half for Darwin's theory or that anything else could be needed was missing from biographies and commentaries, many scientists detected an underlying fault line. They seldom put it as a matter of completing Darwin's theory. And certainly almost none were so rash as to suggest the omission might have anything to do with morality.[54] But throughout all of the 20th century scientists in a number of fields pointed to various shortcomings in what came to be known as neo-Darwinian theory—which the neo-Darwinians kept assuring themselves and everybody else was the one and only true blue, thrice-blessed theory for evolution. This questioning began early in the century. Some of the same holes and flaws in the cloth being woven to garb the emperor we can see here at the start of the 21st century were noted with great distress by Darwin's closest disciple and protégé as early as 1897. This was the worshipful youngster who trekked between London and Down to spend time with Darwin during his final years, George Romanes.

Year by year young George steadily became to Darwin like another son, but with a special importance beyond that of a son. For Romanes had a much greater capacity to understand the deeper and long-term significance of Darwin's work than any of his own flesh and blood. Indeed, this may also be true in relation to Thomas Huxley, Darwin's famous "bulldog," or Hooker, Henslow, or any of the other pals of the *Origin* days that all the biographies focus on. The more one looks into it, the more it seems likely that Romanes may have been the only person in Darwin's own time who not only began to glimpse, but even bothered to read, his larger vision! At his death, Darwin left to this adoring and despairing young man all his notes on psychology. Romanes then went on to become an important British biological psychologist, expanding Darwin's original rather informal insights into a full-scale study of the evolution of mind in prehumans and ourselves.

By 1897, Romanes was appalled by what was already happening to the "real" Darwin. How could they already be burying him, Romanes practically thunders out of the pages of his great tribute *Darwin and After Darwin.*

How, for example, could they so soon ignore that the man himself had "stoutly resisted the doctrine that natural selection was to be regarded as the only cause of organic evolution?"[55]

Why was there already a move afoot to "hide certain parts of Darwin's teaching, and give undue prominence to others?" he asks. Whether "the misrepresentation be due to any unfavourable bias against one side of his teaching, or to sheer carelessness in the reading of his books," it was inexcusable that the neo-Darwinians—for in this book Romanes first coined the phrase—should "positively reverse" Darwin's teachings. All too often ostensible Darwinians were "unjustifiably throwing over [their] own opinions the authority of Darwin's name," Romanes charged.[56]

"I myself believe that Darwin's judgement with regard to all these points will eventually prove more sound and accurate than that of any of the recent would-be improvers upon his system," Romanes predicted way back then—a prediction I believe this book at last, over 100 years later, finally bears out.[57]

Again and again, as we will glimpse in Chapter 8 and elsewhere, the need for Darwin's "invisible discovery" of what I call organic choice to explain evolution has been perceived. Scientists have given it a variety of names, but for lack of a rationale for connecting it to Darwin or basic evolution theory, it keeps disappearing from the scientific literature and discourse. And this is only the most obvious among concepts that scientists in many fields have offered to account for a more adequate picture of evolution that have been given short shrift or entirely done in.[58] Outside the boundaries of small symposia and specialist journals with very limited circulations, their observations are seldom reported. Moreover, through the working of what elsewhere I explore as the dynamics of paradigm defense,[59] all too soon there is a small-scale replay of what happened to Darwin. As with the fate of those who would question repressive regimes in Chile, Argentina, or Guatemala, most of these alternative suggestions "mysteriously" disappear from the scientific literature.

Darwin's theory of the moral sense, however, is another matter. For despite the fact he focuses on it an astounding 90 times in *Descent*, it never seems to have gained enough attention to be thought worth the effort to "disappear" it. In scientific writings as well as biographies and commentaries, very rarely does one find it even mentioned that Darwin might have said something about "morality" in *The Descent of Man*. So glaring is this omission that the introduction to the Princeton University Press edition of *Descent*—which most American scholars and the scholarly concordances key to—only once in passing even bothers to hint that anything of this sort lies ahead. Moreover, whenever the authors of Darwinian books stray into this forbidden territory that lies beyond the borders of the Great Invisibility, what they bring back is usually a misleading garble or a highly selective skip-reading.[60] Yet with the exception of the fragments from Darwin's long unpublished private notebooks, what he writes out about the moral sense—which we explore at length here in Chapters 6 through 17—has been sitting there in plain sight in *The Descent of Man* for over 100 years!

When I finally caught on to what was going on here it was somewhat like waking up to the fact of something else up there alongside the giant stone portraits of Washington, Jefferson, Lincoln, and Teddy Roosevelt on the face of Mount Rushmore. As if one day one happens to look up and notice that a portrait of Jesus or Gautama has all along been up there looking out sadly upon our world. Or more to the point, it is like the figures that in psychological tests are hidden in plain sight within a perceptual maze.

How this happened involves the story of three burials. The first was burial by the generally unseen but incredible power of paradigm. The second burial was by historical circumstances. But the third burial, most complex and haunting psychologically, was by Darwin himself. We will also look at the strange sequence of unlikely events that led to this rediscovery of Darwin's lost theory, and how it has been reconstructed to make it accessible both to scientists and everybody else with a personal stake in what is revealed here.

The Heavy Hand of Paradigm

First, burial by that universal seizure of mind we call ideology or paradigm.

For a long time, many scientists, writers and other observers have been telling us that our minds are caught within an outmoded paradigm in science.[61] It has been variously characterized as objectivist, positivist, reductionist, materialist, cold, mechanistic, valueless, soulless, patriarchal, chauvinistic, inhuman, inhumane, and robotic. As the work of political theorist Michael Lerner, social philosopher Cornel West, theologian Hans Kung, sociologist Robert Bellah, or cultural evolutionary theorist Riane Eisler currently makes evident, the problem is that much more than science is involved in such cases of burial by paradigm.[62] It is a problem also involving politics, economics, education, religion, community, above all child raising—indeed everything that bears on the shaping of our minds.

The net result, according to Eisler, is that we are caught in the "trance" of what she characterizes as the "dominator model," from which we have for 300 years been trying to awake.[63]

One of the most striking things about this "trance," in which we are so often encased like sleepwalkers, is how it has diverted not only science, but also the minds of all of us shaped by the science of our time—as conservative moralists accurately perceive[64]—away from anything to do with the "moral."

We are reading a book, let us say, or leafing through the shelves in a library. At the slightest cue that the "moral" or the "ethical" is about to rear its head, is it not true that the eyes and minds for most of us mysteriously glaze over, and we quickly skip on to something more sure to be of interest? Multiply this by millions of us with minds similarly glazing over, extend this back over all the generations of the 20th century, and you find what seems to be the main answer to the question of why Darwin's lost theory has been buried away in plain sight all these years.

In other words, as long as Darwin is probing the amazing sex life of the barnacle, or the curious twining of the tendrils of the wild cucumber, we are with him. But let him stray into the fusty chamber of "the moral sense," and prompted by the paradigm that insists this is no longer of interest, most people reading *The Descent of Man* have for over 100 years simply skipped these pages.

This is the basic problem, with all the ramifications we are to encounter throughout this book.[65] But much more is involved here—and it is important for us to understand how this vast and seemingly inconceivable devouring of significance works in order to protect the thoughts and causes that matter to us, if not indeed ourselves, from a similar oblivion.

The Heavy Hand of History

Perhaps the most important aspect of the burial by historical circumstance was that after Darwin's death, well into the 20th century, it was all his successors could do to get everybody to swallow *Origin*, much less *Descent* for dessert, as it were.

Though hard to realize now, in the early days of Darwinian science those who later came to guard the prevailing scientific paradigm so ferociously were up against the similarly ferocious guardians of the earlier controlling paradigm of religion. In the aftermath of the scientific and social bombshell of *Origin of Species*, the result was a battle royal that absorbed both the bulk of scientists and their avid readerships so completely they had little time or interest left over for whatever Darwin might have said in *Descent*.

What we collapse today into the seemingly stark and simple machine of Natural Selection and Random Variation emerged out of a wrangling diversity of thought and experiments during what, in retrospect, looms as modern biology's Golden Age. As Ronald Clark's biography **The Survival of Charles Darwin** brilliantly captures, the science of the late 19th and early 20th centuries following Darwin's death fairly bubbled over with the ingredients for everything from the adventure tale to the detective and mystery story. In particular, during this time when Darwin's "comparatively simple approaches were, necessarily, complicated,"[66] the saga of science during this great feeding frenzy of biological creativity became an absorbing entertainment for the readers of the newspapers and popular magazines as well as scientific journals. The clash of strong personalities, strange quirks of fate and coincidence, stories of wondrous discoveries that later fizzled, stories of eventual triumph, the awarding of prestigious prizes—it was all there attached to the names of the heroes of the hour: Gregor Mendel, William Bateson, Walter Weldon, Karl Pearson, Ronald Fisher, J.B.S. Haldane, Julian Huxley, Theodosius Dobzhansky, and Thomas Hunt Morgan and the abiding fascination of **Drosophila melanogaster.**[67]

Drosophila melanogaster was the official name for the fruit fly used in the multiple thousands by Morgan. Year by year, devoted readers followed the progress of Morgan in the sanctum of the famous fruit fly room at Columbia University. Breeding and observing generation after generation of the quick-breeding *drosophila*, Morgan fleshed out the genetic and the mutational part of what eventually became, in the theories of others, a new level of ingenuity for the biology of neo-Darwinism and what became known as the "synthetic theory."

Had our species been composed of 150-pound fruit flies, it is possible the scientists of that time might have been impelled to look into **Descent** for the clues to this fascinating albeit frustratingly slow-breeding creature. But we humans posed a level of complexity that the biologists of that time concluded they were neither equipped nor scientifically ready for yet. This caution was to radically change with the rise of the biological popularizers of rough-and-ready Darwinism at the human level and the late 20th century sociobiologists.

Another problem of historical circumstance is insufficiently remarked but of pivotal importance. This is what might be termed the lopsided or radically imbalanced evolution of our understanding of evolution. Because of the power of both the original liberation and the succeeding enslavement of first-half Darwinian theory, for most of us, if we bother to think about evolution at all, our minds automatically fall into the slot for the first-half Darwinian story. But in trying to understand who we are, where we came from, and where we may be headed, over the years our species has actually come up with at least fourteen primary kinds of stories and theories about our own evolution.

Beginning with the theories and vast story of our cosmic evolution that the late Carl Sagan so expertly dramatized on television, these attempts to explain our great journey through space and time range on upward, outward and inward through the levels thereafter of biological, cultural, personal, social, economic, political, and technological evolution. As well as moral and spiritual evolution. The evolution of consciousness. And the idea of human intervention in evolution—or us taking action, as in the American Revolution, for example, to try to shape the course of evolution to realize our ideals.

Of these, only the first three have been emphasized in the science and education of 20th century Western mind—with the overwhelming focus on *biological* evolution. The Darwin of the lost theory has nothing to tell us of cosmic evolution. Nor, having made his pivotal contribution in *Origin* and elsewhere, does he tell us much here about biological evolution, other than as the foundation for what he is now going to explore. But in regard to cultural evolution and the evolution of an individual over his or her own lifetime, or personal evolution—which over the 20th century became known as the field of developmental psychology—he lays some vital cornerstones. As for moral evolution and the evolution of consciousness, he is loaded with surprises as well as the grounding for what must inevitably become major fields of study for the 21st century. Moreover, out of his own agonizing over the problem, he even suggests an acceptable perspective for the scientist on the usually alien idea of spiritual evolution.

Still another aspect of the pressure cooker of history involved in the burial of Darwin's lost theory is what might be called "evolution theory and story lag." This is the problem of the lag in comprehension between the general or "popular" understanding and the advanced scholarly understanding of evolution theory. The extreme case here is the gap between Darwinian science in any form and the holy-rolling anti-Darwinism of the Creationists.

In other words, as in the case of the flat earth theory, a segment of people are fixated on a mindset of around 300 years ago, unable to move on. The conservative form of this lag is familiar because of the widely publicized political alliance of conservatism with Creationism's rightwing religious adherents. Liberal "evolution theory and story lag," however, has been almost wholly unexamined—and was and is, I believe, an equally serious problem.

Without really thinking about it, many liberals tend to be locked into the rigid defense of unreconstructed neo-Darwinism or sociobiology because of a profound antipathy for the rightists. Also, as I suggested earlier, unless one is impelled to become an evolutionary scientist, we tend to believe whatever we were taught in college about evolution. And what is taught in college? Overwhelmingly, standard neo-Darwinism—which is hard enough to implant in young minds obsessed with sex and how to get more money from the "old man" without considering confusing alternatives. So this lockstep liberal mindset, replete with overtones of the good old days on campus, leads many of us to feel that any questioning of the wholesale operation of natural selection at the human level—or anything so "far out" as a concern with morality or spirituality—surely must be some form of closet Creationism.

Yet it is this questioning of the operation of natural selection and the concern with morality and spirituality at the human level that for Darwin was central in the construction of his lost theory.

Still another factor—also dictating what does or doesn't figure in our minds—is what might be called historical embedding. That is, our situation at any point in history is such that only so much can emerge or be comprehended at any one time. The revolution of **Origin** was, simply put, all that Darwin's age could take.

It is hard for us to realize today, but in Darwin's time the idea of God as the all-purpose answer for everything threatened to stop dead in its tracks not only pursuit of an adequate theory of evolution but also many other aspects of science. Against this long-entrenched power of religion, first-half Darwinism was all that Darwin and his fervent supporters could push through at the time. It was further all that his successors could handle well into the 20th century. The second revolution of **Descent** was just beyond the capacity of his time—as well as most of our own time—to absorb.

Delayed for over 100 years, now, however, it is the great possibility that opens before us as we enter the 21st century. For all the reasons we will explore in this book, it is a revolution whose time has come.

The Inner Qualms of Person and Psychology

In searching for an answer to this truly mind-boggling question of how and why a theory of such power and consequence could be overlooked by practically everybody for over 100 years, I believe the crunch of paradigm is the best explanation. Historical circumstance then comes in second. But the third main reason for the burial of Darwin's lost theory is perhaps the most fascinating because of what it reveals of Darwin personally and his creative situation. The inescapable question is why he himself also buried what over the long run history must surely, in justice, credit as his second great achievement. It is an involved tale as haunting and as inspiring as anything else I know of.

As it deserves a chapter all its own, let us next return to his situation at the time he wrote **The Descent of Ma**n, shortly before and within the years prior to the ill-fated book's publication in 1871.

CHAPTER FOUR

THE AGONY OF DESCENT

At the time of the complex challenge of what was to be his first, last, and only statement on the nature and destiny of our species—homo sapiens sapiens—Darwin was already prematurely aging. Shortly before writing *The Descent of Man*, 13 years before his death, he had so rapidly aged— going from an appearance of considerable vigor to the pale, and even yellowed old man with mournful face and eyes and the long white beard of the favored picture today—that he had to introduce himself to old friends who could not recognize him.

For many years he had suffered from the mysterious stomach ailments that made it impossible to work for weeks and months at a time. From shortly after his marriage until some brief good years toward the end, the generation of an enormous amount of experiments and manuscripts alternates with episode after episode of being bedridden or barely able to function. Often convinced he would die soon, in search of a cure, with family, servants and pets in tow, he would drag himself off to what in those days were called quack doctors, but which today we would call alternative medicine. Atop all this were the inevitable demands of the world upon one of its most famous people. Though he refused to speak in public, thereby avoiding one source of potential enormous drain on his time and energy, there was the inevitable stream of visitors and the volume of correspondence to keep up with—over his lifetime, 14,000 letters to and from others, by one estimate.[68]

All this meant that, although he had a backlog of notes and great chunks of manuscript not used in *The Origin of Species* to draw on, he could not bring to *The Descent of Man* and the dream for the completion of his theory anything approaching the time or energy he had given to his earlier masterpiece.[69]

But above all there was his peculiar isolation in regard to the subject he is to take up in *Descent*. By then "the moral sense," although still of interest to philosophers such as Herbert Spencer, was already of little interest to the new scientists of his time, including his closest scientific friends. Botanist Joseph Hooker did at least aver that "morals and politics would be very interesting if discussed like any branch of natural history."[70] But to the biologists, geologists, and assorted naturalists who were both his cohorts and formed the *Origin of Species* defense team, the idea of a "moral sense" was bosh.

They felt then—as their counterparts today still do—that it was something once talked about by fusty philosophers gathering dust on the shelves, such as Hume and Adam Smith, but was of no relevance to the scientific task at hand. Worse yet to the eyes of his scientific peers were the works of theologians in which one found this old-fashioned phrase "the moral sense." Not only were these the dullest books ever written, but also the most dangerously misleading. With their hands full defending Darwin against the Church and its outraged agents, out to wholly free themselves and humanity of religion's old hold on the mind, to Darwin's scientific defenders then—as well as for 100 years thereafter—the idea of a "moral sense" was at best a dated bit of the past they were busy shedding, and at worst a matter of threat that called for maximal suspicion.

At the same time, Darwin could of course look to no support from religion. The subject was of great interest to the theologians and a handful of other scholars to whom Darwin had in his youth been close during the years he was preparing for the ministry. Indeed, one of them, the great Sir James Mackintosh, to whom he was related by marriage, with whom he used to go for long walks and talks, had been the greatest single influence on his thinking regarding the moral sense.

As we will see, the roots for Darwin's core concept of the origin and dynamics of morality can be found in one of the notes he jotted down while reading Mackintosh at the usual site of their walks. "Looking at Man," Darwin wrote over thirty years before he began writing *Descent*, "it must be concluded that he has parental, conjugal and social instincts," which reflect "a feeling of love and benevolence," which in turn lead to such "active sympathy that the individual forgets itself, and aids and defends and acts for others at its own expense."[71]

But now Mackintosh and the rich and lofty excitement of that earlier world of being young at Christ's College at Cambridge and the works of Hume, David Hartley, Dugald Stewart, and all the others who puzzled over these matters, were long gone. He was on his own, wholly alone. To the generation of theologians now living, Darwin was perceived either as an unwelcome interloper in their territory, or as a controversial person they could not afford to be associated with. In chagrined recognition of this barrier, while *Descent* was underway, he wrote to the pal of his youth, his cousin, the minister William Darwin Fox, with whom he had shared many joyous hours in the search of exotic beetles. Alarmed, cousin Fox had reported hearing "sad tales" about what Darwin was writing. It "will disgust you and many others,"[72] Darwin sadly warned.

Knowing now what was at work within him, it is haunting to read through the letters he wrote others during the time he worked on *Descent*. Earlier, while working on everything up to and including *Origin*, and then after *Descent* as he wrote his last works, his letters dance and fairly bubble over with his questions and all that he is sharing with his vast range of correspondents. It is like a great mouse chortling over and eager to share with everybody else the discovery of a great mound of cheese. But during the writing of *Descent*—not a word other than to laconically note a beginning for the effort, and occasionally thereafter a single sad line to lament the difficulties, as with his letter to Fox.

The Lost Heart and the Lost Mind at Work

And so, in what must in retrospect be seen as a lonely but magnificent isolation, he poured out the deep feelings and thoughts about the human condition as he had observed and suffered it over nearly sixty years.

In what was to pour from him we now find the other side to the voyage of the Beagle. In contrast to the sunny, upbeat observation of flora and fauna that Darwinians have come to cherish, now we find overtones of what he had found to be the wholly abhorrent depravity of the natives of Tierra del Fuego. When food was scarce they would kill and eat the old, presumably useless women, he had earlier noted with horror. Or there was the barbarous cruelty of Brazilian slave owners given to the use of whip and thumbscrew, or the gleeful Indian-slaughtering of the Gauchos of Argentina. But more often, again and again in *Descent*, we find overtones of the goodness he had found in the mentors and exemplars of his youth and the friends of his advancing years, and in his own children. We also find something that puts into a new light the charge of his sexism—the celebration of goodness in women in contrast to men, of which I also write more extensively in *Darwin in Love*.

Most striking of all, however, is the vast outpouring of his feeling for the heroes and heroines of the animal world. In his tales of monkeys who save their keepers, of old orangs who rescue young ones from dogs, of rabbits who stamp their feet to warn their fellows of danger, of pelicans who feed the aged and crippled, he writes as if to again and again ask us to consider this. "If there is all this evidence of the impulse and even the roots of conscience in so many exemplars among the so-called lower species," the underlying rationale for *Descent* goes, "why do we find it so hard to believe in or to honor the moral sense as innate within ourselves? And why does our own species display such a horrifying range between the caring and the sublime and the depraved and the degraded?"

On one hand, Darwin seems to have had the advantage—with one exception that I will come to—of no great body of people through whom he felt compelled to run either his ideas or their writing. In this way, he seems to avoid the fuzzying of points that riddled successive editions of *Origin* in response to many critiques by others. Other than what happened during its editing and the psychological complexities that further drove him to hide his light under an obfuscating bushel, what emerges here seems mainly dimmed only by his own caution and haste, but through which the revolutionary boldness of his mind could here and there burst via his disarming skill as a writer.

Also advantageous must have been his great pleasure in developing this second part for his theory that he had been sitting on for thirty years. The fear of religious reaction that made him keep secret the first half of his theory of evolution for nearly eighteen years is well known.[73] Still generally unknown are the multiple layers of additional complexity, which I explore in *Darwin in Love*, that made him keep secret his theory of the moral sense almost until the very last.

We may also intuit how great was his sense of the future as he wrote about what were to become major concepts for the fields of psychology and the other social sciences as well as the core perspective for systems science. Although remarkable in all he anticipated, he could only toy with but still deeply appreciate what was yet to come. But most of all is the sense he expresses of the future for his own species—this most difficult and disappointing yet at the same time most wondrous of all the incredible diversity of species that he loved with such an all-consuming curiosity and with such intensity.[74]

On the other hand were the realities of the time. Here was the followup book to *Origin* to be completed. Here was a readership waiting for this new book—to most of whom what he had to say about the moral sense would be baffling, confusing, or infuriating. This in part is what lies behind the strange way he opens *Descent*.

He tells us, we have seen, that he has "been led to put together my notes, so as to see how far the general conclusions arrived at in my former works were applicable to man." But shortly before this something very revealing happens. It also seems, to some degree, to account for why this book has been ignored for all these years.

He tells us that he has held back for a long time what he will now lay before the reader because of fear that it "would add to the prejudices against my views."[75] He then seems to invite us to skip the whole thing as really not worth bothering with! The formidably long and turgid book ahead, he tells us, "contains hardly any original facts."[76]

Not until he is well into the book, sure that he has lured the wary reader into it, does the first brief hint appear of what he hopes to do without bringing on the wrath of the Powers That Be—scientific, on one hand, but also religious, let alone the hypothetical God of thunderbolts and wrathful wholesale devastations.[77]

Again and again his agony and misgivings come through. "I can see that I shall meet with universal disapprobation, if not execution," he wrote to one potential critic.[78] Of the book another letter ventured, "I dare say many will decry [it] as very wicked."[79] When at last the proofs went off to the publisher, he doubted that it was "worth publishing."[80]

A Fearful Prophecy

It was clear to him, then, that the moral sense and completion of theory in the book were likely to be rejected or passed over as nothing but the fumblings and rumblings of a quaint interloper in the territory of others. And this indeed, after a brief flurry of fad interest, turned out to be the case. So amid the twenty-one chapters of *Descent*, he tucked away what he had to say about the moral sense and completion of theory into Chapter 3, with a few vital touches in Chapters 2, 4 and 5 and at the conclusion.[81]

And what does he fill the rest of the book with? From the chunk of still unpublished or ongoing manuscript, he had two choices. He could fill *Descent* with the colorful ins and outs of sexual selection. Replete with fine engravings of exotic birds and other animals, filled with the varieties and the oddities of male-female relationships from ants to antelope, this was sure to grab a readership.[82] But it would also blur the picture. Yes, yes, of course, one can picture his mind at work. It would also, most certainly, protect him from criticism by pushing all the baffling, confusing, and even dull "moral stuff" back into the cognitive wallpaper of the general mind.

His other choice was to flesh the book out with the close relationship of his probe of morality to his pioneering work on the development of emotions in the human. Again, he had on hand some appealing illustrations to use—a particularly good set of photographs of gifted actors registering emotional differences in facial expression ranging from puzzlement and sadness to anger and rage.

Such a move would have both aesthetically and scientifically made *Descent* a far better book. And so what does he do? He opts for the choice best calculated to obscure and hide what he has felt and thought about so deeply over the years in private, but about whose reception he has such overwhelming fears and misgivings. He opts for sexual selection—and separately, a year later, in *The Expression of the Emotions in Man and Animals*, he brings out what in any less stressful circumstances would have gone into *Descent.*

It is for this reason that, although it remains a subject of great importance explored at length in *Darwin in Love,*[83] almost nothing further will appear in this book about sexual selection. It is time for "the moral stuff" to re-emerge from the wallpaper. But then in ending *Descent,* Darwin seems to have felt compelled to overcome his fears and, hang it all, say what he thought should be said, come what may. So in Chapter 21 we are given a few last magnificent fragments of his vision. These include the observation that departs so dramatically from what his successors were to put together and call "Darwinian theory," where he rejects "blind chance" as an idea the mind must find revolting.[84]

But even where he clearly flags what he is writing of—and even with the skill at his disposal of the uncommonly good science writer that he was—we are not yet out of the woods. For Darwin so further buried his light in an additional bushel of problems as to make its rediscovery improbable without the unusual circumstances that, as we'll next examine, led me to this document.

CHAPTER FIVE

REDISCOVERY, RECONSTRUCTION, AND THE PROBLEMS OF EDITING DARWIN

In science, as in everything else, few things pop whole from our heads as supposedly the goddess Athena did from the head of Zeus. In other words, without certain paths and offbeat stepping stones, I would never have strayed into the dark woods wherein lay buried Darwin's lost theory. But for fate, Karma, luck, or whatever, I would have gone blithely on my way past those woods along with the thundering herd for 20th century science.

I was led to the notebooks and *The Descent of Man* by paths provided by three scholars who received prestigious prizes for their work. But then, as is typical for those who even in the mildest of ways attempt to go against the prevailing paradigm, they were dropped back into obscurity except for a trickle of continuing attention by heretics such as I. These were the pioneering studies of psychologist Howard Gruber and biologist Paul Barrett and the psychologist and historian of science Robert C. Richards at the University of Chicago.

After nearly a century of the almost exclusive possession of Darwin and the Darwinian paradigm by biologists and other natural scientists, it looked as though his protégé George Romanes' prediction that the voice of Darwin himself would in the end prevail was a forlorn and improbable hope. But then came publication of Gruber and Barrett's *Darwin on Man* in 1974, which won the National Book Award. And then in 1987 came

Richards' book with its long, intriguing title *Darwin: The Emergence of Evolutionary Theories of Mind and Behavior*, which won the Pfizer Prize of the History of Science Society.

These were the breakthrough books to "the other Darwin."[85] Here, for the first time since the death of Romanes almost a century earlier, we find the portentous shift of focus to Darwin the pioneering social and systems scientist and even humanistic psychologist, who soars beyond his age in such an astounding way.

Also led back to the "other Darwin" by Gruber and Barrett and Richards were five other people I have been able to identify who, after the lapse of over a century, began to read and write of this lost theory.

As noted earlier, I had carefully sampled more than 100 Darwin biographies and books on evolution theory spanning practically the whole of the 20th century.[86] Beyond this was my personal knowledge of several hundred other books and articles on evolution theory. Out of all these books I could find only a dozen or so offhand or cautious mentions of Darwin's theory of the moral sense. And in only eight instances did I find clear evidence of scholars who had gone beyond the slight mention to actually read something of the moral parts of *Descent* and the private notebooks and write of it!

The first, and for a long time lone, venturer was the amazing Russian prince, naturalist, and anarchist philosopher Peter Kropotkin. His reading of *Descent* (but not the notebooks, for these weren't published until almost three quarters of a century later) became the basis for Kropotkin's famous celebration of the evolutionary power of cooperation rather than competition in his classic *Mutual Aid*. And where did he get this title? Yes, of course, it too was right there in plain sight in Darwin. Later, Kropotkin further briefly explored the "lost Darwin" in his little-known but great book *Ethics*, posthumously published in 1925 and ever since then out of print until recently.[87]

Thereafter followed twenty-seven years of oblivion. Then in 1952 anthropologist Ashley Montagu—dedicating his book to Kropotkin—tried to break through the crust with *Darwin: Competition and Cooperation*, which again touches on the "lost Darwin." But as Montagu himself warned me—ruefully but sternly trying to get me to drop the research and then, when I persisted, the writing of this book—so powerful was the prevailing paradigm that his own "book fell stillborn from the press."[88] Then in 1974 came Howard Gruber's pointing of the way for Robert Richard's pioneering 1987 re-exploration of Darwin's moral theory, along with the moral theories of Herbert Spencer, William James, and many other long-forgotten evolutionary moral theorists.

In 1993 political scientist James Q. Wilson made use of Richards' sketch of Darwin's theory in the book he called *The Moral Sense*, as did journalist Robert Wright in *The Moral Animal* in 1994.[89] Wilson, however, used only a single page on Darwin to bolster the case for his title, with the rest of the book given over to an exploration of recent social scientific studies. And Wright—in a worshipful paean to sociobiology and evolutionary psychology that most surely would have sickened both Romanes and Darwin—grossly distorted the new Darwin in a misleading hop, skip, and jump dabbling for his own questionable purposes.[90]

One of the best new Darwinian books to come out of this late 20th century revival of interest was Adrian Desmond and James Moore's *Darwin*. Originally published in 1991, the Desmond and Moore biography takes what might in other hands have been handled as a staid and conventional life and brings it to life in a lively, vivid way. Their book is also in a class by itself in its rare attention to Darwin's interest in morality.[91] Characterizing *Descent* as "an armchair adventure of the English evolving," however, it dismisses his moral theory as of little consequence.[92] In sharp contrast, first published in 1990, is moral philosopher James Rachels's *Created From Animals*. Prompted solely by Gruber's book, this was the result of Rachels's own reading of the original source material rather than derived from Richards's brilliant but at times rather ambiguous sketch.[93]

The result was the first—and possibly the only—book in the century to perceive that the moral theory of *Descent* was not just a quaint afterthought.

"It is of one piece...one view, held together by a sense of how the elements of one's thinking must be mutually supportive, and how they must fit together, if one's outlook is to form a reasonable and satisfying whole," Rachels noted.[94] Coming at the end of a book covering much else, however, Rachels only provides a few tantalizing pages for what the reader will find here requires not only this whole book but also, so far, at least a trilogy.[95]

Through the Looking Glass, or the Mystery of Coincidence

Though Howard Gruber did not explore Darwin's moral theory, given the potential consequences of this rediscovery for the 21st century, history may record that this was an epochal case of much being set in motion by a single book. Gruber's book was of special interest to me, as I was a student of his in graduate school.[96] At the time, it was rumored that he was at work on a book on Darwin.

I can still remember how we budding psychologists wondered why our professor, who otherwise seemed a rational and sensible person, could possibly be interested in something as dated and far removed from our field as Darwin. There Gruber was, undeniably modern and full of the proper recent references to the rat research, which he abhorred, and to the exploration of optical illusions, which were his delight. And yet after we found out about his obsession with Darwin, he seemed an anachronism there at the blackboard—a character more out of Dickens than of this century. When his book came out years later, I read it, and then later with mounting excitement, Robert Richards' book. But still I never would have seen what was buried in *The Descent of Man* except for a unique prior set of circumstances.

To understand what Darwin has to tell us, one needs to bring to the job of rediscovery and reconstruction an acquaintance with the most advanced scientific thinking and discovery for our own time. In particular, one must have become involved with brain research, systems science, and advanced biological and evolutionary theory. One also needs to be more than usually sensitized to the range of problems—environmental, social, political, etc.—that our species faces at this juncture. At the same time, one also has to get into a moral place in mind that not only passed out of scientific but also general consciousness many years ago.

It so happened that I came to Darwin at the end of an unusual ten-year period of research in all of these directions. On one hand, I had been involved as a psychologist with a multidisciplinary evolutionary research group composed of biologists, physicists, astronomers, mathematicians, sociologists, historians, systems scientists, philosophers, and other scholars from Europe and Asia as well as the U.S. As further described in Appendix A, drawing on chaos, self-organizing and complexity theory and the rest of the heady mix of thought in our time, we were involved in the development of the new field of general evolution theory.[97]

On the other hand, I had been independently exploring the long-ignored moral studies of the great founders of modern social science. This lineage—also mainly lost to us today—begins with the scientist-philosopher Immanuel Kant, who precedes Darwin. Thereafter, it includes Marx and Engels and Herbert Spencer, who were Darwin's contemporaries and admirers. Then come the key shapers of modern social science who were Darwin's successors as well as pioneering moral theorists—Sigmund Freud in psychology, Emile Durkheim in sociology, and Jean Piaget in child and cognitive psychology. I had also studied in depth the later important contributions to moral studies of the psychoanalyst Erich Fromm and psychologists Milton Rokeach, Lawrence Kohlberg, and Carol Gilligan.

Out of this research I had developed my own theory of moral development and evolution and had begun to write a series of books generated by this research.[98] So when I came at last to read Darwin, I had been unusually primed by fate to recognize the significance of what he had to say. But what I was not prepared for was the astonishment that seized me.[99]

As I began to edit, releasing from burial what the reader will find in Part II of this book, it soon became apparent that here was more than just another old book, however quaint and charming. Here was not only the rough map and landmarks for the completion of Darwin's theory of evolution. Here, too, was the most comprehensively grounded of all scientific theories bearing on the vital guidance system for ourselves as people and for our poor, floundering species, of what was right for us, and what was wrong for us, or of morality.

I also soon discovered another reason so few had bothered to read him in all these years—these sections of Darwin were mangled in peculiar ways in both their expression and the editing. What had apparently happened took a good bit of time to piece through and figure out, but the complexities further explain why this pivotal contribution could remain buried all these years.

One reason for such widespread neglect could have been the lack of clarity, or fuzziness, deriving from Darwin's ambivalence toward what he was discovering as a naturalist and toward the society into which he had been born and had shaped him. In attempting to make sense of the complex interplay of both views he alternates between a hard-nosed macho stance ("so it's brutal and bloody but that's the way it is, so like it or lump it") and the recognition of an inescapably valid higher and better side both to nature and to ourselves that appealed to his own gentle and highly moral nature. As the simple device of my word counting demonstrates, it is the "higher" side that prevails in *Descent*. But as observations of the first kind fit with Origin, they were seized up by the ready minds of most devout Darwinian readers. As for the "higher side," it was just brushed aside as one might deal with an unwanted gnat buzzing around one's head.

In *Darwin in Love* I go into the formative struggle in the young Darwin between the "hard" view of natural selection and the "soft" view of love as the primary force in evolution. Revealed through his letters and the private notebooks, it is quite a story—with the "hard" view winning until the need to write *Descent* forced him back in time to the memories, insights, and aspiration of his youth.[100]

Even more important, however, closely intertwined with this complexity, was a fundamental and too seldom noted factor in Darwin's personal makeup. The more basic problem is that—in comparison to the blunting of affect and the blinding of eye that passes for normality among most of us—Darwin was a man of abnormal sensitivity to others.

As many of his biographers bring out, he couldn't bear to hurt anyone's feelings. In the writings that lie ahead this seems to accounts for some of the confusion resulting from the way his thoughts go back and forth, as though he were trying to please everybody and accommodate all points of view. Yet here he was in this historical situation where, in order to go where the intensity and honesty of his mind was taking him, he must not only offend the bulk of the religious leaders and scientists of his time, but also his wife, Emma, to whom he was deeply devoted and loved with fervor.

Over the years many commentators, including psychologists such as myself, have tackled the question of why Darwin was sick so often. Psychiatrist John Bowlby, especially, has probed the problem in depth in his very useful Darwin biography, offering a wide range of theories.[101] In addition to Bowlby's conclusions, it seems to me that it was Darwin's unusual sensitivity to the feelings of others that continually tied his stomach in knots, as they say, driving him to the sick bed week after week and sometimes month after month. That is, he could not bear to hurt the feelings of others—but yet, if he was to pursue where he was going in science, and speak out, and lay his bombshell before both science and society, he had to! Even then the situation was more complex than usually portrayed.

If one does not know much about his wife Emma, the stereotype of the unappreciated genius may tempt one to think she was probably a subgrade religious bigot from whom he had to conceal his heretical theories. In fact, she was a highly intelligent, well-educated and musically gifted woman who had studied piano with Chopin.[102] Moreover, at critical junctures, unable to be dishonest with her, he had revealed his heresies. She, in return, bent over backwards to find some reconciliation with her own deep but liberal religious views. Even so, in the writing of *Descent* both her liberality and his sensitivity to her feelings were tested to the limit.

His fear of hurting her feelings definitely seems to account for the occasional blunting and distortion of his writing, as well as some mangling of the book's editing whenever he deals with religion and morality. A more direct source of this mangling, however, according to the biography by Desmond and Moore, was his daughter Henrietta. As Darwin worked "through the long hard winter" at Down to finish the sections on the moral sense, he sent them on to twenty-seven-year-old Henrietta, then basking in sunny France at Cannes. "A stylist and petty moralist, she touched up his prose and guarded the proprieties," Desmond and Moore note.[103]

What this may have meant becomes apparent if one compares the differences between the original edition of Darwin's *Autobiography*, which came out soon after his death, with the new Norton edition in which his granddaughter Nora Barlow restored all the cuts Emma had insisted on in the sections dealing either with morality or religion.[104] Now here, a decade earlier, already the family protection society was in operation.

Publication of *Descent* "might injure the family," Desmond and Moore report. "Henrietta had to ensure that the wrong inferences would not be drawn. As she preened the text, her own guardian angel—Emma—jogged her. The treatment of morals and religion might be 'very interesting,' Emma wrote, but she would still 'dislike it very much as again putting God further off.'"[105]

What was left may have then, I surmise, been subjected to the neglect of some poor editor at Darwin's publishers who had been properly intimidated by the family to touch not thereafter. So what Darwin had to say whenever the subject is morality or religion is all crammed together. The sentences are strung together with seemingly endless semi-colons. This tight-packed filigree is encased in paragraphs that go on forever. And then to help guarantee that no one today will ever read him, we are provided with minimal subheading. It makes reading Darwin on morality or the completion of theory in the original like having to swim underwater for about a mile with only three breaks to come up for air.

The Challenge of Restoration

If one compares these sections of *Descent* with the easy flow of his less "sensitive" biological writings, Darwin also has two bad habits that bear out not only the difficulty of the material, or the historical circumstances, but also Henrietta's role as Emma's agent and Darwin's fear of hurting Emma's feelings. It is as though he has been afflicted with a form of psychohistorical stage fright, where one freezes up, or ever so often mumbles, or says the wrong thing. Indeed, the problem is best explained in terms of two symptoms that aspiring actors must learn to avoid. For Darwin "steps on his lines" and he "drops his lines."

Actors soon learn that whenever they have something to say that they want to be sure the audience hears and retains, they must pause ever so slightly before going on. If they race on without such a pause, it is said they are "stepping on their lines," and no one gets the point they needed to make.

The other problem is well known to anyone who has ever acted as either an amateur or professional—that horrible moment, all too often unrealized by any but one's mystified co-players, when one's memory fails to supply, and so one drops a chunk of dialogue essential for comprehension of what is yet to come. This is known as "dropping one's lines." And so, all too often, Darwin in the original either steps on his lines or drops his lines, thus failing to provide the reader with the necessary clarifications, summaries, transitions, and all the other little touches that in a line or two make all the difference between comprehension of what one is reading or being quickly out at sea.

There is also the problem of his language. By modern standards, his is overwhelmingly sexist. Everything is mind-numbingly "man," "he," "him," "mankind," etc. His use of the word "savage" everywhere for anyone not properly civilized is also guaranteed to set the teeth of the multiculturally sensitive on edge. He also occasionally uses words like "disapprobation" where today we would use "disapproval," or "whilst" where we would use "while." This seems a minor matter, but such is the ahistoricity, parochialism, and intolerance of our vaunted modernity that on such slight grounds we speedily reject anything from the past today as not worthwhile.

To top off all this there is the problem of what Darwin's scholarly guardians of both long ago and recent years have done with *Descent*. Alas, considering all this, how is it the poor man ever got even a single reader for his vision over the years!

The most startling fact in this regard is further testimony to the power of paradigm. For although Darwin actually writes of moral development and morality 90 times in **Descent**, there is only a single entry for the word in the official index!

In other words, for over 100 years all those who zip in and out of books with scholarly efficiency by reading a book by index rather than text have been given the impression he only took up the subject once—and apparently not one of them ever saw fit to question or change this situation.

If this weren't bad enough, the problem is even further compounded by his modern caretakers. As indicated earlier, the standard edition to which are keyed the concordances is the Princeton University Press printing of the first edition of 1871.[106] What the racing guide is to the gambler at the horse track, the concordance is to the scholar. Available in either great fat books or slim CD's these days, the concordance is the invaluable key word indexing linked to pages and sources for everything one wants to track throughout some weighty reference. Now, should you possess one of these things, which most people don't, it would lead you to all 90 places where Darwin takes up the moral sense. But you would still be out of luck in key regards because of what *isn't* in the Princeton edition.

As Darwin himself tells you—should you escape the official tour and wandering about discover his Preface to later editions of *Descent*—the later editions contain "several important corrections" and "a surprising number of new facts and remarks," all prompted by "the fiery ordeal through which the book has passed."[107] And so, indeed, I found the later editions do contain additions bearing on both his moral theory and his attempt to complete his theory as a whole. As the notes reflect, this forced me to work with the headache of having to bounce back and forth between editions. The problem is best dramatized, however, by my discovery in the Preface to a later edition the clue to Darwin's startling perception over 100 years ago of one of the main tenets of modern chaos theory.

"...nor must we forget what I have called 'correlated' growth," he writes in what is missing from the concordanced and thereby basic Princeton edition, "meaning, thereby, that various parts of the organisation are in some unknown manner so connected, that when one part varies, so do others; and if variations in the one are accumulated by selection, other parts will be modified."[108]

Here we see what in his computerized analysis of weather patterns, the Nobel Prize Winner Edward Lorenz identified in 1960 as in part the operation of the strange attractor in chaos theory! More popularly, this is known as the Butterfly Effect.[109]

There is a good bit more to the story here, but the rest of the problems must be detailed in the General Guide to Selections at the end of this chapter.[110] Only by happenstance did I wander on this preface in which the clue to chaos theory is prefigured. On the bookshelf in my study for years, gathering dust unopened, was a beloved first edition of an 1879 printing of the 1874 edition passed down to me from my great-great-grandfather.[111] On impulse one day, I took it down—and there it was. Chaos theory, by gosh!

The cover is stained with no doubt the sweat of many thumbs over the years, and the pages are yellow and crumbling, but at least it sits there on my shelf intact after all this time—safe from the vagaries of Darwin's scholarly guardians and modern publishing.

All this, I hate to mention, still only scratches the surface of the difficulties for anyone trying to rescue Darwin from the clutches of the paradigm, but as

William Blake wrote, *Enough or too much!* It all adds up to something similar to the long time layer of grime and smoke so obscuring an old painting that one can no longer see that here we have a Michelangelo. So my textual editing has chiefly been directed to taking care of all these problems. I use the later edition to fill in the gaps in what has become the standard edition. I have practically done away with the semi-colon in order to provide both Darwin and his modern reader with the relief of modern sentence structure, paragraphing, and subheading. I have further modernized Darwin's language for gender sensitivity and dropped a good bit of the material dealing with "savages" in the original. I have also straightened out or shortened and smoothed an awkward or ungraceful line here and there.

There are Darwinian scholars to whom any such changes will of course be considered the kind of heresy for which burning at the stake would be mild punishment. But to paraphrase what Mark Anthony said of Caesar, my purpose here is to liberate Darwin from his friends, not to further bury him. For those who want to find out precisely what he said in the original, this is clearly, if not indeed doggedly, indicated in the notes. I believe scholars will also find there everything else they may want to know.

The Challenge of Building the Better Theory and the Better Story of Evolution

As for my step-by-step reconstruction of Darwin's magnificent theory of the moral agent and first steps toward completion for the larger theory, this too I believe is adequately explained in the text as well as the notes.

This reconstruction will of course be closely scrutinized by those with an investment in clinging fiercely to—as well as those interested in broadening and liberalizing—both the prevailing picture and theory of Darwin. With the needs of both parties in mind, it is important to realize that what we are dealing with here is not a completed theory with everything in apple-pie order. Again in musical terms, I think Darwin's theory of the moral agent is like Mozart's Requiem, a majestic fragment that others have attempted to finish from Mozart's notes, or like Schubert's Unfinished Symphony, which critics revere for what is there rather than fault for what is not.

As for the completion of his theory of evolution, I think what is here is akin to the fragments of a Rosetta Stone, which made it possible for archeologists and linguists to at last translate the lost language of the Egyptians.

These are more than fragments, but less than the whole thing. The task, as I see it, calls for an investment by three kinds of people interacting over the years ahead. First is the need for the completion of a full spectrum, action-oriented Darwinian theory by the science of the 21st century. Second is the need for completion of a full spectrum, action-oriented story of evolution by the writers, artists, and musicians of a new generation. Last is the use of both theory and story as a guide to a better way of life by the readership for the "new" Darwin that the publication of this book at long last makes possible.

Briefly projected in Part III, using what is here both as the groundwork and as a partial framework for the larger theory of evolution in keeping with Darwin's vision, it is the task for the hundreds if not thousands of biologists who are already trying, in a situation of great difficulty, to move in this direction. But even more decisively, it is the task for the psychologists, sociologists, and other social scientists who long ago abandoned this quest, but now, of pivotal importance, must again take it up. And it is the task for the systems scientists, who provide the liberating perspective for and vital bridge between the two.

In regard to this most urgent of undertakings for both science and society, I do not attempt to tie up all the loose ends. In both my commentary throughout Part II, which contains Darwin's writings, and the very brief Part III, which lays out what Darwin's lost theory seems to mean for the science and society of the 21st century, my purpose is mainly to try to make it possible for others to arrive at their own conclusions and completions of theory.

This includes very much the everyday reader, the nonscientist—that is, for most of you out there who will read this book, for whom I have worked very hard to make it both readable and enjoyable. This is information that I believe must be rapidly and widely shared if it is to be used to help construct the better future we must gain for our children, their children, and for all species, including ours, before our time runs out.

It is a thrilling thought that after all these years of being bottled up by the multifaceted prevailing paradigm, as well as by the vicissitudes of recent years in trying to find a publisher bold enough to at last reveal what is here uncovered, the breaching of the barricades is at hand.[112] Through the happenstance of a publishing venture combining Internet with bookstore distribution, the full power of Darwin's vision can now leap over and otherwise bypass all the old barriers to find a global readership via the World Wide Web as well as through the bookstores. Had there been the free flow of information on the Internet 100 years ago—with its potential for high flight over the quicksand of paradigm—could this better half of Darwin been lost?

This kind of breakthrough for the liberation of the greater mind is a hopeful sign for the future. But it is only the first step in a long journey we must now compress into the shortest possible stretch of time. It is only the first step for the rebuilding of theory and story we must now undertake to make up for all the time we have lost, and now with the clock running out.

A General Guide to Selections from The Descent of Man.

1. *Selections are from two sources.* The 1871 edition published by Princeton University Press, to which most concordances are keyed, has become the standard edition for most scholars. Darwin, however, made many important changes in and additions to the revised edition of 1874, which—although this leads to some confusion—I decided to draw on also

as it is superior to the earlier edition, including useful data and observations beginning to disappear from scholarly sources that key solely to the 1871 edition. It includes a table to all additions made to the earlier edition and Darwin's addition of an important essay by Thomas Huxley comparing the brains of apes and humans. Some idea of the advantage of the later edition can be gained from Darwin's observation that he is able here "to introduce several important corrections," having "endeavored to profit by the fiery ordeal through which the book has passed," also adding "a surprising number of new facts and remarks" provided by his correspondents.

The copy of the later edition I key to was published in the Encyclopedia Britannica-University of Chicago Great Books series— which provides neither the fact that this is the later edition of 1874 nor the important Preface Darwin added, but does include both *Origin and Descent* in a single volume, which is handy (see references).

2. *Page referencing.* As practically everybody works with the Princeton edition, endnote numbers at the end of each subhead key to the page number in this edition, indicating the page where the selection or selections under each subhead begin. *Unless indicated otherwise, page numbers are for the Princeton edition.* Wherever inserts are made of Darwin's later addition of data or observations, endnote numbers within the text key to page numbers for the Great Books edition.

3. *Differences from the original.* For the reasons given in the Introduction, although most of the writing is unchanged, its exclusively male referents have been changed to gender-neutral equivalents. As also explained in the Introduction, other changes to make Darwin accessible to the modern reader include new and frequent subheading, new and frequent paragraph breaks, and occasional rewriting of a sentence or two to untangle garbled or unintelligible passages (see Introduction re Darwin's difficulties). These selections also vary from the original in being *excerpts.* That is, I have cut material that risks becoming boring or excessive, doesn't fit the subhead, or for reasons of the readership sensitivities explained in the Introduction.

PART II
The Theory

CHAPTER SIX

THE BIOLOGY AND THE VISION

Like an old letter in the attic from a forgotten ancestor to some forgotten friend, Darwin's theory of "the moral sense" is by now, as we have seen, so slight a thing within the modern mind as to barely register. Because of the new meaning it takes on in terms of the science of the 21st century, and a surprising activist thrust, it is overdue for renaming. Accordingly, this reconstruction is of what may more appropriately be called Darwin's theory of the moral *agent*.

Darwin developed this theory of the moral agent in two periods of intense creativity. The first and most basic statement appears in the set of notes he jotted down after his return from the famous voyage of the Beagle. As the private notebooks of his youth were unpublished until comparatively recently, this part was to remain unknown for 136 years.[113]

The theory has three levels: biological, then social and systems scientific, and finally, and primarily, psychological. In their relation to one another, these levels of theory are roughly analogous to the basement, first story, and second story of a house.

There is first the vision of the early notebooks—a primarily biological theory of how over millions of years the moral sense rises out of the evolution of sexual, parental, and social instincts, capped by the development of emotion and reason. This level we will explore in this chapter.

Next, Darwin develops the second level for his moral theory and also attempts to move ahead with his larger, more general theory of evolution, of which the moral theory is to provide the higher motivational thrust. This is the sprawling rumination of *Descent* that foreshadows, as well as in key ways transcends, the development of psychology, sociology, anthropology, and systems science well into the 20th century. It is a theory of how not just natural selection and random variation, but also much else all works together in the development of moral sensitivity and moral agency. Instincts, sympathy, love, pleasure, pain, selfishness, mutual aid or altruism, the acquisition of language, habit, imitation, reason, courage—all this he finds is of driving significance in the evolutionary journey for our species covered here in Chapters 7 through 11. He also finds the surprise of what has long seemed obvious to many people, but has been rigorously left out of Darwin by his successors—the idea that education, religion, and spirituality are also involved in the evolution of our species.

Here, too, we are to uncover what will be either the most controversial or the most exciting of findings for this book—the rediscovery by Darwin of what was possibly first discovered by the ancient Chinese, then repeatedly rediscovered, refined, and renamed throughout the 20th century. This is the multiple discovery of "organic choice" as a core self-organizing drive for evolution comparable in impact to that of natural selection.

Last comes the surprise that ends Part II of this book, with Chapter 11. Leaping ahead nearly eighty years, Darwin anticipates the psychology of health and love we associate today with Abraham Maslow and humanistic psychology—as well as a psychology of moral transcendence still to be realized.

A Brief Historical Perspective

Before we get underway, we must first ground ourselves and the future in the relevant past. As we take up the three levels for this theory over the next several chapters, we will be looking at them in relation to at least four great streams for the development of science between Darwin's time and ours. Here is a quick sketch of what they are.

One stream is the development of scientific theory that began with the earlier period of big, exciting, all-purpose theories we are about to return to. Just as the voyage of the Beagle, Stanley's search for Livingston in Africa, and Heinrich Schliemann's discovery of ancient Troy captured one compartment of the imagination of that time, so did the Really Big Theories take over another part of mind. It was the 19th century of the holistic macrotheories of thinkers such as Darwin with Natural Selection, Marx and Engels with Dialectical Materialism, and Herbert Spencer with various Big Theories that have long since died on the vine.[114]

Sustained into the 20th century by Freud with Psychoanalysis and Einstein with Relativity Theory, this macro thrust was followed by the proliferation of all the smaller, special-purpose microtheories that have bubbled up from the stream for science over most of the 20th century. Field theory, cognitive dissonance theory, bootstrap theory—they all had their day and created their own pools of excitement, but in comparison to what preceded them they often seemed like the darting about of schools of minnows after the sportive splashing of dolphins or the mighty plashing of whales.

Now, as we move into the 21st century, a new kind of theory rises from this stream that combines the bold size and scope of 19th century thinking with the more cautious and detailed understanding of parts of the whole that characterized the science of the early and mid 20th century. Here, for example, we find the theories of thermodynamicist Ilya Prigogine, biologists Stuart Kauffman and Vilmos Csanyi, and systems philosopher Ervin Laszlo. This new kind of theory—which we will begin to get into in Chapter 7—rose from the House that Jack Built development of systems science, which led to general systems theory,[115] which in turn has led to the development of what is known as general evolution theory.[116]

A second stream—by and large walled off from sight by the towering concrete of the prevailing scientific paradigm—is of the development of scientific theories of morality. These range from the 19th century pioneering of Immanuel Kant, Marx and Engels, and Herbert Spencer into the 20th century with Sigmund Freud in psychology and Emile Durkheim in sociology through J.M. Baldwin, Jean Piaget, Erich Fromm, Lawrence Kohlberg, and Carol Gilligan in psychology.[117]

A third stream is the enticing, ever fascinating flow of new discoveries in brain research, with high points such as the uncovering and substantiation of the *active* brain by Karl Pribram and Alexander Luria, and the *moral* brain by Paul MacLean.[118] A fourth stream is the development—going far beyond the database available to Darwin at the time of one of his most uncanny intuitions—of an understanding of the biology of the emergence and the dynamics of sex in evolution prefiguring the theories of biologist Lynn Margulis as well as biology more generally.[119]

It is these last two streams we will dip into in exploring the first tenets of Darwin's theory of the "moral agent."

A Statement of the First Level for The Theory of the Moral Agent

"May not the moral sense arise from our strong sexual, parental, and social instincts." This is what Darwin jotted down in the M Notebook in 1838. He was only 29 at the time—two years after returning to England from the famous voyage of the Beagle.[120]

He further speculates: "May not this give rise to 'do unto others as yourself' and 'love thy neighbour as thyself.'"[121]

Still later he completes the track for his thinking: "Therefore I say grant reason to any animal with social and sexual instincts and yet with passion he *must* have conscience."[122]

Whatever all this means, one has to admit it is impressive for a 29 year old—or of any other age.

At first reading it may seem to be no more than a peculiar juxtaposition of Jesus and the Bible with, of all things, sex. Yet in these three terse notes, jotted down by Darwin soon after he returned from the pivotal voyage, he makes a striking statement of scientific theory.

Admittedly, this is at first difficult to see. But when, through reconstruction, we can bring to these long-lost passages the perspective out of which they emerged, they loom as a first statement of theory not unlike Einstein's $E = mc^2$ in its capacity to pack much into a small space.[123]

Within science the strategic importance of this first-level statement is that its sexual base, or point of origin, is rooted in biology. It also provides the long-lost link between the first and the second halves for Darwin's theory. That is, it provides a link between the primarily biological theories of natural selection and (as later developed by others) random variation, with which Darwin is almost exclusively identified today, and his higher-level theory of moral agency.

To reconstruct the first level for Darwin's lost theory, I will restate it here in the form of the step-by-step propositions or "tenets" once commonly used in building scientific theory.

Tenet I:
"May not the moral sense arise from our strong sexual, parental, and social instincts."

Here Darwin first states his hypothesis that we are impelled toward goodness by a specific sequence of events, or evolutionary stages, which gradually, within trillions of creatures over billions of years upon this planet, embed within us the drive of the "moral sense," or moral sensitivity, as we would call it today.

Sex and Morality

This developmental sequence is rooted—first, most fundamentally, and with a range of ramifications—in the emergence of sex about a billion years ago, an event establishing what Darwin defines as the sexual instinct.[124]

What we know today greatly amplifies but does not change the priority and precise grounding of Darwin's original intuition. In numerous ways he anticipated the groundbreaking work of biologist Lynn Margulis and brain scientist Paul MacLean, whose far more detailed work with a modern database of fossils, living organisms, and the structural wonders of our own brains corroborates Darwin's original intuitions and discoveries.

From the work of Margulis and others, we know that prior to the billion-year-ago emergence of sex differences, life perpetuated itself through asexual reproduction, including forms of self-division whereby an organism would in effect make a copy of itself.[125] Though opinions vary today among biologists as to why "fully" sexual or meiotic reproduction came into being, two things about this emergence are notable.

The first is that by joining the subtly different genetic structures of two separate beings through mating, this biological innovation vastly increased the possibilities for generating the variability, diversity, and complexity of species that has produced the richness that is the wonder of life on this planet.[126]

In other words, out of a more sterile earlier time of self-reproducing "clones," reproduction by sexual coupling released an explosion of creativity through a process compelling a sexual partnership with another organism.

Secondly, if we carefully consider the situation at that time—before sexual reproduction emerged—as far as the basic need for life to perpetuate itself was concerned, each organism existed in a state of comparative self-sufficiency and isolation from other organisms.

I say comparative self-sufficiency because, as the pioneering work of biologist Lynn Margulis points out, there were numerous arrangements for the symbiotic involvements of one organism with another. One organism, for example, would provide the housing for another. Or the waste products of one would provide food for another. Most dramatically, according to Margulis, one component of what we think of as sex today may have originally emerged from a predator-prey relationship—of the cannibalism of one organism eating another and the eaten creature remaining alive within its host.

This may seem a strange beginning point for one evolutionary track for the build-up of the symbiotic relationship. But as Margulis notes—recapping what we can now see lay at the core of the Darwinian vision—"Partnership between cells once foreign and even enemies to each other are at the very roots of our being."[127]

Darwin specifically anticipates Margulis in a long-ignored observation on the last page of *The Origin of Species*, which he further pursues in *Descent*. As we will explore in the context of self-organizing processes in Chapter 8, this is his observation that the "mutual relation of organism to organism" lies at the core of evolutionary process.[128]

Within *Origin* this seems no more than a casual observation. But within the context of his work as a whole, behind this observation lay an immense body of his own work often thought to be merely the escapist diversion that delayed the writing and publication of *The Origin of Species*. This was his detour into the study of the sex life of barnacles. [129]

Beginning as no more than the plan for a single article, barnacles became the eight-year obsession and two-volume set of books that almost allowed Wallace to preempt the discovery of the principle of natural selection.[130]

One of the things that most fascinated Darwin about barnacles was the existence of tiny males that lived within the females of some species. As he vividly put it, "half embedded in the flesh of their wives," in some cases little more than an "enormous coiled penis," they lived within a pocket in which "she kept a little husband."[131] This was a relationship Margulis further defined, pointing it in the same direction as Darwin in her interpretation of a long-range meaning for the evolution of organisms culminating with the development of moral sensitivity in ourselves.

Such symbiotic relationships, benign and otherwise, Margulis and others have shown, provide the path to the jump in evolution represented by the development of meiotic sex—or the first coupling for the first transitory act of sexual union.

Now prior to this first sexual coupling, the organism certainly had to be intimately aware of "the other" in prior situations of symbiosis—particularly if one had been eaten and from within the host had to find some way to survive. And in the very fact of symbiosis—that is of the cooperative need of one organism for another in order to survive—the basis for caring for another was biologically established. This is also the motif of Margulis' theory of symbiogenesis, as the generation of new life forms through the merging of species.[132]

At the same time, it seems evident that before this decisive stage of sexual coupling, each organism, in a profoundly basic way, was impelled to *care* mainly for itself. The organism would have been aware of, and in some dim way beginning to care about the existence of the other, but it seems unquestionable that prior to meiotic sex caring for oneself would have remained the overwhelming consideration.

Within the complexity of this context, it further seems evident that the emergence of meiotic sex must have represented the pivotal crystallization, or step upward, of the idea of *caring for another*.[133] With the emergence of dependency on sexual reproduction for the perpetuation of life, organisms would have been forced out of themselves in this particularly enticing new way.

They would have been forced out of their previous comparative isolation to periodically feel an urgent new need for another organism of a very special type—an organism very much like themselves in general appearance, but at the same time subtly differing from themselves in sexual equipment.

They would have been, for the first time, for however brief a moment—even for a second in a tiny lifetime—forced to consider intimately the separate nature and separate needs of another organism. In other words, they would have been forced to assign the special value to another that today we would call *caring for another*.[134]

They were, in short, impelled to cross the barrier between organisms to form the symbiotic bridge of sexual connection that becomes the grounding for the special connectivity of life to life that for Darwin was the prime drive for evolution at our level. In this tracking of a development over at least one billion years by modern biological research and theory, we may find confirmation for Darwin's long buried theory. Out of sex there rose up the evolutionary basis for what eventually became moral sensitivity. And out of this thrust there eventually came to rise up and walk upon this earth the moral intelligence and the moral agency that, in turn, became the basis for the better part of what we know today as morality.

Does this mean that every time we have sex we are being moral? Or that every act of sex from a kiss to rape is moral? Of course not. It simply means that, in terms of *evolutionary beginning points*, what eventually became morality began with the hunger, search for, and discovery of the glory of the sexual connection.

The Parental Instinct

Once an origin for the stream of development we are examining had been established with the innovation and imbedding of the "sexual instincts," the next step up for the biological evolution of the moral sense seems to have emerged out of the result of trillions upon trillions of matings over many millions of years.

For a long time the vast birth of multi-billions of new beings was characterized by one very revealing thing: *They had to be able to immediately care for themselves in order to survive.*

Not only did newborn organisms provide food for all the roaming hordes of well-established foragers and predators. Often, as we may still see today, for example among species of reptiles, unless they were by instinct clever and quick in getting the hell out of the way, their own parents ate them. But eventually came the new turning point that Darwin characterized as the development of *the parental instinct*, where organisms are instinctively impelled to protect and nurture their offspring.

As the work of brain scientist Paul MacLean and others reveals, although foreshadowed earlier, this capacity for the parent to care for the child appears for certain with the emergence of the reptiles.[135] In work both anticipated by and corroborating the 29-year-old Darwin's intuition, MacLean found that for organisms to reliably care for their offspring, their brains must be developed to the point where they contain a certain necessary part of what is known as the limbic system. This structure, known as the septal subdivision, first reliably appears with the emergence of the reptiles.

We can see this new capacity for the evolution of life upon this planet—the caring for the offspring by the parent—operating most dramatically in museum representations and in movies of the dinosaurs. In the movie *Jurassic Park*—or in the fascinating animated children's film *The Land Before Time Began*—we may see touching reconstructions of how 235 million years ago the dinosaurs cared for their offspring in building nests, and in sitting upon to warm, or otherwise protect, the eggs out of which the new being is to emerge.

The Social Instincts

Finally, atop the prior emergence and evolutionary embedding of the sexual and the parental instincts, again after more millions of years, we have the situation that gives rise to the *social instincts*.

Out of all this coupling and parental caring driven by the sexual instincts and parental instincts—out of this vast process of gene-swapping and the "mystery dance"[136] of variability—millions of different kinds of organisms of widely varying kinds and developmental levels had spread over the planet. Stage by stage they emerged: jellyfish, sea pens, flat worms. Trilobites, clams, snails. Jawed fishes. Insects. The first trees, the first amphibians. And at last the dinosaurs.[137]

Now began the grounding of this third step in evolution, the innovation and imbedding of the "social instincts" that Darwin repeatedly focuses on in his analysis of the operation of natural selection, and of what lies *beyond* natural selection.[138] For more millions of years all these organisms clustered together by species, not only preying upon one another but also sharing warmth, mates, sometimes food, and protecting one another.

In this sense, they were displaying a rudimentary but fundamental degree of caring for one another. But about 216 million years ago, with the appearance of the first mammals, the development of the "moral sense" took a decisive step upward. For now appeared a new kind of creature with an unusual capacity for the special valuing of others—even the deep driving need for, and cherishing of, their company—that we call sociability.

These were what become known as the social animals—the step up from the so-called cold-blooded species of fish to dolphins and whales, or from land animals to the higher reptiles and mammals, including ourselves.

In searching for a way to account for this move to the next level up in the development of the moral sense, Darwin originally came up with an ingenious idea of how moral sensitivity expanded with the emergence of our particular kind of species. This was a special application of the principle of natural selection today called *group selection*.[139] The prevailing idea had been—and still is—that natural selection not only shaped the species but also the individual in the sense of differences in our color of eyes, skin, hair, height, and so on. But this wouldn't work for moral advancement, other theorists in Darwin's time decided. Moral evolution just could not be explained by natural selection.

For example, wouldn't the moral individual, caring for others and thereby more vulnerable and open to attack, always be prey for the predators who were "more fit" according to the requirements of survival of the fittest? Wouldn't the good and their children be stamped out, rather than advance and even sometimes prevail, in evolution?

It is a question that still comes up today—for example, in relation to the cultural transformation theory outlined in *The Chalice and the Blade and Tomorrow's Children* by evolution theorist Riane Eisler.[140] In Chalice,

Eisler tracks the struggle throughout our species' history of people orienting to the peaceful, equalitarian, and morally sensitive "partnership model" to survive in a world filled with others all too often orienting to the violent, hierarchic, and morally insensitive "dominator model." The practical question that comes up again and again is: are the partnership people always doomed to be conquered, or otherwise put down, by the more callous, uncaring, and potentially vicious dominators?

While laying the foundation for the moral sense in writing *Descent*, a solution came to Darwin. What he saw—adding this in a touch to the fifth edition of *Origin*, which he was working on at the time—seemed to override the impact of natural selection pitting individual against individual. What about the impact of group pitted against group, tribe against tribe, or community against community? Yes, indeed, here such qualities as loyalty and all other forms of caring for one another would bind the members of a community together. This would so strengthen the good community that it could prevail against its enemies, and thereby prevail in the survival of the fittest, and goodness would advance among us over time.

We will see what he specifically said about this in the next chapter. We will also take a look at why—although group or community selection remains both a good argument and a potential source of comfort to partnership people trying to prevail within dominator systems today—there is a problem with this explanation. Something more powerful is needed to account for the next step up in the development of the moral sense. Here Darwin also knew the answer—but lacking something else we only know today, going solely by intuition, he didn't know he knew it at the time.

That "something else," again, was modern brain research. In terms of brain development, the work of Paul MacLean reveals how with the arrival on this planet of the social animals, the capacity for moral sensitivity advances with the emergence of the third of the three main parts of the limbic system—the structure given the jawbreaking name of thalamocingulate division.

Few other brain structures so dramatically reveal the evolutionary building of the moral sense, or the power of Darwin's visionary understanding of the origin and foundational nature of what he called "the social instincts."

In 1937, the noted brain scientist James Wenceslas Papez first observed that a structure within this third, and newest, part of the limbic system "may be looked on as the receptive area for experiencing emotion."[141] Other suggestive things about this area were noticed. Humans with injuries to this area were subject to wild fits of laughter or uncontrollable crying.[142] Monkeys so injured "showed no grooming or acts of affection" and would walk over their cage mates "as though they were inanimate."[143]

The most striking thing that Paul MacLean found in his own studies of reptile and mammalian brains, however, was that this particular structure was not found in reptiles. It only appears with the emergence of the mammals in evolution.

Looking more closely at this third part of the limbic system, he found that it added three highly suggestive new capacities to the animal behavioral repertoire. To the earlier rudimentary capacity for parental caring found at the reptile level, it now (1) added a new capacity for the more prolonged and intimate function of the nursing of the infant primarily by the mother—and, at times, also by the father.[144] It also (2) added the capacity for maintaining an ever-vigilant "audiovocal" contact between infant and parent. In other words, there were—as parents can quickly identify with—special arrangements for mother and child to stay within sight and hearing of one another. This advance, in particular, gave rise to the development of the "separation cry" by the infant as a signal to the mother for help.[145] But most suggestive of all to MacLean was the addition, for the first time in evolution, of (3) a new capacity for that wonderfully sportive enjoyment of one another that we call play.

The first two of these new capacities laid down the evolutionary basis for the establishment of the family as the basic social unit. But it was play that MacLean surmised must have "served originally to promote harmony in the nest, and then later in life, affiliation among members of social groups."[146]

What a far cry this is from the grim picture of our evolution that first-half Darwinism so successfully sold humanity throughout the 20th century! Instead of the cartoon picture of cave people clustering to the Chief for protection while arming to become the best killers and exploiters of others, this evokes the picture of youngsters rolling about in the meadow, or some early intertribal game of what over time became the American Indian stick ball game.

"From the standpoint of human evolution, no behavioral developments could have been more fundamental" than this brain capacity for play, MacLean tells us, because it "set the stage for a family way of life with its evolving responsibilities and affiliations that has led to world-wide acculturation."[147]

This "social bonding," in turn, seems "to have favored the evolution of the human sense of empathy and altruism."[148]

So we have this situation so far:

Strung together aeon by aeon, generation after generation, is this vast chain linking of *caring for one another* that over billions of years, acting through the lives of multi-billions of predecessor organisms, lays down the basis for the "moral sense" in our planetary ancestors.

Now let us move ahead to ourselves—to the life of each one of us, white, black, red, yellow, or brown, woman or man, rich or poor, living in all the vastly differing places of this earth. Now we may see how from the moment of the joining of sperm to egg in our own conception, to the moment of our birth, to the moment of our first suckling at the breast, to the moment of the first clustering of relatives and friends to beam down upon us in the crib, and to talk to us, and to take us up in their arms to hold us and to look upon us with love—the evolutionary foundations for this "moral sense" are further laid down within each of us today, and into the reach for our species into the future.

CHAPTER SEVEN
EMERGENCE OF THE GOLDEN RULE

So we have come a long way from the first mating within the ooze of the past. We have come all this long journey that at a more advanced level is recapitulated in the conception and birth that becomes each of us on this earth.

We have plumbed the first of the three tenets for the first level of Darwin's theory, with Tenets II and III to consider now.

Tenet I, as we have seen, was based on young Darwin's perception of the biologic of a step by step emergence of the sexual, parental, and social instincts among prehumans in establishing the foundation for the moral sense within humanity.

The next step for his thinking—or more properly, his intuition, for the thinking mainly came over the years ahead—was based on his observation that among groups of humans, scattered out and evolving at different rates over many regions of this planet, had emerged what we know today as the Golden Rule.

Here, again, is what he jotted down:

Tenet II:
"May not this give rise to 'do unto others as yourself' and 'love thy neighbour as thyself.'"

Here we have the leap of youthful intuition that joins in mind the earlier Darwin, who left England a troubled divinity student, with the new Darwin, who returned from the voyage of the Beagle a budding naturalist.

Out of that voyage that took him to the Galapagos Islands and his ponderings on species, and to the dramatic and pivotal encounter with the natives of Tierra del Fuego later to figure in these pages, came a new vision.

The billions of years of the biological embedding of the moral sense via sexual, parental, and social instincts in earlier species leads over only a few million years—he surmises—to the final stages of the biological evolution and the early stages for the cultural evolution of our own species.

So what happens next?

Young Darwin saw that out of the experience of this radically new kind of organism in forming groups and building societies that require rules for interacting with one another there would logically, over time, emerge a Rule of Rules. Yes, of course, this rule-making experience would have led to the grand guideline, ethical principle, social standard, or coding for the moral sense that we know today as the Golden Rule.

The most striking support for this aspect of Darwin's theory—which in a single sentence vaults from the biological to the cultural level—comes from a scientific perspective on the study of religion.

Given the first step in his thinking, it was evident the universality of the Golden Rule could not be merely coincidental. For out of every region, varying only in the language and specific wording, the same concept has emerged and re-emerged.

Out of India and Hinduism at least 4,000 years ago comes "Do naught unto others which would cause you pain if done to you."[149]

Some centuries later, also out of India and Buddhism, comes "Hurt not others in ways that you yourself would find hurtful."[150]

Out of this period—roughly the sixth century B.C.E., when within 100 years of one another there emerged Gautama and Buddhism in India, Zarathustra and Zoroastrianism in ancient Persia, and Lao Tsu and Taoism, and Confucius and Confucianism in China—comes this from Confucius: "What I do not wish men to do to me, I also wish not to do to them."[151]

About 570 B.C.E., working with precepts earlier ascribed to Moses, the man known today as Leviticus composed the book of the Old Testament bearing his name, which out of the Middle East gives us "Love thy neighbor as thyself"—later widely attributed to Jesus.[152]

Next, in the third century B.C.E., out of Greece and the moral philosophy of Aristotle, comes the precept that we should act toward our friends "as we would that they should act toward us."[153]

Next comes the well-known statement attributed to the Middle Eastern Jesus—and by now it is surely evident that this so-called Golden Rule is not merely some nice little saying for Poor Richard's Almanac, or for some quaint and homey stitchery on the wall. Rather, it is a fundamental and universal law for our species.

"Therefore all things whatsoever ye would that men should do to you, do ye even so to them: for this is the law and the prophets."[154]

Five centuries later, out of Arabia, Mohammed counsels, "No one of you is a believer until he desires for his brother that which he desires for himself."[155]

Then out of the years of the Enlightenment—during the 18th century with its rallying cry of freedom and equality, and the transition for our species out of tyranny into the enormous expansion of political, economic, and educational opportunities that characterizes modern times—comes the restatement of Immanuel Kant's famous Categorical Imperative.

This is of considerable importance in this context, as it is not coincidental that Darwin, as we will see in the next chapter, evokes Kant in his discussion of the evolution of the moral sense.

As I develop elsewhere in detail,[156] Kant was one of the leading scientists of his time before he became better known as a philosopher. Kant was also a predecessor of Darwin in evolutionary theory—he wonders how "an orang-outang or a chimpanzee" might develop into the "articulated structure of a human being."[157] He was also the first to attempt to translate the Golden Rule into the language and scientific perspective of "modern times."

"Act only on that principle which thou canst will should become a universal law," Kant first tells us.[158]

To restate it in terms of "natural laws," he rephrases it this way:

"Act as if the principle of thy action were to become by thy will a universal law of nature."[159]

And then once again from still another perspective—for Kant was a professor in the little North German town of Koenigsburg, and he knew how often one had to drill the point into one's students to make sure they got it:

"So act as to treat humanity, whether in thine own person or in the person of another, as an end withal, never as a means only."[160]

It is no wonder, then, that it is with a quote from Kant that Darwin opens the great later statement of his theory of the moral sense, of moral intelligence, and of moral agency in *The Descent of Man*. He knew where he came from historically as well as where he hoped to go. As Kant had pinned his theory to the universality of the Golden Rule, so he Darwin would now both corroborate Kant's insight and pin his own theory to its evolutionary foundation.

Tenet III:
"Therefore I say grant reason to any animal with social and sexual instincts and yet with passion he must have conscience."

Now we come to the final stage for the biological level of Darwin's theory of the evolution of the moral sense. Again, as with the earlier tenets, seldom has so much been compressed into a single line.

Tenet I states his conviction that the moral senses arises "from our strong sexual, parental, and social instincts." In embedding the sexual, parental, and social instincts within all organisms, including ourselves, he is emphasizing that by doing this evolution succeeded in laying the biological *foundation* for the moral sense. But now we are to consider how upon this foundation is built the *superstructure*. We move from the realm of the first half to that of the second half of his theory of evolution.

This shift is reflected in the note quoted above and in another closely related passage in the youthful notebooks in which Darwin jotted down his thoughts on returning from the voyage of the Beagle.

If we look at the dog—he ponders in one of these notebooks—we can see this division between animal and human that must seize the mind.[161] We share with the dog and all other social animals this foundation of sexual, parental, and social instincts. But although our dog can obviously love us, as we can love him or her, the emotional range for the dog is radically limited in comparison to ours.

Likewise, although our dog (or the monkeys, elephants, bears, rats, fish, and the vast range of other species he looks at in the next chapter here)[162] can display intelligence and reason, again, this capacity is radically limited in comparison to ours.

Similarly, if we compare the dog with ourselves as a moral being, we come upon the same limitations.

Certainly the dog can display many qualities we associate with morality, such as faithfulness, loyalty, courage, caring, and love. The dog can further even display the rudiments of a conscience (as Darwin later develops). But when it comes to a full-blown capacity for differentiating right from wrong or good from evil—such as becomes possible for a majority of humans—again we come upon a fundamental difference.

But what if through magic the dog (or any comparable animal) were suddenly provided with both our emotional range and our intellectual capacity, what then? Would the dog similarly have this full-blown capacity for differentiating right from wrong, or a conscience much as ours?

To this, Darwin's answer ("Therefore I say grant reason...and yet with passion he must have conscience") is a most emphatic yes.

Again his power of observation and intuition is confirmed by modern brain research. For what brain research finds is the following complex but revealing picture. Though we share with dogs and comparable animals all of the three major structures for the limbic system—which accounts for the foundational range for our emotions—our limbic development is already considerably advanced over earlier species in evolutionary sophistication.[163]

Now if to the "emotional brain" of the limbic system is added the phenomenal expansion of the cerebrum and cerebral cortex so striking with our species—particularly the expansion of the frontal brain lobes—the gulf between ourselves and prior species dramatically widens both in brain physiology and in capacity for feeling, thinking, and behavior.

What happens with this late evolutionary addition to the basic brain for prior organisms are two key developments.

One is the arrival of an enormous enrichment in emotional variety and intensity. This enrichment of emotion Darwin indicates with his use of the word "passion." Immediately following *Descent*, he goes on to develop this train of thought in *The Expression of the Emotions in Man and Animals*.[164]

The other development, he is telling us, with corroboration by modern brain research, is an escalation of *reason*—the capacity long seen as most characteristic of our species that in its departure from what led to it is like a rocket soaring out of nature.

The intricacies of this expansion for emotion and reason are played out both in the difference in size and complexity of the neuronal interlinking between the limbic system and the cerebrum of our human biology.

In particular, we find the ascendancy in relation to the frontal regions of the brain involved in the operation of moral sensitivity—that is, the *moral sense*. We may further perceive how this capacity is interlinked to other brain areas for storage of the memories of what turned out to be right, versus wrong, for everything we did in the pastor—which becomes the stored learning for our *moral intelligence*. Finally, we can see how the "messages" from these areas shoot on to the belt of the "motor areas" that horizontally cross the top of our brain, to result in the *moral action* or behavior that constitutes moral agency.

The work of many brain researchers—for example, Pribram, Luria, Halstead, Freeman, Damasio, Elliot[165]—quite literally "fleshes" out this quick sketch, but the relationships were first seen, and are easiest to follow, in the work of Paul MacLean. Two passages from MacLean best suggest key aspects of this interrelationship.

MacLean observes that it is in the prefrontal areas of the brain adjacent to the limbic system that we find the neuronal capacity "to see with feeling" that makes possible "planning for ourselves and others."[166]

All in all, from a footing in the hypothalamus, then step by step rising through the limbic structures into the cloudlike configuration of the prefrontal cortex of frontal "higher" brain, MacLean beautifully captures the lyrical ascendancy of this evolutionary thrust from the deep past into the aspirational future. He speaks of "a neural ladder, a visionary ladder, for ascending from the most primitive sexual feeling to the highest level of altruistic behavior."[167]

It is also at this prefrontal cortex level—as the brain research of Karl Pribram and Alexander Luria defined[168]—that our highest, most complex and forceful capacity for decision-making and initiating action exists.

In other words, here atop all the other rungs in the brain for the ascendancy of moral sensitivity up this neural ladder we find the brain substrata for *moral agency*—or the thrust to take action on the behalf of others.

And here again, over 150 years ago, 29-year-old Darwin, fresh off the boat from going around the world, anticipated all these findings!

This brain-driven insistence on action is the necessary thrust of *will*, or intentionality—which Darwin alludes to with his striking use of the word "passion" in this third tenet for the biological level of his theory.

"Therefore I say grant reason to any animal with social and sexual instincts and yet with passion he *must* have conscience," he tells us.

Passion implying the thrust of emotion, yes, but also passion implying the thrust of moral agency.

Thus, here in the brain research that has provided so much of the excitement in science during the 20th century—typically, all of it dealing with our moral capacities even yet almost wholly ignored—can be found the long-delayed corroboration of this first of the three levels for Darwin's lost theory.

Here in the most solid and hypothetically least disputable kind of finding for science—in the visible, tangible, testable structures revealed by modern brain research ranging from surgery to electronic mind mapping—can be found the point-for-point substantiation of the first, and most foundational, level for Darwin's theory of moral sense and moral agency.

Tenet I, Tenet II, and Tenet III—they all "stack up" and make sense after all these years. The first and foundational level for his theory "checks out," as we would say today.

In other words, prior to and during Darwin's time there were others, for example David Hume, Adam Smith, and various theologians, who had theories about "the moral sense."[169] For this reason, it has been assumed that Darwin's contribution was probably not original, or at best only a naive and unlettered intrusion into philosophy or religion. But as we have seen, modern science—in particular, systems science, brain research, much ignored or peripheralized social science, and a modern biological understanding of the evolutionary emergence of sex—shows that the long lost observations of young Darwin provide us with a rock-firm foundation for the first well grounded, scientific theory of what makes us good and drives us to do good in the world.

Moreover, rather than being only a theory of moral sense—or the capacity to resonate to the ills of this world—Darwin also identifies in his later writings the territory and way stations for a theory of moral *intelligence* and moral *agency*, or what drives and gives us the courage to confront the ills of this world and take action to remedy them. For now, after many pages to explain what the young Darwin managed to pack into three terse sentences, we are almost ready to move ahead thirty years to Darwin at age 60, as he returns to develop the second and third levels of the theory of the moral agent.

I say "almost" because we must explore another part of the story before we move on to the next level for this second half for Darwin's theory.

It is a story with a twist as consequential as any I know of, as well as a moral in more ways than one.

Goodbye to Sex

It took me a good bit of time to detect this, and then much longer to figure out what it meant. For from this point on Darwin will never again link the sexual instinct to the moral sense. Nowhere in his published writings do we find this pivotal observation—nor in his letters, or even in a single unguarded remark picked up by those who cluster about the famous, jotting down notes on what they say for later reporting.

In other words, between the time young Darwin shared this dangerous thought with his private notebooks and the expansion of his moral theory in *The Descent of Man* thirty years later, he wrote hundreds of pages on practically every other aspect of sex as it relates to evolution. Indeed, one might say the subject became almost as obsessional for Darwin as soon it was to become, more notoriously, for Sigmund Freud.

For Darwin sexual selection was a major force, along with natural selection, in the evolution of all species. Besides attention to this factor in *The Origin of Species* and many other publications, in *Descent* he gives roughly seven times as much space to sexual selection as to the moral sense—thirteen chapters and parts of two others. But in all these pages that are fairly bathed in every other aspect of sex, and even though his original insight at age 29 was of pivotal scientific and social importance in linking the billion-year-old emergence of sex with the later rise of morality, no longer are we to detect even a hint that he ever had so rash a thought as to link sex in evolution to Jesus and the Golden Rule.

This remained the scandalous secret of his private notebooks for over 136 years.

Why did he bury this pivotal insight throughout the rest of his lifetime? The reason is not hard to understand within the context of the science and society of his own time.

Much has been made of the fact that Darwin waited so long to publish his own basic natural selectionist theory of evolution—so long that Alfred Wallace nearly beat him to it. But Darwin did not keep his basic theory to himself for 18 years because he was slow-witted or super-cautious. The storm of protest and outrage that descended upon him when finally he was forced to publish the earlier theory of *Origin* indicates the power of disapproval that he knew awaited him. And this had not been just the disapproval—or disapprobation, as he would have put it—of livid ministers and theologians condemning him to eternal hellfire or labeling him the Anti-Christ, as the reaction is usually portrayed. Also involved was the opposition, severe questioning, and rejection of his theory by many of his scientific peers, which called forth the resounding voice and lectern-pounding of the mighty Thomas Henry Huxley to act in his defense as "Darwin's bulldog."

If such a storm could follow the announcement that human beings are descended from much lower animals, most recently a form of ape, what awaited him this time? Consider what would have happened had Darwin simply marched his earlier moral theory out of the private notebooks without omitting, as he did, the pivotal but titillating and horrifying connection to sex.

The cataclysm of *Origin* would have been nothing in comparison with the firestorm in Victorian England—where not only women, but even piano stools were, out of "sexual modesty," draped in long skirts. Sex the beginning point for morality? Heat up the tar! Get out the feathers! Look for a rope and the nearest tree!

Small wonder he decided that his rash youthful indiscretion must forever remain in the closet. In *Descent* he skips the vital beginning point to discreetly pick up the story next with the evolutionary sequence of parental instincts, social instincts, et cetera for the development of the moral sense. Yet how different our world might have been today if his guilty secret had been known, and faced, at the outset, over 150 years ago. For it is the rooting in sex that links the moral second half to the biological first half for his full spectrum theory of evolution.

Had the connection been made openly—had it been there, inescapable, fairly shoving itself upon them—it is hard to see how the biologists and other natural scientists could have avoided the implications of the theory of the moral sense for Darwin's theory as a whole.

A biologist or any other natural scientist could write off the stuff about parental and social instincts as nothing more than outdated language for what seemed to them then—as all too often even now—the woefully non-scientific territories of psychology and sociology. But sex was different. This fascinating basic activity whereby all the creatures little and big of the biologists' scientific passion proliferated over millions of years put the matter squarely within their own territory.

Had fate ruled otherwise—had Darwin simply hauled up the earlier theory wholesale, sex and all—indeed what a difference it might have made. It is hard to see how science could have gone on to fail throughout the whole of the 20th century to give humanity the theory of evolution it needed and deserved—the biologists and other hard scientists by taking over and excluding the levels of science dealing with what Darwin had gone on to insist was of the greatest importance at our level of evolution, the rest of science by letting them get away with it and by failing to take responsibility for moving its end of it ahead. In the next nine chapters, we will see what he was trying to tell us in his own words.

CHAPTER EIGHT
OUR ANIMAL HERITAGE

The Descent of Man was published in 1871, twelve years after *The Origin of Species.* As we saw in the chapters of Part I, Darwin's long ignored but avowed purpose in writing *Descent* was to go beyond the prehuman or first half theory of *Origin* to complete his theory of evolution by probing the superstructural nature of our species. Beyond the lockstep clasp of natural selection and variation, he wanted to probe possibilities for other evolutionary processes and principles at this higher or second half for his theory. This exploration swiftly centered on the pivotal question for him of the origin and nature of the moral sense—and thereby the question not just of human origins but also of the human destiny.

Darwin was 60 by then. Possibly with him on the Isle of Wight were some of his notebooks from thirty years earlier. Certainly we encounter many overtones, even whole phrases from earlier. But in the long-bypassed parts of *Descent* immediately ahead in this chapter, there is—starkly and wholly contrary to what we have been told by all avowed Darwinians who apparently who never bothered to read him on this matter—also much that is new. For Darwin is now setting out on the long-delayed, but second great intellectual journey of his life. Beyond all that he has previously pondered as a naturalist, and wanted to share about the shaping of life into all its fascinating forms, he now wants to range on beyond what he and his particular scientific circle are comfortable with into unfamiliar territory.

For now he must venture into the higher reaches of mind and behavior both for prehumans and for ourselves—a culmination of earlier trends that practically everybody he is close to is highly motivated to avoid, except for the raw young recruit George Romanes, soon thereafter to appear.

As we are to join him first in his probe of the moral world of the animals, we must be prepared to deal with two things that, although they may pose no difficulties for most of us, will be jarring to those securely indoctrinated by 20th century science. For 20th century science has regarded anthropomorphism, or the attribution of human qualities to animals, as a great sin. The other sin of sins is anecdotal evidence. As was the custom for the naturalists of his time, Darwin fairly wallows in both.

It is important to know that the other side to the coin of avoiding "anthropomorphism" and "anecdotal evidence" was the rise of the kind of cold-hearted objectivity that prevailed in the often horrendously brutal animal research of the 20th century. This is now rapidly going out of fashion, with a reversion among leading primatologists and other naturalists to the warm-hearted empathy that Darwin displays. Also, use of the anecdote, while anathema to 20th century "hard science," has long been a respectable aspect of research in anthropology, sociology, and psychology, as well as ethology. In my own experience during the 20th century, I saw the phrase "only anecdotal evidence" chiefly used either by very narrowly trained scientists or by non-scientists to try to discredit any approach to wisdom other than their own.

It may seem that Darwin also wanders a good bit from one subject to another. Sometimes he also contradicts himself. As is known by those familiar with the way he built up the earlier part of his theory in *The Origin of Species*, this is the discursive method, which can be a befuddlement but is also a great strength of Darwin's theorizing. He may wander a bit, but always he is steadily building up the database and case for his summary in Chapter 10 here of the second level for his theory of the moral sense and of moral agency.

To return to an earlier analogy, in the last two chapters he excavated and poured in the concrete for the biological foundation of his theoretical "house" of mind. In this and the next chapter, in terms of the animals preceding our species in evolutionary development, he is bringing in the materials with which he will construct the first above-ground story of this "house".

What follows is Darwin himself speaking. After the opening section, I will drop the quotes and interrupt only to *insert paragraphs, subheads, and an occasional explanation or comment in italics,* as I indicate here. **Bold face will be used to occasionally emphasize observations by Darwin** that are particularly notable or important to the further building of his theory. For a general guide to selections, see the preamble to Notes for Chapter Five.

Getting Underway

"I fully subscribe to the judgement of those writers who maintain that of all the differences between ourselves and the lower animals, the moral sense or conscience is by far the most important," Darwin writes in opening the argument that, after the gap of thirty years, is to lead to his statement of the second level for his theory of the moral agent.[170]

"This sense, as Mackintosh[171] remarks, 'has a rightful supremacy over every other principle of human action.' It is summed up in that short but imperious word *ought*, so full of high significance," he tells us.

It is the most noble of all the attributes of our species, leading us without a moment's hesitation to risk our lives for those of our fellow-creatures, or after due deliberation, impelled simply by the deep feeling of right or duty, to sacrifice our lives in some great cause.

Of this deep feeling of right or duty, Immanuel Kant exclaims, 'Duty! Wondrous thought, that workest neither by fond insinuation, flattery, nor by any threat, but merely by holding up thy naked law in the soul, and so extorting for thyself always reverence, if not always obedience.'[172]

This great question has been discussed by many writers of consummate ability. My sole excuse for touching on it is the impossibility of here passing it over, and because, as far as I know, no one has approached it exclusively from the side of natural history. This investigation possesses, also, some independent interest as an attempt to see how far the study of the lower animals throws light on one of the highest psychical faculties of our species.

The following proposition seems to me in a high degree probable— namely, that any animal whatever, endowed with well-marked social instincts, the parental and filial affections being here included, would inevitably acquire a moral sense or conscience, as soon as its intellectual powers had become as well, or nearly as well developed, as in our species.

This of course we can recognize as a restatement of our "old friend" from the private notebooks of thirty years earlier— minus so much as a hint of the forbidden connection to sex.

And so without further ado, Darwin moves on to explore the similarities and differences in the moral sense in humans and prehumans.[173]

The Early Glimmering of Conscience[174]

I do not wish to maintain that any strictly social animal, if its intellectual faculties were to become as active and as highly developed as in our species, would acquire exactly the same moral sense as ours.

In the same manner as various animals have some sense of beauty, though they admire widely different objects, so they might have a sense of right and wrong, though led by it to follow widely different lines of conduct.

If, to take an extreme case, we ourselves were reared under precisely the same conditions as hive-bees, there can hardly be a doubt that our unmarried females would, like the worker-bees, think it a sacred duty to kill their brothers, and mothers would strive to kill their fertile daughters, and no one would think of interfering. Nevertheless, the bee, or any other social animal, would gain in our supposed case, as it appears to me, some feeling of right or wrong, or a ***conscience.*** For each individual would have an inward sense of possessing certain stronger or more enduring instincts, and others less strong or enduring.

Thus, there would often be a struggle as to which impulse should be followed. And as past impressions were compared during their incessant passage through the mind, satisfaction, dissatisfaction, and even misery would be felt.

In this case an inward monitor would tell the animal that it would have been better to have followed the one impulse rather than the other. The one course ought to have been followed, the other ought not. The one would have been right, the other wrong.

> *Here Darwin has rather quickly gone to the core of the key observation he will repeatedly bring up in the context of our own moral evolution. As we will see again very soon, it is an observation with extraordinary implications for advanced modern evolution theory. For easy reference when we come upon it again, it is the first glimpse of the working within pre-humans of Darwin's discovery (or more properly speaking, rediscovery) of "organic choice.*"[175]

The Moral World of the Social Animal[176]

Animals of many kinds are social. We find even distinct species living together—for example, some American monkeys, and united flocks of rooks, jackdaws, and starlings. We ourselves show the same feeling in, for example, our strong love for the dog, which the dog returns with interest.

Every one must have noticed how miserable horses, dogs, and sheep are when separated from their companions, and what strong mutual affection horses and dogs, at least, show on their reunion.

It is curious to speculate on the feelings of a dog, who will rest peacefully for hours in a room with his master or any of the family, without the least notice being taken of him. But if left for a short time by himself, he barks or howls dismally.

We will confine our attention to the higher social animals and pass over insects, although some of these are social and aid one another in many important ways.[177] The most common mutual service in the higher animals is to warn one another of danger by means of the united senses of all. Every sportsman knows, as Dr. Jaeger remarks, how difficult it is to approach animals in a herd or troop. Wild horses and cattle do not, I believe, make any danger signal, but the attitude of any one of them who first discovers an enemy warns the others.

Rabbits stamp loudly on the ground with their hind feet as a signal. Sheep and chamois do the same with their forefeet, uttering likewise a whistle. Many birds, and some mammals, post sentinels, which in the case of seals are said generally to be the females. The leader of a troop of monkeys acts as the sentinel, and utters cries expressive both of danger and safety.

Social animals also perform many little services for each other. Horses nibble, and cows lick each other on any spot that itches. Monkeys search each other for external parasites. And Brehm states that after a troop of the *Cercopithecus griscoviridis* has rushed through a thorny brake, each monkey stretches itself on a branch, and another monkey sitting by "conscientiously" examines its fur, extracting every thorn or burr.

Franz de Waal's book **Good Natured** *provides a fascinating recent update on animal moral sensitivity and animal morality and what it reveals of our own roots. De Waal's book is not only the most important scientific work on morality of recent years, but also destined to become a classic in this* *unfortunately small field. Again, in point after point, de Waal's observations were both anticipated by Darwin and corroborate this aspect of the grounding of Darwin's lost theory. Jeffrey Masson's book* **When Elephants Weep** *also provides recent updates on animal morality, as also does Peter Kropotkin's turn-of-the-century classic* **Mutual Aid.**[178]

Stories of Courage and Moral Action[179]

Pelicans fish in concert. The Hamadryas baboons turn over stones to find insects, and when they come to a large one, as many as can stand around, turn it over together and share the booty.

Social animals mutually defend each other. Bull bisons in North America, when there is danger, drive the cows and calves into the middle of the herd, while they defend the outside. In Abyssinia, Brehm encountered a great troop of baboons who were crossing a valley. Some had already ascended the opposite mountain and some were still in the valley when the latter were attacked by dogs. Immediately, the old males hurried down from the rocks, and with mouths widely opened roared so fearfully that the dogs quickly drew back.

The dogs were again encouraged to the attack. But by this time all the baboons had re-ascended the heights, excepting a young one, about six months old, who, loudly calling for aid, climbed on a block of rock and was surrounded.

Now one of the largest males, a true hero, came down again from the mountain, slowly went to the young one, coaxed him, and triumphantly led him away—the dogs being too much astonished to make an attack.

I cannot resist giving another scene witnessed by the same naturalist. An eagle seized a young *Cercophithecus*, which, by clinging to a branch, was not at once carried off. It cried loudly for assistance, upon which the other members of the troop, with much uproar, rushed to the rescue, surrounded the eagle, and pulled out so many feathers that it no longer thought of its prey, but only of how to escape.

This eagle, as Brehm remarks, assuredly would never again attack a single monkey of a troop.

Moral Behavioral Ups and Downs[180]

It is certain that associated animals have a feeling of love for each other, which is not felt by non-social adult animals. But how far in most cases they actually sympathize with the pains and pleasures of others is more doubtful, especially with respect to pleasures.

Mr. Buxton states that his macaws, which lived free in Norfolk, took "an extravagant interest" in a pair with a nest, and whenever the female left it, she was surrounded by a troop "screaming horrible acclamations in her honour."

It is often difficult to judge whether animals have any feeling for the sufferings of others of their kind. Who can say what cows feel when they surround and stare intently on a dying or dead companion? Apparently, as Houzeau remarks, they feel no pity.

That animals sometimes are far from feeling any sympathy is certain, for they will expel a wounded animal from the herd, or gore or worry it to death. This is almost the blackest fact in natural history, unless the explanation that has been suggested is true: that their instinct or reason leads them to expel an injured companion lest beasts of prey, including the predators of our own species, should be tempted to follow the troop.

In this case their conduct is not much worse than that of the North American Indians who leave their feeble comrades to perish on the plains, or the Fijians who, when their parents get old, or fall ill, bury them alive.

Many animals, however, certainly sympathize with each other's distress or danger. This is the case even with birds. Captain Stansbury found on a salt lake in Utah an old and completely blind pelican. This pelican was very fat, so it must have been well fed for a long time by its companions. Captain Stansbury also gives an interesting account of the manner in which a very young pelican, carried away by a strong stream, was guided and encouraged in its attempts to reach the shore by half a dozen old birds.[181]

Mr. Blyth tells me he saw Indian crows feeding two or three of their companions which were blind, and I have heard of a similar case with the domestic cock.

So what are we to make of instances such as these so far? What might they foreshadow of a fully developed moral agency in ourselves? Darwin turns to the debate among the great authorities of his time.

Speculations Back and Forth[182]

We may, if we choose, call these actions instinctive, but such cases are much too rare for the development of any special instinct.[183]

Mr. Bain[184] gives a list of twenty-six British authors who have written on this subject, whose names are familiar to every reader.[185] Sir B. Brodie, after observing that man is a social animal, asks the pregnant question, "Ought not this to settle the disputed question as the existence of a moral sense?"

Similar ideas have probably occurred to many persons, as they did long ago to Marcus Aurelius. Mr. J.S. Mill speaks in his celebrated work, *Utilitarianism*, of the social feelings as a "powerful natural sentiment," and as "the natural basis of sentiment for utilitarian morality." Again he says, "Like the other acquired capacities above referred to, the moral faculty, if not a part of our nature, is a natural out-growth from it; capable, like them, in a certain small degree of springing up spontaneously."[186]

But then in opposition to all this, Mill also remarks, "If, as in my own belief, the moral feelings are not innate, but acquired, they are not for that reason less natural."

It is with hesitation that I venture to differ from so profound a thinker as Mr. Mill, but it can hardly be disputed that the social feelings are instinctive or innate in the lower animals. And why should they not be so in ourselves?

Mr. Bain and others believe that the moral sense is acquired by each individual during his lifetime. The general theory of evolution indicates this is at least extremely improbable.

The ignoring of all transmitted mental qualities will, it seems to me, be hereafter judged a serious blemish in the works of Mr. Mill.[187]

Pioneering economist, bold advocate of gender equality, and moral giant for his time, John Stuart Mill was widely considered the smartest man of mid-century England. This courtly exchange is pivotal for Darwin. In keeping with Mill's belief, a majority of social scientists, educators, and most of us whose minds have been shaped by first half Darwinism still believe today that we arrive on this planet with no inherent capacity for or drive toward goodness within us—that we must all be taught right and wrong from the ground up with nothing there initially to build on. Over and over again Darwin demonstrates there is this inherent drive toward goodness to build on—which makes a profound difference in what we believe of the chances for our species not only to survive but to live up to its incredible potential.

Focusing on sympathy, Darwin now returns to the animals to continue to develop his case for the existence of the moral sense in animals as the grounding in evolution for the same in ourselves.

Evidence of Sympathy at Work in Animals[188]

I have myself seen a dog, who never passed a cat who lay sick in a basket, and was a great friend of his, without giving her a few licks with his tongue, the surest sign of kind feeling in a dog.

It must be called sympathy that leads a courageous dog to fly at any one who strikes his master, as he certainly will. I saw a person pretending to beat a lady who had a very timid little dog on her lap. The little creature instantly jumped away. But after the pretended beating was over, it was really pathetic to see how perseveringly he tried to lick his mistress's face and comfort her.

Brehm states that when a baboon in confinement was pursued to be punished, the others tried to protect him. It must have been sympathy in the cases above given which led the baboons and Cercopitheci to defend their young comrades from the dogs and the eagle.

I will give only one other instance of sympathetic and heroic conduct. This is the case of a little American monkey. Several years ago a keeper at the Zoological Gardens showed me some deep and scarcely healed wounds on the nape of his own neck. These were inflicted on him, while he was kneeling on the floor, by a fierce baboon.

The little American monkey, who was a warm friend of this keeper, and lived in the same compartment, was dreadfully afraid of the great baboon. Nevertheless, as soon as it saw its friend in peril it rushed to the rescue, and by screams and bites so distracted the baboon that the man was able to escape, after, as the surgeon thought, running great risk of his life.

A Hymn to Love, Maternal Affection, and the Sense of Humor[189]

The love of a dog for its master or mistress is notorious. As an old writer quaintly says, "A dog is the only thing on this earth that luvs you more than he luvs himself."[190]

In the agony of death a dog has been known to caress its master, and every one has heard of the dog suffering under vivisection, who licked the hand of the operator—this man, unless the operation was fully justified by an increase of our knowledge, or unless he had a heart of stone, must have felt remorse to the last hour of his life.

> *This issue, the cutting up and killing of animals for scientific research, was a difficult one for Darwin. Here we see how greatly the process disturbed him in one part of his mind. Indeed, two of the things that most disturbed him were humans in slavery and cruelty to animals. As an old man, he became known for his fierce interventions on the behalf of horses being beaten by their drivers or dogs being abused. But when his daughter Henrietta became a crusading advocate for ending vivisection, he felt compelled to come out in support of the practice. He could see no other way for science to continue to advance in areas of benefit to the health and welfare of our species without continuing it.*

> *Once again the issue presses on us today as increasingly we find our fate bound to that of other species and as science discovers alternatives.*

As Whewell has well asked, "Who that reads the touching instances of maternal affection, related so often of the women of all nations and of the females of all animals, can doubt that the principle of action is the same in the two cases."

We see maternal affection exhibited in the most trifling details. Thus, Rengger observed an American monkey (a Cebus) carefully driving away the flies that plagued her infant. And Duvaucel saw a Hylobates washing the faces of her young ones in a stream. So intense is the grief of female monkeys for the loss of their young that it invariably caused the death of certain kinds kept under confinement by Brehm in North Africa.

Orphan monkeys were always adopted and carefully guarded by other monkeys, both males and female. One female baboon had so capacious a heart that she not only adopted young monkeys of other species, but also stole young dogs and cats, which she continually carried about. Her kindness, however, did not go so far as to share her food with her adopted offspring, at which Brehm was surprised, as his monkeys always divided everything quite fairly with their own young ones.

An adopted kitten scratched this affectionate baboon, who certainly had a fine intellect, for she was much astonished at being scratched, and immediately examined the kitten's feet, and without more ado bit off the claws.

For the purpose of discrediting my work, a critic, without any grounds, disputes the possibility of this act as described by Brehm. Therefore I tried, and found that I could readily seize with my own teeth the sharp little claws of a kitten nearly five weeks old.[191]

Most of the more complex emotions are common to the higher animals and ourselves. Everyone has seen how jealous a dog is of its master's affection, if lavished on any other creature, and I have observed the same fact with monkeys.

This shows that animals not only love, but desire to be loved. Animals manifestly feel emulation. They love approval or praise, and a dog carrying a basket for its master exhibits in a high degree self-complacency or pride. There can, I think, be no doubt that a dog feels shame, as distinct from fear, and something very like modesty when begging too often for food. A great dog scorns the snarling of a little dog, and this may be called magnanimity.

Dogs show what may be fairly called a sense of humor, as distinct from mere play. If a bit of stick or other such object is thrown to one, he will often carry it away for a short distance and then squatting down with it on the ground close before him, will wait until his master comes quite close to take it away.

The dog will then seize it and rush away in triumph, repeating the same maneuver and evidently enjoying the practical joke.[192]

Conscience and Fidelity[193]

Besides love and sympathy, animals exhibit other qualities connected with the social instincts, which in us would be called moral. For example, **I agree with Agassiz**[194] **that dogs possess something very like a conscience.**

Dogs possess some power of self-command, and this does not appear to be wholly the result of fear. As Braubach remarks, they will refrain from stealing food in the absence of their master. Dogs have also long been accepted as the very type of fidelity and obedience. But the elephant is likewise very faithful to his driver or keeper, and probably considers him the leader of the herd.

Dr. Hooker tells me that an elephant that he was riding in India became so deeply bogged that he remained stuck fast until the next day, when he was extricated by men with ropes. Under such circumstances elephants will seize with their trunks any object, dead or alive, to place under their knees to prevent their sinking deeper in the mud. The driver was dreadfully afraid that the animal would seize Dr. Hooker and thereby crush him to death. But the driver himself, Dr. Hooker was assured, ran no such risk.

This forbearance under an emergency so dreadful for such a heavy animal seems a wonderful proof of noble fidelity.[195]

Pleasure and Pain as Moral Motivators[196]

With respect to the impulse that leads certain animals to associate together, and to aid one another in many ways, we may infer that in most cases they are impelled by the same sense of satisfaction or pleasure that they experience in performing other instinctive actions—or by the same sense of dissatisfaction as when other instinctive actions are checked.

We see this in innumerable instances. It is illustrated in a striking manner by the acquired instincts of our domesticated animals. Thus, a young shepherd dog delights in driving and running around a flock of sheep, but not in worrying them. A young fox hound delights in hunting a fox, while some other kinds of dogs, as I have witnessed, utterly disregard foxes.

What a strong feeling of inward satisfaction must impel a bird, so full of activity, to brood day after day over her eggs. Migratory birds are quite miserable if stopped from migrating. Perhaps they enjoy starting on their long flight, but it is hard to believe that the poor pinioned goose, described by Audubon, which started on foot at the proper time for its journey of probably more than a thousand miles, could have felt any joy in doing so.

Some instincts are determined solely by painful feelings, as by fear, which leads to self-preservation, and is in some cases directed toward special enemies. No one, I presume, can analyse the sensations of pleasure or pain. In many instances, however, it is probable that instincts are persistently followed from the mere force of inheritance, without the stimulus of either pleasure or pain.

A young pointer, when it first scents game, apparently cannot help pointing. A squirrel in a cage who pats the nuts which it cannot eat, as if to bury them in the ground, can hardly be thought to act thus, either from pleasure or pain. Hence the common assumption that we ourselves must be impelled to every action by experiencing some pleasure or pain may be erroneous.

A habit may be blindly and implicitly followed, independent of any pleasure or pain felt at the moment. But if it be forcibly and abruptly checked, a vague sense of dissatisfaction is generally experienced.

And so it goes. Laying down the database for building his theory, Darwin roams the great bank of stories and observations picked up through his voluminous correspondence with other naturalists from all over the world. Typical of his capacity as a psychologist and his foreshadowing of the development of this field is this last observation—of the motivational effect of being checked before completing something we want to do. As with the lover put off from seeking a kiss, or the insurance salesperson initially rebuffed in trying to make a sale, the impulse remains bottled up within us seeking the opportunity to persist and complete the impulse or act. Here his ruminations point ahead sixty years to work in the golden period of the 1930s for psychologist Kurt Lewin and his students with what became known as the Zeigarnik effect.[197]*

It would be helpful also at this point to say something about Darwin's use of the word "instinct," which is beginning to appearing with some frequency. In the last chapter we became acquainted with his use of the word to identify the "hardwired" programming for behavioral sequences laid down in animals over millions of years—for example, the sexual, parental, and social instincts. But here, all of a sudden, he is talking about the "acquired instincts" of sheep dogs and fox hounds—or "instincts" requiring not millions of years to implant, but only some training and selection over lesser periods of time.

What we are beginning to encounter is Darwin's all-purpose use of the word "instinct" for processes later defined with other words by his successors in science—e.g., "drive" for psychologists, or "innate behavior" by biologists.[198]

But onward, and let us see where he is going with all of this...

CHAPTER NINE

CLOSING THE GAP

So he ruminates, searching, searching, searching for his grounding points. He is not worrying very much about whether he has the reader with him because, although perhaps he has a dim hope otherwise, his good sense sadly tells him what history will prove. Practically everybody, he knows, will skip over his probing of animal morality in order to keep reading what for that time of upper-class repression were the "racy" sections on sexual selection.

He is mainly talking to himself and a readership among his naturalist cronies, such as Brehm of the heroic monkeys or Captain Stansbury of the blind and fat old pelican. At least Brehm and Stansbury will stick with him because, storytellers themselves, they will cherish the way he has polished their anecdotes.

What all this is giving him is the warm up exercise for the heavy-duty thinking he has been avoiding for a long time, but now must engage. But now well underway, he is beginning to relish the task.

Now we are to see him take up themes that have come back to interest our times. What is this about mothers? What is involved in the power of the maternal instinct? And bringing in the males, what about the parental instinct more generally?

Now he is to engage the theory builder's problem of the differences between the first half and the second half. Just how much of what happens is determined by natural selection? Where and how does the power of sympathy and love take over? And how does this new idea of "community selection" fit in?

Now he also moves into the territory of the debate between the sociobiologists and evolutionary psychologists of our time and those who feel we are impelled by higher motivations. How selfish really are we? How altruistic?

What he tells us, I can guarantee, will both confuse and dismay those who want to think we are exclusively one way or the other—and who think that he will be *our* champion, rather than the impartial judge trying to honestly sort his way through our mix of both motivations.

It is also important to read him with an understanding of his personal position in the history of the evolution of thought and mind for our species. Wherever he can he tries to ground himself in the thoughts and observations of the great minds of his time and earlier—in Kant, in John Stuart Mill, in Alexander Bain. But it is most important to realize the ultimate boldness of his venture—how he is acting as our scout into unknown territory, how he is to serve our species as the great evolutionary outrider for his time and centuries to come.

For now he must turn from what the outer eye sees—from what can be seen, weighed, dissected, or otherwise measured—to the world of the inner eye that deals with the felt, the intuited, and the unseen, but which no less powerfully impacts and shapes us.

By the nature of his task, and the demand from within himself for completion of his theory, he must now proceed as the sky diver leaps from the airplane, and plunging through the open air gives himself or herself over to the language of the winds—and at times what emerges from Darwin reads as though he is writing from a waking trance. For he must range not just backward into the past, difficult as that may be, but also out of the present into the enticing but at the same time frighteningly open-ended future, no longer in search of human origins but now also of the human destiny.

We begin with a pivotal passage revealing the difference between first half and second half Darwinism—or where he is headed in trying to complete his theory.

The Conflict of Instincts[199]

It is impossible to decide in many cases whether certain social instincts have been acquired through natural selection, or are the indirect result of other instincts and faculties, such as sympathy, reason, experience, a tendency to imitation, or are simply the result of long-continued habit.

So remarkable an instinct as the placing of sentinels to warn the community of danger can hardly have been the indirect result of any of these faculties. It must, therefore, have been directly acquired.

On the other hand, the habit followed by the males of some social animals of defending the community, and of attacking their enemies or their prey in concert, may perhaps have originated from mutual sympathy. But courage, and in most cases strength, must have been previously acquired, probably through natural selection.

In other words, here—in striking contrast to the biological determinism of the sociobiologists—Darwin specifically points to the difference between motivations and behavioral sequences that are determined primarily by natural selection, or by first half Darwinian theory, and those that result from other processes that become more powerfully impelling in evolution at the level of the higher mammals and ourselves, our species.

Here he has specifically identified sympathy, reason, experience, imitation—or the power of "modeling" ourselves after the example of others—and the incredible accumulating power of habit as more important than natural selection at our level.

In other words, for a space age analogy, natural selection was the big booster rocket that launched us, but now we shoot on through space and time on a variety of second stage rockets toward our unknown destination. However, the difficult point that Darwin will repeatedly make is that this is not a matter of choosing up sides, or an either/or situation. In the totality of our life functioning, we are both first half and second half Darwinians.

Of the various instincts and habits, some are much stronger than others, **he continues.** That is, some either give more pleasure in their performance, and more distress in their prevention, than others—or, which is probably quite as important, they are through inheritance more persistently followed without exciting any special feeling of pleasure or pain.

We are ourselves conscious that some habits are much more difficult to cure or change than others. Hence a struggle may often be observed in animals between different instincts, or between an instinct and some habitual disposition. We see this, for example, when a dog rushes after a hare, is rebuked, pauses, hesitates, pursues again, or returns ashamed to his master. Or we see this struggle in the case of the love of a female dog for her young puppies and for her master—for she may be seen to slink away to them, as if half ashamed of not accompanying her master.

But the most curious instance known to me of one instinct getting the better of another is of the migratory instinct conquering the maternal instinct.

The former is wonderfully strong. A confined bird will at the proper season beat her breast against the wires of her cage until it is bare and bloody. The migratory instinct causes young salmon to leap out of the fresh water, in which they could continue to exist, and thus unintentionally to commit suicide.

We can perceive that an instinctive impulse, if it be in any way more beneficial to a species than some other or opposed instinct, would be rendered the more potent of the two through natural selection, for the individuals which had it most strongly developed would survive in larger numbers. Whether this is the case with the migratory instinct in comparison with the maternal instinct may be doubted. The great persistence of the former at certain seasons of the years may give it for a time paramount force.[200]

Every one knows how strong the maternal instinct is, leading even timid birds to face great danger, though with hesitation, and in opposition to the instinct of self-preservation. Nevertheless, the migratory instinct is so powerful that late in the autumn swallows, house martins, and swifts frequently desert their tender young, leaving them to perish miserably in their nests.

Among several careful observers, Mr. Blackwell, for example, over two years, observing nests in late autumn, found these results with thirty-six nests.[201] Twelve contained young dead birds and five contained eggs on the point of being hatched.

Many birds not yet old enough for a prolonged flight are likewise deserted and left behind.

Natural Selection and the Origin and Power of the Parental and Social Instincts[202]

It has often been assumed that animals were in the first place rendered social, and that they feel as a consequence uncomfortable when separated from each other and comfortable while together. But it is more probable that these sensations were first developed in order that animals, which would profit by living in society, should be induced to live together, this much as the sense of hunger and the pleasure of eating were, no doubt, first acquired in order to induce animals to eat.

The feeling of pleasure from society is probably an extension of the parental or filial affections, since the social instinct seems to be developed by the young remaining for a long time with their parents—an extension that may be attributed in part to habit, but chiefly to natural selection.[203]

With those animals that benefited by living in close association, individuals that took the greatest pleasure in society would best escape various dangers, while those that cared least for their comrades, and lived solitary, would perish in greater numbers.

With respect to the origin of the parental and filial affections, which apparently lie at the base of the social instincts, we know not the steps by which they have been gained, but we may infer that it has been to a large extent through natural selection.

Certainly natural selection must have been at work in the unusual cases of hatred between nearest relations, as with the worker bees that kill their brother drones, and the queen bees that kill their daughter queens—in these cases the desire to destroy their nearest relations having been of service to the community. In contrast, however, we find parental affection, or some feeling that replaces it, has been developed in certain animals extremely low in the scale, for example, in star fishes and spiders.

Parental affection is even occasionally present in a few members alone in a whole group of animals, as in the genus Forficula, or earwigs.[204]

> *Earwigs? If you are a gardener trying to save your roses from those ravenous jaws it must stretch the limits of belief to think of earwigs as affectionate little parents. And yet here Darwin aligns himself with the ethos of Buddhism and Deep Ecology in an expression of the interconnected meaningfulness of all life.*

The Dynamics of Community Selection

> *Earlier we outlined how Darwin used the idea of community selection in trying to track the development of the biological foundation for moral sensitivity. Here is the argument.*

With strictly social animals, natural selection sometimes acts indirectly on the individual through the preservation of variations which are beneficial only to the community.[205] Although a high standard of morality gives but a slight or no advantage to individuals and their children over others of the same tribe, yet an advancement in the standard of morality and an increase in the number of well-endowed people will certainly give an immense advantage to one tribe over another. There can be no doubt that a tribe including many members who—from possessing in a high degree the spirit of patriotism, fidelity, obedience, courage, and sympathy, were always ready to give aid to each other and to sacrifice themselves for the common good—would be victorious over most other tribes, and this would be natural selection.[206]

> *This sounds good, of course, and here is the outcome that Darwin thought would prevail:*

At all times throughout the world, tribes have supplanted other tribes, and as morality is one element in their success, the standard of morality and the number of well-endowed men will thus everywhere tend to rise and increase.[207]

> *There is just one problem here—and it seems a pretty big one. What Darwin called community selection and modern Darwinists call group selection has undoubtedly worked to the good in many cases in our past, and continues to work in many places to our advantage today. This has been amply proven by the work of biologist David Sloan Wilson, who battled uphill for thirty years against efforts by more traditional first-half Darwinists to also bury this original insight by Darwin into the dynamics of goodness.[208] But if we take a good look at the big picture in terms of the work of evolution theorist Riane Eisler, we can see how at times group selection seems to have also accounted for some of the worst recorded evolutionary regressions in ancient as well as modern times.*

> *The problem, Eisler's work shows, is the havoc wreaked by "community selection" when coupled to the dominator model for human relations. Hers, and the work of archeologist Marija*

Gimbutas and others, shows how such appealing values as patriotism, loyalty to, and most certainly sympathy for, one another, bound together both the early Kurgan and Indo-European tribes and the modern Nazis in their devastating drives of conquest.[209] *My own development of Evolutionary Action Theory also probes the pro and con dynamics involved here in terms of partnership and dominator model differences.*[210] *Notable for both the Indo-Europeans and the Nazis was their fierce and overbearing conviction of their own moral superiority over the "weak" and "immoral" people—that is, for the Nazis, Jews, gypsies, homosexuals, and everybody foolish enough to believe in democracy. The result was that the early Indo-Europeans were seen by scholars and the Nazis saw themselves as the "fittest" displacing the "unfit" and the "misfit" in what was proclaimed an advance for evolution.*

One also only has to look around our world—and let us hope not one's neighborhood today—to see the same force or mindset of "negative" or "subhuman" group selection working against moral advancement in the case of the Mafia, terrorist, right-wing militia, and other right-wing and comparably anti-human communities. I also think the same dynamics are at work in all other cases where the "bad eggs" gradually take over a country, a company, a church, or any other group—including all too many causes that start out with noble purposes.

The Majesty and Mystery of Sympathy[211]

The all-important emotion of sympathy is distinct from that of love. A mother may passionately love her sleeping and passive infant, but she can hardly at such times be said to feel sympathy for it. The love of a man for his dog is distinct from sympathy, and so is that of a dog for his master.

Adam Smith formerly argued, as has Mr. Bain recently, that the basis of sympathy lies in our strong retentiveness of former states of pain or pleasure. Hence, "the sight of another person enduring hunger, cold, fatigue, revives in us some recollection of these states, which are painful even in idea."

We are thus impelled to relieve the sufferings of another in order that our own painful feelings may be at the same time relieved. In like manner we are led to participate in the pleasures of others.

This is a point made in the first and striking chapter in Adam Smith's *Theory of Moral Sentiments*[212] and also in Mr. Bain's *Mental and Moral Science*. "Sympathy," Mr. Bain states, "is, indirectly, a source of pleasure to the sympathizer." He accounts for this through reciprocity. "The person benefited, or others in his stead, may make up, by sympathy and good offices returned, for all the sacrifice," he says.

But if, as appears to be the case, sympathy is strictly an instinct,[213] its exercise would give direct pleasure in the same manner as the exercise of almost every other instinct.[214]

I cannot see how this well-known view of Smith and Bain explains the fact that, for example, sympathy is excited in an immeasurably stronger degree by a beloved than by an indifferent person. The explanation may lie in the fact that, with all animals, sympathy is directed solely towards the members of the same community, and therefore toward known and more or less beloved members, but not to all individuals of the same species.[215]

> *Here Darwin's observations clearly support the doctrine of sociobiology—in this instance, the theory of "kinship selection" advanced by W.D. Hamilton to account for altruism by attributing it not only to selfishness but to selfishness confined to one's own kin. That is, the contention is that we act on the behalf of others in order to protect the gene pool to which we belong.*

As earlier noted, this kind of perspective has been extended beyond the kinship link by Robert Trivers with the idea of "reciprocal altruism"—or that we do good for others because we expect thereby to receive good in return. In other words, this is a sociobiological basis for the Golden Rule.[216]

Darwin continues...

This fact is not more surprising than that the fears of many animals should be directed against special enemies. Species that are not social, such as lions and tigers, no doubt feel sympathy for the suffering of their own young, but not for that of any other animal.

With our species, selfishness, experience, and imitation probably add, as Mr. Bain has shown, to the power of sympathy. It seems true, as he and Mr. Smith have argued, that in many instances we are led by the hope of receiving good in return to perform acts of sympathetic kindness to others. Sympathy of this kind would also be much strengthened by habit. But basically my point is that in however complex a manner this feeling may have originated, as it is one of high importance to all those animals that aid and defend one another, it will have been increased through natural selection.

This seems probable because communities that included the greatest number of the most sympathetic members would flourish best, and rear the greatest numbers of offspring.[217]

So we conclude with the positive view of "community selection"—which works, I am convinced, when coupled with the partnership model but not the dominator model for relationships and morality.

To those to whom the most important thing about evolutionary theory is whether the neo-Darwinians and sociobiologists or their critics are winning, however, the most important question at this point will be "What's the score?"

For those who line up conservatives and first-half Darwinians on one side, and liberals and potential second-half Darwinians on the other, the score card at this point reads: First-Halfers, 2; Second-Halfers, 0.

Certainly, after going back and forth on the question, the Great Halfback seems to have scored a touchdown for the first-halfers, as Darwin winds up his section on the moral sense in animals by coming down hard on the side of the self-ishness side of the debate—or that goodness, or altruism, doing good for others, is primarily motivated by selfishness.

Moreover, the triumph for first-half Darwinism is further sweetened by Darwin's prediction that this finding of good-ness driven by selfishness among the animals also applies to ourselves. In part, the same motivational structure applies to our species, he is telling us, as to the prehumans.

As we will see in what is to come, however, his position—as well as the evidence—is more complex. Yes, we ourselves as well as the prehumans are motivated to do good in the world by the "selfishness" of hoping for a reward. Prefigured in Darwin's observations, we are motivated both by the "kinship selection" of sociobiologist Hamilton and the "reciprocal altruism" of sociobiologist Trivers.

We are also motivated to do good in the world through the impact of "community selection"—but when linked to the dominator model of social organization this also seems to work in the other direction.

But what about this other powerful underlying factor that Darwin has set in motion? What about this instinctively embedded moral sense that works in prehumans as well as humans? What about this force both reflected in and functioning through the massively established empirical shaping of our brain structures, but which also exists in prehumans? What about this force that drives not only us, but also the prehumans, to transcend all possible motivations of personal gain?

How do we resolve the conflict of this self-transcendent drive with the beloved selfishness solution for sociobiology? And how might it clarify the complication of positive and negative kinds of community selection?

Isn't there a rather large measure of conflict here? How are we to resolve this? Where is Darwin's first level vision of a basic underlying biological drive toward goodness to fit in, and where is it to take us?

CHAPTER TEN
THE DRIVE FOR FULFILLMENT

We have examined the amazing range of what Darwin identifies as moral behavior in animals. From throughout the world he has pulled together these observations out of which he will now construct the first floor of his theoretical house of mind. As both architect and builder, he will now do something that, in speed and economy, if this were an actual house under construction, would be somewhat of an overnight miracle.

In Chapters 6 and 7, we saw how—holding everything from the first impulse of the organisms known as the eukaryotes toward sex,[218] to the first inclination of a reptile to seek another for warmth, to the first nursing of an infant by a mother mammal—he would put the "basement" in place.

In Chapters 8 and 9, out of his own remarkable range of experience and personal contacts with other naturalists at work throughout the world of his time, he has pulled together what he now needs for constructing the next stage for his theory. Out of his memories of the forests of Brazil, the mountains of Chile, the Galapagos Islands and all the other places where the Beagle put ashore during its famous voyage; out of zoos in England where he loved to sit and watch hour after hour; out of scores of visits to the contests of pigeon fanciers and stables of horse breeders; and out of hundreds of letters with foreign stamps from what had become "the Darwin club" among naturalists throughout the world, he has drawn together the materials in his mind for constructing the next step upward for the evolution of morality.

In the original, the statement that provides the keystone for this level of construction comes in a brief passage that goes by so swiftly that, unless you knew what you were looking for, you might hardly notice it. No doubt he worried it over a bit later, editing and polishing. But in all probability it was dashed off in no more than an hour or so in a burst of special energy on a particularly good day with his stomach not churning as much as usual.

Afterwards, he must have sighed in relief. That was that, thank goodness! Very likely there was a bit more of a snap to his step as he set off with cane and favorite dog for his customary stroll up and back through the woods near his house on the well-worn path that Darwin and family called "the Sandwalk."

So here it is, his distillate of thousands of stories and observations expressed as a short stream of tenets.

The Second Level of Darwin's Theory of the Moral Agent[219]

In the first place, the social instincts lead an animal to take pleasure in the society of its fellows, to feel a certain amount of sympathy for them, and to perform various services for them.

The services may be of a definite and evidently instinctive nature. Or, as with most of the higher social animals, there may be only a wish and readiness to aid their fellows in certain general ways. But these feelings and services are by no means extended to all the individuals of the same species, only to those of the same association.

Secondly, as soon as the mental faculties had become highly developed, images of all past actions and motives would be incessantly passing through the brain of each individual. *Out of a comparison of past and present*, the feeling of dissatisfaction, or even misery, which invariably results from any unsatisfied instinct, would arise.[220]

Third, after the power of language had been acquired, and the wishes of the community could be expressed, the common opinion of how each member ought to act for the public good would naturally become the guide to action.[221] (But it should be borne in mind that however great weight we may attribute to public opinion, our concern for the approval and concern about the disapproval of our fellows depends on sympathy, which, as we shall see, forms an essential part of the social instinct, and is indeed its foundation-stone).

Lastly, habit in the individual would ultimately play a very important part in guiding the conduct of each member, for the social instinct, together with sympathy, is, like any other instinct, greatly strengthened by habit, and so consequently would be obedient to the wishes and judgement of the community.

A Restatement in Terms of Modern Psychology and Systems Science

As my commentary in this chapter will take more space than Darwin's terse statement, I am reversing the relation of margins that to this point have been used to set off the different voices. His text has been pulled in from the sides. Mine, for the time being, will spread to the standard margin.

Again, we have seemingly little to go on. But this time at least we have what are four whole paragraphs in *Descent*, rather than only the three sentences of the notebooks we had to work with earlier. In terms of modern science, let us see how, through translation of this fragment, we may further unlock the lost secrets of the evolution of ourselves and moral mind.

To position ourselves for this intriguing task, three things will be helpful. The first is to be clear about where we are in terms of the relation of first-half to second-half Darwinian theory. He has told us the moral sense rises out of the sequential development of our sexual, parental, and social instincts, topped with emotion and then reason. Having laid down a foundation for moral evolution in biology, he will now erect the superstructure in psychology, sociology, and anthropology.

This relation, explored throughout the rest of Part II, is shown in Table 10.1.

Table 10.1

The Two Halves of HoloDarwinian Theory

First Half	Second Half
Biological	Cultural/Psychological
Foundation	Superstructure

Second, we need to clarify a source of possible confusion. Is Darwin talking here about us, or about "the animals"?

He is talking about both of us, but primarily he is constructing this level of his theory out of his stories and observations of prehumans. What is confusing is that this is the kind of language that today most of us would only apply to ourselves. His theory is, in fact, about what prehumans and humans share, but also about the evolutionary transition from one to the other. For a time here, he will have a foot in both worlds, before he moves on to consider the greater complexities of our species.

A third point to note before we move on is indicated by the line Darwin adds to his observation of how the social instincts lead to sympathy, and how both in animals and ourselves this underlies our pleasure in serving others. He indicates an increase in the "wish and readiness" to help others as we move up the evolutionary scale. But then he adds that this is limited to those "only of the same association."

This again supports the position of the sociobiologists—that altruism only extends to our close kin, to whom we are genetically related.[222] To some degree it also supports the idea that altruism is driven by selfishness.[223] So one might say the score now reads: First-half Darwinians, 3; Second-half Darwinians, 0.

But of course we are only in the early quarters of this theoretical game. We must keep in mind that we are looking primarily at *pre*human behavior here, and what humans and prehumans share. The most complex and exciting play still lies ahead. Who knows what may happen when our own species is called up full time from the bench to enter the game.

Now, point by point, let us examine this four-paragraph fragment of lost wisdom in terms of modern science. Again, from the perspective of what we know today, Darwin has packed a staggering amount of information into a few lines.

I. The Power of Caring

"In the first place, the social instincts lead an animal to take pleasure in the society of its fellows," Darwin tells us. In other words, at the developmentally earlier as well as more advanced animal level, we are impelled to feel sympathy and perform services for each other.

At the more advanced level, this "wish and readiness" to aid one another becomes widespread, or as Darwin puts it, it prevails among animals "in certain general ways."

Here, so swiftly we can easily miss it, he covers the fundamental relation of foundation to superstructure to which, heavily influenced by him, the founders of modern social science were soon to turn their attention.

Today the influence of Sigmund Freud on the shaping of 20th century consciousness is well known. And what did Freud center his view of the mind of our species on? Much of his reconstruction of the field of psychology is in terms of the relation between the unconscious mind as foundation and the conscious mind as superstructure. Also casting their theories in terms of the foundation to superstructure relation were Emile Durkheim in sociology, Vilfredo Pareto in economics, and Ivan Pavlov in neurophysiology.[224]

The same pattern holds for later theorists. On one hand Darwin calls the social instincts foundational. On the other hand is the rise upon this foundation of something ever more refined and advanced as the other mammals and we ourselves evolve. This is the superstructure of our "higher" capacities for sympathy, altruism, and of caring for and feeling responsibility for the well-being of one another, as corroborated by the work of sociologist Pitirim Sorokin, anthropologist Ashley Montagu, psychologist Carol Gilligan and many others.[225]

II. The Power of Reflection

"Secondly, as soon as the mental faculties had become highly developed," Darwin tells us the situation arises where "images of past actions and motives" shape decisions and actions for both prehumans and humans in a critically important new way. For here he focuses on a pivotal difference between biological evolution and psychological or personal as well as cultural evolution for both prehumans and humans.

As indicated by the italics, I added the line "out of our comparison of past and present" to provide the needed context for what he is saying here. Already at work in the prehumans, this comparison of past and present is of skyrocketing importance in the case of our own species. For it is out of a comparison of who we have been in the past, and who we are now in the present—and, most decisively for our own species, *who we can become in the future*—that the "feeling of dissatisfaction" rises that drives us to try to improve ourselves.

And isn't this drive to improve ourselves—seen within this larger context for the meaning of our lives—our drive to evolve? Isn't it about time this thrust familiar to every one of us who has ever aspired to "make something of ourselves" in school, on the job, in being a good parent, as a creative writer, artist, or composer, or in serving any of hundreds of "good causes" be recognized as a major factor in evolution?

In discerning this basic dynamic to the thrust of personal and cultural evolution, Darwin anticipates the thrust of a vast range of work in psychological theory and practical psychotherapy. Classically, he prefigures Alfred Adler and Carl Jung as well as Freud.[226] Out of the 1930s and 1940s came further development of this type of insight by Kurt Lewin, Gordon Allport, Hadley Cantril, Kazimierz Dabrowski, and Eric Berne in psychology, and thereafter countless schools for the human potentials movement into our day.[227] Quite a bit of corroboration one might say for the power of the theory that this amateur psychologist, unsure of it himself, wondering whether it would ever make sense to anyone or have any enduring value, spun "out of his head" there in the isolation of his study at Down amid the chatter of the children nearby.

Here we have a glimpse, as with the door slightly ajar, into the vast chamber of "organic choice," or the discovery that Darwin never named that we will look at in the next chapter.

III. The Power of Language

"Third, after the power of language had been acquired, and the wishes of the community could be expressed"—here Darwin discerns how out of the opinions of others as well as ourselves emerges the consensus on how we are to act for the benefit or good of all.

This is an immensely impactful step upward. At the earlier stages, the organism could only signal to others in various ways. The flower could send forth on the wind the fragrance telling of a certain readiness for pollinating. Or the partridge could join its fellow males in rushing about in the frantic circle signaling a readiness for mating.[228] But now, at the mammalian level, with the emergence of our own species, the organism finds the ability to construct words, sentences, whole books, thousands of libraries—and eventually the world-encircling excitement of email and the World Wide Web.

With Darwin's consideration of the rise and perfection of language we are moving from cognitive psychology's concern with the acquisition of language to the concern of social psychology and sociology with how "the wishes of the community" are expressed—or the impact of language on the development of moral sensitivity and moral agency.

Today what Darwin anticipated about the acquisition, development, and nature of language fills many libraries. In the work of linguists such as Noam Chomsky, Benjamin Whorf, Alfred Korzybski, and in the field of semiotic theory, we again find a general corroboration for his lost theory.[229] Yet in the end all this work only adds vital detail to the function for language within both general and moral evolution that again Darwin accurately perceived and recorded over 100 years ago while laboring away at his desk during the long cold winter of 1868-69.

IV. The Power of Habit

"Lastly, habit in the individual would ultimately play a very important part in guiding the conduct of each member."

Today we think of habit as no more than the routine fact that we daily brush our teeth on arising. Or after putting on our clothes, we make the coffee and look for the newspaper in the driveway, or feed the cat. But Darwin has in mind the immense work over many thousands of years that brought us to the point where we can do such things routinely and safely today—that is, the span of evolution and the weight of history that lies behind even the smallest of habits today.

The repetitive power of habit—or "replication," as evolutionary theorists today prefer to put it[230]—plus the drive of sympathy and the social instinct, would create, Darwin tells us, an increasing mutuality of moral guidance and purpose between the individual and the community. Or, to put it another way, through habit the network of morality—which is the most basic of all social safety nets—was not only created, but is also maintained.

In ending this fragment for his theory with its seemingly humdrum focus on habit, Darwin again foreshadows the development of one of the most absorbing of concepts for psychology during the early part of the 20th century. Darwin's contemporary, the British psychologist Alexander Bain—whose work he will refer to later here—began the study that led to American psychologist William James' brilliant articulation of the force of habit on our lives. James, in turn, inspired other psychologists who applied the concept to learning theory and American education. At the same time, the idea of the power of habit took hold in Russia through the work of Ivan Pavlov with conditioning, and in America through J.B. Watson, the "father" of behaviorism, leading to B.F. Skinner and the *zeitgeist* for the whole field of computer-guided education today.

Against this backdrop, the vital difference between the bulk of 20th century science and what seized the mind of Darwin likely on the Isle of Wight is arresting. Working through the ramifications of the concept of habit was to shape the course for much of social science throughout the 20th century. This involved thousands of psychologists drawing inspiration from and spurred along by one another. But almost alone—in isolation, by himself there at the outset—Darwin had the vision to apply this concept to the larger questions of what is our purpose here on earth, what is to be our destiny, and how do we expand the vision, range, and responsibility of science to link the evolution of our species with the evolution of morality.

Charles Darwin, Systems Scientist

So far we have focused on various parts of Darwin's lost vision, but it is the whole that is most significant and fascinating—or how he is putting the parts together, one by one, and what they add up to at the end.

What is so uncanny is the sophistication of Darwin as a systems scientist. Freud and the others are known today as great psychologists. The same is true for Durkheim and the others as sociologists, Chomsky and the others in language studies, and Skinner and others for the focus on habit in learning theory.

They all occasionally attempted to branch out and fit their specialty into the larger picture for the life of our species on this earth. But Darwin's sure, mature, and understated mastery of this kind of effort is unrivaled. Because of the nature of his mind and the task he had set for himself, he alone was capable of this giant leap into the future to operate at the level science was only to reach during the closing decades of the 20th century. Already, over 100 years ago, he was operating as a modern systems scientist, who picks and chooses from many disciplines to try to achieve an understanding of whatever is at hand as a well-rounded whole.

The difference can be seen in an example at this point very close at hand—namely one more look at his four part perspective on the morally-oriented evolution of the human mind. First most notable about Darwin's approach as a pioneering systems scientist is the sequence, or the order in which he sets forth his thoughts.

This is not the focus on only one of the four parts to the exclusion of others—or on only the first part to his own theory as a whole, ignoring its second and completing half, as has crippled all too many scientific studies. Nor is it someone saying, "Well, what I think is going on here seems in some way to involve things like caring, reflection, language, and habit." Darwin is quite specific in saying that first comes the drive of emotion— this *caring* for what happens to ourselves and to others on this earth.

This would have led our earliest ancestors to encounter much that calls for *reflection*, which forces us to reason our way through the encountered problem to decide what to do about it. And what comes next? As we are social animals—as we do not and cannot live alone, but are by our nature dependent on others—our ancestors would have turned to others, as we do today, for help in deciding what to do and for aid in dealing with the problem.

But we must be able to speak with one another if we are to solve our problems together, Darwin reasons, so this systems approach tells us that next, most basically, comes *language*. But then he doesn't stop there, as most of us would. For what builds and holds all this together and gives it meaning over time? What goes into the crafting and building of a higher form of ape into a woman as gracious, talented, and caring as his wife Emma? Or into children as wondrously varied in personality and prospects as his own, some of whom are still living there with him, the others gone. Or to a man like himself able to think at this level of thought?

Is it not *habit?*

Yes, that is it. Just as we learn in our lifetimes through doing the same thing over and over again, so our species has grown into what it is today, and what it promises for the future, through doing the same things over and over and over again together over thousands and thousands of years.

It is this humdrum thing, habit, when added to caring, reflection, and language that has brought us to where we are.

Within the context of his time, and his struggle, and his historical meaning for humanity today, there is also a prime factor for him at work in the drive of his rounded systems analysis of what takes us out of the past into the future. It might be put this way.

All the admonitions of preachers and parents about morality and getting along together were not handed down to us inscribed on mighty stones by God, Darwin is telling us. That is only the myth to explain a much more complicated reality. Nor did this requirement for our species in any other way mysteriously appear on our plate with no struggle. *It is the inheritance of much human blood, sweat, and tears, and to preserve it requires a comparable commitment from us today.*

It was given to us by the struggle of those who saw the necessity for weaving the fabric of our life together of the toughest threads that could be found—of all the norms, customs, rules, laws, standards, and ethical precepts and commandments that morally and practically hold us together, as well as the soaring figurations of the ideals and the dreams that drive us both to form and change all these rules to live by. It was the struggle to weave this fabric against the counter purposes of those who prefer to make their own rules and hang the rest of us—or who work to tear apart this fabric overnight for their own ends.

In a time that seems to have forgotten how we got here, or what is at stake, it is a reminder of how precious and in some regards how fragile is the 100,000 year investment in the evolution of our species, and how much it is our responsibility to preserve and advance.

CHAPTER ELEVEN
ORGANIC CHOICE

In getting underway with his stories and observations of life among the animals in Chapter 8, we saw how almost immediately Darwin moves to seize our attention with a little story of how conscience may have begun to emerge even as early as among insects.

This comes up in his gory tale of the reality of life among the little honeybees that so pleasantly buzz about the garden. As a result of a place and function in nature crafted by the operation of natural selection, he tells us that if "we ourselves were reared under precisely the same conditions as hive-bees, there can hardly be a doubt that our unmarried females, like the worker bees, would think it a sacred duty to kill their brothers, and mothers would strive to kill their fertile daughters, and no one would think of interfering."

With this horrifying little domestic drama he makes sure, of course, that he has captured our attention so effectively that at the mention of anything to do with the dreaded M-word we will not dash on ahead to the more enticing parts of *Descent* about sexual selection So thus protected he goes on to make this observation about the rise of morality.

"Nevertheless, the bee, or any other social animal, would gain in our supposed case, as it appears to me, some feeling of right or wrong, or a *conscience*. For each individual would have an inward sense of possessing certain stronger or more enduring instincts, and others less strong or enduring.

"Thus, there would often be a struggle as to which impulse should be followed. And as past impressions were compared during their incessant passage through the mind, satisfaction, dissatisfaction, and even misery would be felt.

"In this case an inward monitor would tell the animal that it would have been better to have followed the one impulse rather than the other. The one course ought to have been followed, the other ought not. The one would have been right, the other wrong."

This was our first look at the basic brain-behavioral "loop" I identified as the working of "organic choice." Since then I have pointed to how, in his statement of a second level for his theory, this particular kind of observation and train of thought has come up in two more places.

A kind of psychic bell rings in the mind of the trained researcher on finding what in detective work would be called a clue. Usually at the time one has no idea of what it is a clue to, or what it really means. It is just a sense that behind whatever it is lies something of potentially considerable meaning.

What one suspects is not the murder or the swindle, as in the detective story. In science it is a sense of a possible *connection* between one thing and another, or across many fields. It can be the intuition of a chain linking of findings that may pull together many fragments of insight into something that could be of help in reaching a new level of understanding.

This bell kept ringing as I worked on—I will flag the places as we come to them in chapters ahead.

It wasn't until well through the fourth draft of this book that I finally saw what the ringing was all about. This understanding came by stages that I believe in recounting them will best reveal to the reader what excited my interest and lured me to persist until I had found what I am now convinced is the solution to this mystery story.

The first thing I noticed was a curious similarity between Darwin's observations and the dialectical theorizing of Karl Marx and Friedrich Engels.

In Darwin, for example, focusing on how the mind of bee or "man" works, he observes this sequence of (1) the intake of information, (2) a comparison of the memory of the past and the observation of the present, (3) the discovery of a conflict between perception of past and present, (4) concern about this discrepancy, and (5) the drive to resolve the conflict. Underneath an entirely different set of words and in a much different over-all context, in Marx and Engels one can find roughly the same sequence for their dialectical analysis of history, or of human cultural evolution.[231]

This struck me as quite ironic—that Darwin, long considered the "good" conservative patron saint for modern capitalism, should be thinking along the same lines as the "bad" and dreaded patron saints for communism.

I saw that this was probably why Marx so admired Darwin that he wanted to dedicate a volume of *Das Capital* to him—a proffered honor that a leery Darwin deftly side-stepped.[232] I then dipped into Marx and Engels and found a remarkable mirroring, indeed even an expansion, of Darwin's "dialectical" theorizing.[233]

"By thus acting on the external world and changing it, he at the same time changes his own nature," Marx writes in *Das Capital* of much the same dialectical process Darwin has observed.[234]

It was next most fascinating for me to realize that all three were thinking and writing about the dynamics of the *cultural evolution* of our species. This, for Marx and Engels, was old, familiar territory. But for Darwin this was something fresh and new for heavy-duty second half thinking. He had, after all, not only made his reputation but also had been immersed for most of his life up to this point in puzzling through the ins and outs of biological evolution, as recorded in the well-known first half of his theory.

Dialectical theorizing about evolution, however, was already a very old tradition not only before Darwin but also long before Marx and Engels came to it. It goes back thousands of years in Eastern thought to the China of *I Ching*, the Book of Changes.[235] This kind of theorizing generally involves so many words and such escalating complexities that few but the devotee will bother with it. Out of its great slippery basket of wonderments, however, one can extract some essentially simple basic ideas.

Change in our lives, for example—which in fact is the basic characteristic for life itself—often involves a three-step process of roughly the following sort. We want something and do something to try to get it. There is a reaction to what we do. To this reaction, then, we must adjust our reaction—and so it goes on as we further pursue, modify, or abandon our objective.

You want to buy a new suit or dress, let us say. You go to the store and see what you want and tell the sales person this. But the price the sales person quotes seems too high. You set that dress or suit aside and look about for a cheaper alternative, but there is nothing else in that store that captivates you. You go to another store and see something you think might work. But now the price quoted is so low you think there must surely be something wrong with it. So you go to another store—or simply go home and forget about it.

It is the cognitive lawfulness underlying both such familiar and more exotic little dramas of life that the dialectical theoretician tries to identify and puzzle through. According to ancient Chinese evolution theory, for example, out of the dialectical interaction of Yin and Yang pours forth the ever-shifting stream of change of all aspects of our lives. As sociologist Pitirim Sorokin makes clear in an extensive probe of the roots of dialectical theory in sociology, dialectical evolution theory also goes back in Western thought to Aristotle and the earlier Greek philosopher Heraclitus, who said, "You never step into the same river twice."[236]

But it isn't only ancient thought that is involved here. Again from the point in time where Darwin was puzzling this through on the Isle of Wight and at home in Down we can leap ahead into our own time and our own future, and find more of the same.

For the same stream of basic insights into evolution processes—ever given new faces, new names, but always at the heart the same—moves forward into the fields of systems science, and into the advanced biological, chaos, and general evolution theory only coming into their own as we move out of the 20th into the 21st century.[237]

Here too Darwin back then was stepping in a mighty way into this stream—but without calling attention to it, as if he had gone off swimming by himself in a forbidden place and didn't tell anybody. Or rather he was fascinated by this particular finding, and kept trying to tell everybody about it, but nobody was listening.

The Chaos and Cybernetic Revolutions

Darwin's long hidden plunge into this ancient stream of evolutionary theorizing can be most quickly grasped in terms of the re-emergence of the stream of dialectical thought in modern systems science. Though few today acknowledge this heritage, dialectical thinking is both grandfather and grandmother to the chaos and cybernetic revolutions of the 20th century. Of the two, chaos theory would, I believe, have been most appealing to Darwin because of the way it links a rich mix of imagery to mathematics to provide a new language for the kind of mental probing he delighted in.

As I have indicated, he was so intrigued by his observations of what we know today as "the strange attractor" and "the butterfly effect" that he identified them at work in *Origin* as well as *Descent*.[238] Who knows what he might have gone on to do with the basins, saddles, braids, octave jumps, or Birkhof's Bagel, Rossler's Funnel, or the Blue Sky Triplet of chaos theory had he had them to play with in his day?[239]

Darwin's kinship with the future is, however, easier to follow with certain ideas out of the revolution in modern science that came before chaos theory. For at the heart of Darwin's analysis of our evolution as a species lies the concept of the feedback "loop" articulated during the 1940s and 50s by Norbert Wiener with cybernetics and cybernetic theory.[240]

Two concepts basic to modern systems science, widely known by now, are those of *feedforward*, or the drive of what we seek, and *feedback*, or the response to whatever we do to try to get it.

Long before these concepts were finally articulated through a massive investment in theorizing sparked by the development of early computers, Darwin is already at work applying this line of thought to his observations.[241]

In the case of the foundation for our moral evolution in biology, for example, he perceives that it is built up over millions of years through the *feedforward* thrust of sex, which leads to parenting, which leads to socializing, which leads to the expansion of emotion, and finally reason. But reason, emotion, and socializing, in turn, have a *feedback* impact on sex and parenting.

If this is the way the foundation is built, what do we find at work in the construction of the superstructure for moral evolution?

Again, we find this step-by-step process for an upward driven cycling operating at a higher level in the cultural evolution of our species. In terms of the four components of evolution that Darwin identified in his brief statement of the second level for his higher theory, is not this what is going on at this higher level where psychology comes into play and we are entering the wonderland of a significant expansion for the human mind and our everyday consciousness?

Are we not looking at how the feedforward power of *caring* leads to the power of *reflection*, leads to the power of *language*, leads to the power of habit? And in the long-lost analysis of this pioneering systems thinker, from each stage comes the feedback that makes of this interaction the basic cycle of *learning* whereby we both evolve and advance into the future.

That is really something to think about. We must not rush on too quickly. It is a thought not to let go of until we must.

For what this indicates is that after all these years of being taught that evolution is only something that happens at the microscopic level of the selfish gene, or through the operation of natural selection that works like the romping and stomping of King Kong among us, something else far more powerful is happening to us and among us.

Something so prevalent at the level of emergence for our species, something seeming so ordinary that we overlook it. Something we everywhere take for granted.

Could it be that reading to our children at bedtime, or studying late at night, or going to school is what makes the big difference at our level? In other words, could it be that *learning* is the fundamental process of evolution at our level of being?

This is a thought we will come back to, but first we need to look at a bit more of the science of our time that we generally know too little about. For now, building on Norbert Wiener and cybernetics, via the biologist Ludwig von Bertalanffy and others, comes one of the most startling and irony-laden aspects of this story. It is the lost Darwinian link to the current discovery and re-evaluation of evolution from the perspective of the "new" concept of *self-organizing* processes.

Although usually explained in terms of concepts requiring many pages or whole books, self-organization basically means just what it sounds like. Rather than being organized from outside itself, an organism or other system is organized from *within* itself. It is shaped by its own needs, integrity, and goals. It is shaped by the life-thrust of its guiding form, *gestalt*, or *self.*

This perception of the power of the *choice* of destiny for both organism and system, while seldom seen or presented in this way, is at the heart of the excitement of much of the work of Ilya Prigogine, Stuart Kauffman, Brian Goodwin, Humberto Maturana, Francisco Varela, Vilmos Csanyi, and others I noted earlier.

A definition by Fritjof Capra captures the concept well in terms of the language in which it is often expressed in science. Self-organization, Capra tells us, is "the spontaneous emergence of new structures and new forms of behavior in open systems far from equilibrium, characterized by internal feedback loops and described mathematically by nonlinear equations."[242] More evocatively but less informational, Stuart Kauffman calls it "order for free."[243]

This sounds quite involved—and at one level it is. But beneath the scientific terms and elaborations lies the pattern familiar to all of us—as over thousands of years has been emphasized in Yoga[244]—of so seemingly simple a thing as eating or breathing. Driven by the feedforward need for oxygen, we breathe in. Driven then by the energy this gives us and the information we take in to guide the feedback of our movements, we exhale and *live—*

and through this cycle of breathing in and out, continually self-organizing and re-organizing ourselves with each breath, we move ahead through time.

As we will see, at the brain level for thinking rather than breathing this continues to be the pattern for both Darwin's observations and his theorizing as we move ahead. But now we must consider the implications of a fascinating fact in this regard.

Unaware of all that I have sketched here—unaware of I Ching in the deep past, or much about Marx and Engels within his own time, or the investigation of self-organizing processes lying ahead in the future—Darwin is repeatedly seized by a sense of a powerful overriding connection with the intimate nature of reality. Relying only on the uncanny power of the creative trance out of which he wrote, Darwin is stopped in his tracks to *repeat essentially the same observation eleven times.*

A New Principle of Evolution?

Gradually I realized there was something quite unusual about this repetition. Ever since Freud, the bit of behavior or thought that is repeated over and over has alerted the clinical psychologist to something to which one should pay special attention. The same thing is true of clues for the detective. Whether psychologist or detective, the repetition tells us that behind it may lie hidden something of immense importance to the person displaying such a compulsion or even obsession.

Now when this happens to a scientist in the course of research, it is welcomed, for in this way we recognize that we have discovered something potentially meaningful—*and to whatever it is we are powerfully motivated to give it a name.*

We label it so that with the economy of a single word or phrase we can put our discovery to work with ease in our own thinking. We also name our discoveries because it makes it easier for us to explain them to others. Also, let us face it, we are powerfully driven to name whatever it is in order to claim credit for the discovery or its naming in the history books for ourselves. But despite all these pressures on him—even though obviously Darwin could see this was a central finding for the development of the second and completing half for his theory of evolution—he did not give this process a name. Why?

I believe we do not have to look far for the answer. As any good biography makes apparent, by the time Darwin came to write *The Descent of Man*, his name, his international reputation, indeed what he as well as others already knew was his great contribution to humanity rested upon his revolutionary formulation of the principle of natural selection. But by the time he wrote *Descent* the reactionary forces of his time in religion and in science had recovered, regrouped, and were mounting an increasingly more ferocious and potentially devastating attack on the concept of natural selection.

Today, to those of us who have no reason to understand the importance of the nature and discovery of the concept, natural selection as routinely explained in the high school biology class may seem rather old and tame. But in Darwin's time it was perceived as dangerously radical a notion as communism—and even more so. Communism merely proposed ending the privilege of the upper classes and elevating the status of the lower classes. But Darwinian Natural Selection not only threatened to displace and destroy God and religion. It was further perceived as the most dangerous of all possible attempts to devalue the status for the whole of our species.

But perhaps even more unsettling was the perception—largely a matter only of intuition, existing below consciousness—that the idea of Natural Selection as the single, overriding Master Principle for both the creation and guidance of everything in this world elevated the uncertainty and chaos of nature into a new kind of brutal divinity beyond influence either by prayer or by doing good in the world. It meant that to prevail on this earth one must worship the power of privilege, money, or the strong man, that nice guys do most certainly finish last. So from all sides this most cherished child of Darwin's mind was being attacked and torn apart.

During the writing of *Descent* two attacks in particular were "extremely disturbing" to Darwin and with mounting frequency "greatly troubled him." One indeed was cause for being unsettled. It was by the leading physicist of his day, who later became Lord Kelvin. For some time afterward Darwin reported that Kelvin's attack continued to haunt him "like an odious spectre."[245]

In both cases history has shown Darwin to be right and his attackers wrong, but that didn't help at the time. For hard upon the Kelvin onslaught, immediately after publication of *Descent*, came the most famous of these attacks historically. It particularly hurt because it was by a former colleague and purported admirer St. George Mivart. This attack gained such a wide reading, and seemed to so effectively riddle the case for Natural Selection for many readers, that Darwin despaired.

Given this historical context, it becomes readily apparent why he did not give a memorable name to his discovery—or rather rediscovery—of cognitive dialectics, or to his prediscovery of self-organizing processes. By giving it a handy name, at that time it could only have provided his critics with more ammunition against Natural Selection.

People back then—as well as most of us still today—were always looking for a single cause for whatever happened.

"Is evolution driven by X or by Y?" they would have cried, tearing at him in journals, by letter, out of the pulpit and lecture platform. "Why can't you make up your mind?"

Moreover, there was the complication of his theory of sexual selection. He was already on tricky ground in *Descent* in trying to gently get across the idea that he felt Sexual Selection was in many cases equal to and even more important than Natural Selection in the evolution of species.

"Okay, is it Natural Selection? Or is it Sexual Selection? Or is it X or Y, Mr. Darwin?" one could hear them cry.

Alas, it was such a difficult task. For all those prior to him, who could simply pass off the difficult questions as dependent on God, it had been so much easier. They, too, had compounded his problem by accustoming "the mind of man" to look for the Single Great Cause of It All. The idea at the core of systems science of multiple causation still lay more than half a century ahead in the future. But back then one had God to either praise or blame for everything. And if one had moved with the times and prided oneself on being progressively scientific, if not God, then Natural Selection, it was as simple as that.

Besides, Darwin was old and sick and the fight was gone from him. Particularly in the opening of *Descent*, it is obvious that, like Chief Joseph of the Nez Percé, he doesn't want to fight any more. He just wants to make peace with his own mind—which, no matter how much Darwin the aging country gentleman would prefer it be otherwise, has insisted on this one last attempt to complete the theory and express his deepest convictions regarding the centrality of morality.

And so for over 100 years, as the bulk of the first-half Darwinians formed their battle lines around Natural Selection, this unnamed and unrecorded love child of Darwin's attempt to complete the second half has suffered a curious fate. It has either roamed the lonely streets of science as an outsider, refused entry to the textbooks or the mainstream thinking of the time. Or it has been used as a battering ram by a phalanx of advanced biological, cybernetic, and chaos theorists trying against much opposition to radically expand the paradigm.[246] In relation to Father Darwin, it has been either the orphan or the lost heir fighting for a place in the development of an adequate theory of evolution.

We will follow the journey of this orphan concept throughout the rest of the chapters of this section. And what are we to call it? As it involves what are historically known as dialectical processes—or, more popular currently, as self-organizing processes—it seems to me that because Darwin's basic focus here is on the factor of *choice of action by the organism to call for the name I suggest of organic choice.*

It also seems evident that in Darwin's repeated observations of organic choice at work he is identifying what has long been seen as a basic principle of evolution in dialectical thinking. But because the word "dialectical" was equated with Marx and communism, throughout the 20th century—particularly during the years of the "cold war"—it was rejected by mainstream evolutionary thought. Had it been perceived as coming from Darwin, however, I am convinced this vital perspective on evolution would long ago have been unequivocally established in general evolution theory. Had it been perceived as coming from Darwin, we would have been at least fifty years ahead of where we are in the development of an adequate theory of evolution.

Instead, as I will pursue in a sequel to this book, whether one calls it dialectical process, or self-organizing process, or organic choice, it occupies the key territory of mind over which the battle rages between the forces of the "old theory" and the "new theory" as we enter the 21st century.

CHAPTER TWELVE

OUR HUMAN SITUATION AND THE FUTURE

With the first story for his house of moral mind in place, Darwin as architect and builder is now ready to construct the second story—or the habitation for our species, and beyond this, for the hope and the quality we have come to call humanity.

There must of course be stairs for this new species equipped by evolution to ascend the heights. Above all, given the elevation that will put the mind of our species significantly above the surrounding land, there must be a bank of windows to take advantage of the view. There should also be skylights so that we may see the stars at night to appreciate our place in the universe and connection with them, and to see and feel the rooms fill with the sunlight that gives life to ourselves and all other species by day.

It has been a long time coming. It has required the investment of billions of lives beyond counting to get us here. It will be a very special dwelling place.

Before we go on, however, we must consider the problems that lie ahead. In chapters eight and nine, dealing with Darwin's view of the moral world of animals, we had a much easier time of it than now faces us. For now we must enter our own world—the moral world of our own species, laden with all the differences of gender, race, class, nationality, ethnicity, creed, and everything else that can radically divide us and lead to sharp disagreement as to what is right and what is wrong, what is good and what is evil, or what is moral and what is not moral.

We must in particular deal with another reason many people have been impelled to avoid or skip-read Darwin on the moral sense over 100 years. Let's call it the irritation/alienation factor.

The Irritation/Alienation Factor

The problem involves at least four kinds of irritation and alienation. The first—ironically, in view of the charm and fascination of Darwin's portrait of the moral world of animals—is that during much of the 20th century such a perspective was roundly condemned by scientists. For a scientist of the prevailing perspective to, by accident, dip into Darwin and come across his section on the moral world of animals, for example, would be enough to drive some to slam shut the book in disgust and immediately wipe the mind clear of everything else Darwin had to say.

As indicated earlier, the scientific sin that Darwin was freely and most shamelessly committing is known as *anthropomorphism*—or attributing human characteristics to animals. One must be wholly objective and simply count, weigh, or otherwise measure and report what the animal does in endless detail—but under the pain of professional death one must attempt no interpretation of what its behavior might mean.

Above all, one must rigorously refuse to in any way empathize or identify with the animal, as this was not scientific. *Moreover, this was also the way one was supposed to conduct all research with humans.* Yes, indeed! We were to be called "subjects," as with those ruled by King or Emperor. Was it any wonder that as the 20th century ended many scandals came to light of human "subjects" who had been experimentally injected with diseases or experimentally exposed to radiation?

This still remains an involved matter involving fierce battles over the proper methodology. Meanwhile, thousands of pet owners and old-style naturalists—as well as increasing numbers of prestigious primatologists—have simply gone on identifying and empathizing with animals and drawing their own conclusions, as Darwin did earlier.[247]

A second source of irritation and alienation driving readers away from Darwin—and here particularly women in droves—has been what has been denounced as his *sexist attitudes and sexist language*.[248] As noted earlier, I have changed his exclusively male referents (he, him, Man for both genders) in order to make him acceptable to a modern readership. This acknowledged, however, it is important to keep in mind the other side. Few men in Darwin's time thought or expressed themselves differently.[249] This has also been true for most men throughout most of the 20th century. And really, when you look into the question in detail, which I do in *Darwin in Love*, it was his honesty in two widely quoted statements that got him in trouble with women today, his respect for women actually was very high, and two of the worst things in the world to him were slavery and the mistreatment of women by men. In fact, as we will see, for Darwin the treatment of women was a major indicator of our degree of moral evolution.

A third source of irritation and alienation was his expression of what are considered *unscientific beliefs* today. What I personally find very impressive is how surprisingly free of this sin he actually is—in instance after instance there is this uncanny anticipation of the science of today and tomorrow. The chief culprit, however, for which some of his successors found it difficult to forgive him, was his waffling on the idea that direct inheritance—including qualities affecting morality—might somehow also account for evolution.[250] Despite the fact that some of the evidence he presents on the hereditary transmission of moral capacities is arresting—and in the light of frontal brain research merits a new look—as I am not a biologist and this idea is wholesale anathema to his biological successors, I have dropped the main offending material.[251]

The fourth source of irritation, if for no other reason than how often it comes up in *Descent*, is the most serious. He was not only wholeheartedly, but, as may be seen in Chapter 15, passionately against slavery. But he was also mildly racist in the way all proper British upper class males were in his time. What we would call today "native" or "indigenous" people are for him "savages."

As these passages would set on edge the teeth of anyone who is multi-culturally sensitive these days, most of this I have cut, or have modified what of necessity must remain. But as the quote regarding racism I give in the introduction indicates, it would be an exaggeration unfair to the complexity of Darwin's attitudes toward tribal peoples to find in him support for the notorious racism of Social Darwinism. "Savage" is his unfortunate all-purpose word, at times meaning a degrading brutality. But most often it is used merely to designate what we would today call tribal people, for many of whom Darwin had a great admiration and of whom he often speaks favorably.

Prior to a century of civilized world wars that out-savaged savagery, almost everywhere he also equates civilization with everything that is good. In fact, for him the movement from "savagery" toward "civilization" became what the neo-Darwinists, as well as many of my friends and other evolution theorists, may find most difficult about this book to swallow. For Darwin to entertain the idea of a *moral* direction for evolution can be forgiven, for all of us are entitled to a little craziness now and then or a few minor peccadilloes. But that he could be so four square convinced of it that he actively measured it along *seven* dimensions—this is too much!

Direction in Moral Evolution

Few things have been as loaded with taboos, or as well-calculated to end one's career as a purported evolution theorist during the 20th century, than to suggest there could be any direction to evolution other than toward greater complexity or diversity.

"In other words, if we flesh out these blithe scholarly abstractions in terms of their practical import for our everyday lives," I characterized this prevailing scientific belief elsewhere, "we are being told that, practically speaking, there is no direction to our lives other than toward becoming ever more ravenous consumers of an ever widening and more complex selection of goods and gadgets."[252]

The problem, basically, is that to maintain there could be any other significant direction to evolution is to go up against the neo-Darwinian worship of the sacred doctrine of a random universe and the wholesale operation of the "blind chance" that—as we have seen—Darwin himself vehemently abhorred!

Yet what is again striking in Darwin is how such a shackling of the mind is blown away by his overriding urge to simply report what he sees. And what he sees in *Descent*—in contrast to the trackless wilderness of *Origin*—is the operation not only of direction in evolution. If you consider the significance of the fact that he insists moral sensitivity becomes the prime drive for evolution at the human level, *Descent becomes his case for the idea that the direction for evolution is moral in its thrust.*

The conclusion is also inescapable that it was Darwin's apostasy in this regard that must also account for why all "the moral stuff" in *Descent* was "invisibilized" or otherwise "disappeared" over 100 years.

I am putting the following table here to help make it extremely difficult to ever again sweep this aspect of Darwin under the rug. It shows the seven dimensions for direction in moral evolution that Darwin will touch on in this and the next three chapters.

Table 12.1

Darwinian Directions for Moral Evolution

Selfishness	Altruism
Moral relativity	Moral universality
Moralism	Morality
Savagery	Civilization
Brutal treatment of women	Respect for women
Slavery	Freedom
Natural Selection	Organic choice and random variation

Evolutionary time line is from left to right

In each case here, as the table indicates, the movement is from an earlier, lower, or less advanced place in evolution, shown at the left, toward the later, higher, or more advanced state of evolution, shown at the right.

The first dimension—*from selfishness toward altruism*—is the one we have been tracking in our imaginary football game between the sociobiologists and their second-half Darwinian critics. And what does the scorecard show at this point? Up until now the sociobiologists have been winning as far as the question of whether altruism is wholly selfish or not is concerned. But now, as we move out of the world of the prehuman into all the "higher" developmental capacities for brain and body in the world of the human, the tide—as the trend in Table 12.1 indicates—is turning.

A new dimension to keep in mind as we read what he has to tell us about ourselves is the evolutionary trend from *moral relativity toward moral universality*. In other words, at the low end of this scale are stories and observations that support the belief in *moral relativity* that prevailed in anthropology and among most academics throughout the 20th century. Things that are moral for one culture are immoral for others. If morality varies so much from culture to culture then the idea of moral beliefs in common, or moral universality, must be an illusion. At the high end of this scale for Darwin, however, is his firm commitment to the perception of an evolutionary convergence toward moral universality—or agreement across religions and cultures on certain basic codes for our personal and social behavior, as we saw in Chapter 7 in the case of the Golden Rule.[253]

Next is the evolutionary shift from *moralism to morality*. Moralism for Darwin, as we will see in Chapter 14, is a fake, exploitive, intolerant, often violent and generally ignorant and self-seeking kind of morality, in contrast to what he defines as true morality.[254]

In Chapter 14 he will also track the controversial movement from *savagery* toward *civilization*. In part he does this to compare cultural stages for his own time. But much more important to him is use of this dimension to assess long span progress from the *origins* toward the hypothetical *destinations* for our species.

As earlier indicated, I selected the movement from *brutal treatment of women toward respect for women* to indicate something seldom remarked, indeed if ever, about Darwin. Four of his 19th century fellow males—the social utopian Charles Fourier, Marx and Engels, and John Stuart Mill— are feminist and humanist heroes for identifying the treatment of women as worldwide the best indicator of how far up the track of evolution our species has risen.[255] Darwin's surprising alignment can be seen in passionate passages in *The Voyage of the Beagle* and *The Descent of Man* expressing his hatred of and contempt for male brutality toward women.[256]

The next dimension, the shift from *slavery* to *freedom*, can be seen in the passion for the cause of abolitionism that was a Darwin family tradition over at least three generations, which Darwin now squarely identifies as still another marker for moral evolution.[257]

Finally, in this chapter and the next can be found what he stresses is the decisive difference between first-half and second-half Darwinian theory. Moral evolution, he tells us, involves the movement beyond the "amoral" working of natural selection and random variation toward the emergence and ascendancy of "higher" processes. This comes out in his stories and observations that show a progression from the ascendancy of *natural selection and random variation toward the ascendancy of organic choice.*

Now let us return to Darwin. Again the writing hereafter is his own. My addition, other than smoothing over the rough places indicated in the introduction, is to add subheads and brief commentaries to make it easier to understand what he is saying.

The Human as Moral Agent[258]

Most people will admit that we humans are social beings.[259] We see this in our dislike of solitude, and in our wish for society beyond that of our own family. Solitary confinement is one of the severest punishments that can be inflicted.

Some authors suppose that our species primevally lived in single families. But at the present day, though single families, or only two or three together, roam the solitudes of some savage lands, they always, as far as I can discover, hold friendly relations with other families inhabiting the same district.

Such families occasionally meet in council and unite for their common defense. It is no argument against the savage being a social animal that the tribes inhabiting adjacent districts are almost always at war with each other, for the social instincts never extend to all the individuals of the same species.

Judging from the analogy of the majority of the Quadrumana, it is probable that our early ape-like progenitors were likewise social, but this is not of much importance for us. We humans, as we exist today, have few special instincts, having lost any which our early progenitors may have possessed.[260] But this is no reason why we should not have retained from an extremely remote period some degree of instinctive love and sympathy for our fellows. We are indeed all conscious that we do possess such sympathetic feelings.[261]

As he seeks for grounding in this complex new moral world of the human, Darwin is feeling his way into it in ways that call for explanation. Regarding both multicultural sensitivities and later science, he exaggerates when he says, for example, that adjacent tribes are "almost always at war with each other." We are also beginning to encounter the confusion of his all-purpose use of the word "savage." It can mean what today we would call "tribal societies" but elsewhere can mean "brutal and degraded people." He will also in some places condemn "savages" for their vices and in other places laud them for their virtues. To provide a fundamental clarification, it is clear that he is generally talking about the two very different kinds of tribal societies that cultural evolution theorist Riane Eisler identifies as orienting either to a peaceful, gender-equalitarian "partnership model" or to a warring, male-dominant "dominator model."[262] Earlier anthropologist Ruth Benedict pointed to differences of "high synergy" and "low synergy" societies.[263] Lacking such a differentiating model, the distinction is—as is still true for many anthropologists and other social analysts today—blurred for Darwin and becomes confusing.

Here Darwin also seeks grounding in the difference for morality as driven by foundational "instincts" and as driven by the superstructural development of "love and sympathy for our fellows"—blurred here again by the problems of his all-purpose use of the word "instinct."

Pursuing the question of why we have this sympathy for others and where it comes from, Darwin continues...

In his ***Enquiry Concerning the Principles of Morals***, Hume,[264] for example, remarks that there "seems a necessity for confessing that the happiness and misery of others are not spectacles all together indifferent to us, but that the view of the former...communicates a secret joy," while "the appearance of the latter...throws a melancholy damp over the imagination."[265] But our consciousness does not tell us whether these sympathetic feelings are instinctive, having originated long ago in the same manner as with the lower animals, or whether they have been acquired by each of us during our early years.

As we are social animals, it is almost certain that we would inherit a tendency to be faithful to our comrades.[266] We would also inherit a tendency to be obedient to the leader of our tribe, for both of these qualities are common to most social animals. We would consequently possess some capacity for self-command. From an inherited tendency we would be willing to defend, in concert with others, our fellow beings. We would also be ready to aid them in any way that did not too greatly interfere with our own welfare or our own strong desires.

The social animals that stand at the bottom of the scale are guided almost exclusively, and those standing higher in the scale largely guided, by special instincts in the aid they give to the members of the same community. But they are likewise in part impelled by mutual love and sympathy, assisted apparently by some degree of reason.[267]

> *Here, aside from the difficulty of his multiple-level use of the word "instinct," Darwin is more importantly making a distinction between the foundation and the superstructure for moral sensitivity.*

Although we have no special instinct to tell us how to aid our fellow beings, we still have the impulse, and with our improved intellectual faculties would naturally be much guided in this respect by reason and experience. Instinctive sympathy would also cause us to value highly the approval of our fellows. As Mr. Bain has clearly shown, the love of praise and the strong feeling of glory, and the still stronger horror of scorn and infamy, "are due to the workings of sympathy." Consequently, we would be influenced in the highest degree by the wishes, approval, and blame of our fellow beings.

Thus the social instincts, which must have been acquired by us in a very rude state, and probably even by our early ape-like progenitors, still give the impulse to some of our best actions. But these actions are to a higher degree determined by the expressed wishes and judgement of our fellow beings, and unfortunately very often by our own strong selfish desires. But as love, sympathy and self-command become strengthened by habit, and as the power of reasoning becomes clearer—so that we can value justly the judgements of our fellows—we will feel ourselves impelled, apart from any transitory pleasure or pain, to certain lines of conduct.

We might then declare I am the supreme judge of my own conduct. In the words of Kant, I will not in my own person violate the dignity of humanity.[268]

> *Here, too quickly to follow, some fundamental points are made. He has told us that "very often" we are motivated by "our own strong selfish desires"—bearing out the sociobiologists. But he has also told us that, as the powers of caring, reflection, language, and habit (to recap our categories for the second level of his moral theory) take over, we are driven to "lines of conduct" providing neither "pleasure or pain"—that is to non-selfish altruism.*

Of critical importance in his moral theory, he further makes the jump from morality as conformity to group norms—which can be quite vicious at times—to morality as most fundamentally dependent on the individual conscience, as the pioneering moral scientist Immanuel Kant pinned his own theory to.

The Love of Praise and the Dread of Blame[269]

It may be asked how within the limits of the same tribe did a large number of members first become endowed with these social and moral qualities, and how was the standard of excellence raised?

It is extremely doubtful whether the offspring of the more sympathetic and benevolent parents, or of those who were the most faithful to their comrades, would be reared in greater numbers than the children of selfish and treacherous parents belonging to the same tribe.

Those who were ready to sacrifice their lives, as many a savage has been rather than betray his comrades, would often leave no offspring to inherit their noble nature. The bravest men, who were always willing to come to the front in war, and who freely risked their lives for others, would on an average perish in larger numbers than other men. **Therefore, it hardly seems probable that the number of men gifted with such virtues, or that the standard of their excellence, could be increased through natural selection, that is, by the survival of the fittest.**

Although the circumstances leading to an increase in the number of those thus endowed within the same tribe are too complex to be clearly followed out, we can trace some of the probable steps. In the first place, as the reasoning powers and foresight of the members became improved, each person would soon learn that if they aided others, they would commonly receive aid in return. From this low motive they might acquire the habit of aiding others. The habit of performing benevolent actions would then certainly strengthen the feeling of sympathy, which originally gave the first impulse to benevolent actions.

Here we have a taste of the fascination for Darwin of the application of the virtues of courage and bravery to what we would perceive as the immoral end of warfare. The difference between then and now is that, while in Darwin's time it was still popular to find virtue in war, following the devastation of two world wars, the over 200 other wars of the 20th century, and the threat of nuclear wipeout for a good chunk of the species, our attitudes have drastically changed. Notably here, however, what Darwin is saying is that the principle of natural selection breaks down here and the increase in people of "noble nature" must be accounted for in other ways.

Along the same line, here he clearly designates selfishness as a "low motive" for doing good for others. Moreover, he also clearly states that altruism is also impelled by a drive separate from selfishness—originating in sympathy "which originally gave the first impulse to benevolent actions."

In other words, we have not one but two significant "touchdowns" for second-half Darwinian theory. The score, by my reckoning, now stands: first-halfers, 4; second-halfers, 3.

But another and much more powerful stimulus to the development of the social virtues is, as I have noted, afforded by the praise and blame of our fellow-humans. As we have seen, we are impelled by the instinct of sympathy[270] to habitually bestow both praises and blame on others—meanwhile loving the former and dreading the latter when applied to ourselves.[271] This instinct no doubt was originally acquired, like all the other social instincts, through natural selection.

At how early a period in the course of their development our progenitors became capable of feeling and being impelled by the praise or blame of their fellows, we cannot of course say. But it appears that even dogs appreciate encouragement, praise and blame. The rudest savages feel the sentiment of glory, as they clearly show by preserving the trophies of their prowess, by their habit of excessive boasting, and even by the extreme care they take of their personal appearance and decorations—for unless they regarded the opinion of their comrades, such habits would be senseless.

We may therefore conclude that primeval humans, at a very remote period, were influenced by the praise and blame of their fellows. It is obvious that the members of the same tribe would approve of conduct that appeared to them to be for the general good, and would disapprove that which appeared evil.

To do good unto others—to do unto others as ye would they should do unto you—is the foundation of morality. It is, therefore, hardly possible to exaggerate the importance during rude times of the love of praise and the dread of blame.[272]

The Crux of Human Moral Agency[273]

We have not, however, as yet considered the main point, on which the whole question of the moral sense turns.

Why should we feel that we ought to obey one instinctive desire rather than another? Why are we bitterly regretful if we have yielded to a strong sense of self-preservation and have not risked our life to save that of a fellow creature? Or why do we regret having stolen food from hunger?

It is evident in the first place that with us the instinctive impulses have different degrees of strength. A savage will risk his own life to save that of a member of the same community, but will be wholly indifferent about a stranger. A young and timid mother urged by the maternal instinct will, without a moment's hesitation, run the greatest danger for her own infant, but not for a mere fellow-creature. **Nevertheless, many of us, who have never before risked our life for another, but full of courage and sympathy, have disregarded the instinct of self-preservation and plunged at once into a torrent to save a drowning person, though a stranger.**[274]

In this case we are impelled by the same instinctive motive that made the heroic little American monkey, formerly described, save his keeper by attacking the great and dreaded baboon.

Such actions as the above appear to be the simple result of the greater strength of the social or maternal instincts rather than of any other instinct or motive, for they are performed too instantaneously for reflection, or for pleasure or pain to be felt at the time. Moreover, if we are prevented by any cause from so acting, distress or even misery may be felt.[275]

Not only has the tide turned on the question of whether altruism is solely driven by selfishness, but now, in game terms, second-half Darwinian theory is winning. In his increasingly forceful argument within the context of the full span for moral motivation—and now with the example of those who will risk their lives to save a drowning stranger, and even a case of cross-species altruism, a monkey rushing to the rescue of a human—out of the lost scientific past Darwin demolishes the argument advanced by the truncation of the evidence and the thinking of the sociobiologists of the 20th century.

In reality, however, science and society are the real winners here as we gain both the economy and potential cohesiveness of scientific and social understanding—rather than grounds for further indulgence in the time-wasting dichotomy of let's-you-and-him fight. For what Darwin is showing is that both motivations operate—and that it is our job now to understand what this means both in terms of science and everyday life.

Some Quibbling and a Rejoinder[276]

I am aware that some persons maintain that actions performed impulsively, as in the above cases, do not come under the dominion of the moral sense, and thus cannot be called moral.

They make the distinction between what they call **material** and **formal** morality.[277] They would confine using the term moral solely to actions done deliberately, after a victory over opposing desires, or when prompted by some exalted motive. But it appears scarcely possible to draw any clear line or distinction of this kind—and I am delighted to find Professor Huxley and Mr. Leslie Stephen take the same view as I do.[278]

Indeed, as Mr. Stephen remarks, "The metaphysical distinction between material and formal morality is as irrelevant as other such distinctions."[279]

As far as exalted motives are concerned, many instances have been recorded of savages, destitute of any feeling of general benevolence toward humankind, and not guided by any religious motive, who have deliberately sacrificed their lives as prisoners, rather than betray their comrades—and surely their conduct ought to be considered moral.

As far as deliberation and the victory over opposing motives are concerned, in rescuing their offspring or comrades from danger, animals may be seen in distress because of the quandary of opposed instincts. Yet their actions, though done for the good of others, are not called moral. Moreover, anything performed very often by us, will at last be done without deliberation or hesitation, and can then hardly be distinguished from an instinct—yet surely no one will pretend that such an action ceases to be moral.

On the contrary, we all feel that an act cannot be considered as perfect, or as performed in the most noble manner, unless it be done impulsively, without deliberation or effect, in the same manner as by someone in whom the requisite qualities are innate.

Those of us who are forced to overcome our fear or want of sympathy before we act deserve, however, higher credit than those whose innate disposition leads them to a good act without effort. As we cannot distinguish between motives, we rank all actions of a certain class as moral if performed by a moral being.

And who is this moral being? Those among us who are capable of comparing our past and future actions or motives, and of approving or disapproving them.[280] We have no reason to suppose that any of the lower animals have this capacity. Therefore, when a Newfoundland dog drags a child out of the water, or when a monkey faces danger to rescue its comrade, or takes charge of an orphan monkey, we do not call its conduct moral.

But in the case of ourselves, who alone can with certainty be ranked as moral beings,[281] actions of a certain class are called moral—and this is so whether they are performed deliberately, after a struggle with opposing motives, impulsively through instinct, or from the effects of slowly-gained habit.

> *"And who is this moral being?" Once again—four times now—we encounter the wording that signals Darwin's preoccupation with the conceptual underlayment for "organic choice." Here, too, behind what on the surface seems no more than philosophical speculation, Darwin's answer foreshadows the findings of modern brain research that both corroborate his observations and reveal to us a critical brain structure for the highest level functioning of "organic choice." For the brain research of Luria, MacLean, and many others shows that this act of "comparing past and future actions or motives" that Darwin describes, and of "approving or disapproving them," is linked to moral sensitivity within the operations of the primarily right frontal brain.*[282]

The Basic Difference Between Moral Agency in Humans and in Lower Animals[283]

Although some instincts are more powerful than others, why is it that with us certain superstructural aspects of the social instincts—including the love of praise and fear of blame—possess greater strength, or have through long habit acquired greater strength, than the more foundational instincts of self-preservation, hunger, lust, vengeance, etc.?[284]

Why do we regret, even though trying to banish this regret, that we have followed one natural impulse rather than another? Why do we further feel that we ought to regret our conduct?

In this respect, we differ profoundly from the lower animals. Nevertheless, we can, I think, see with some degree of clarity the reason for this difference.

We cannot, from the activity of our mental faculties, avoid reflection. Past impressions and images are incessantly and clearly passing through our minds.

Again—five times now—we encounter Darwin's recurring concern with the dynamics of an aspect of the unnamed concept I am calling "organic choice."

Moreover, in the ten paragraphs that follow, Darwin is, through the rambling process of his method for scientific discovery, describing the evolution of both conscience and other aspects of organic choice.

With those animals that live permanently in a community with others of their kind the social instincts are ever present and persistent. Such animals are always ready to utter the danger signal, to defend the community, and to give aid to their fellows in accordance with their habits. At all times, without the stimulus of any special passion or desire, they feel some degree of love and sympathy for the others. They are unhappy if long separated from them and always happy to be in their company.[285]

So it is with ourselves. Even when we are quite alone how often do we think with pleasure or pain of what others think of us? Of their imagined approval or disapproval? And this all follows from sympathy, a fundamental element of the social instincts. Any of us who possessed no trace of such instincts would be an unnatural monster.[286]

By contrast, the desire to satisfy hunger, or any passion such as vengeance, is in its nature temporary and can for a time be fully satisfied. The instinct of self-preservation is not felt except in the presence of danger, and many a coward has thought himself brave until he has met his enemy face to face. The wish for somebody else's property is perhaps as persistent a desire as any that can be named, but even in this case the satisfaction of actual possession is generally a weaker feeling than the desire. Indeed, many a thief, if not an habitual one, after success has wondered why he stole some article.[287]

If we look for highly persistent feelings of this kind, enmity or hatred seems to be perhaps our most likely candidate. To this we might also add envy, as defined as hatred of another for some excellence or success. As Bacon notes, "Of all other affections envy is the most importune and continual."

Dogs are very apt to hate both strange men and strange dogs, especially if they live near at hand but do not belong to the same family, tribe, or clan. This feeling thus seems to be innate. It is certainly persistent and seems to be the complement and converse of the true social instinct.

From what we hear of savages, it also appears that something of the same kind holds good with them. If this be so, it would be a small step to direct such feelings toward any member of the same tribe who had done the savage an injury and had become an enemy. Nor is it probable that the primitive conscience would reproach a man for injuring his enemy in return. Rather, it would reproach him if he had not avenged himself.[288]

By contrast, we have one of the most remarkable of the feelings, motivations, or responses. This is the idea of doing good in return for evil, to love your enemy. To this height of morality it seems highly doubtful the social instincts could ever, by themselves, have led us. Before any such golden rule would ever have been thought of or obeyed, it would have been necessary for these instincts, together with sympathy, to be highly cultivated and extended by the aid of reason, instruction, and the love or fear of God.

We will thus be driven to compare impressions of past hunger, vengeance satisfied, or danger shunned at other people's cost, with the almost ever-present instinct of sympathy, and with our knowledge of what others consider to be praiseworthy or blamable.

This knowledge cannot be banished from our minds and from instinctive sympathy is esteemed of great moment.[289]

CHAPTER THIRTEEN

THE ESCALATION OF ORGANIC CHOICE

Back and forth Darwin roams, from animals to ourselves, from tribal to more civilized people, probing the wide range of both past and present experience and the emotions, thoughts, and behavior involved in the development of both conscience and organic choice—for which we have just encountered a sixth perception.

All this begins to come into focus as—for the seventh time—he centers on the thrust of organic choice elaborated in us in the following analysis of the concept and working of the human conscience.

The Dynamics of Conscience and Organic Choice[290]

At the moment of action, we are no doubt apt to follow the stronger impulse. Although this may occasionally prompt us to the noblest deeds, more commonly it leads us to gratify our own desires at the expense of others. But after their gratification—when past and weaker impressions are judged under pressure by the ever-enduring social instinct, and by our deep regard for the good opinion of our fellows—retribution will surely come.[291]

We will then feel remorse, repentance, regret, or shame—this latter feeling, however, relates almost exclusively to the judgement of others. We will consequently resolve more or less firmly to act differently for the future, and this is conscience, for conscience looks backwards and serves as a guide for the future.[292]

The nature and strength of the feeling that we call regret, shame, repentance or remorse apparently depend not only on the strength of the violated instinct. This discomfort also partly seems to depend on the strength of the temptation, and often still more on the judgement of our fellows.

How far we value the approval of others depends on the strength of our innate or acquired feeling of sympathy,[293] **as well as on our own capacity for reasoning out the remote consequences of our acts.** Another important element here, although not necessary, is the reverence or fear of the Gods or Spirits believed in by each of us. This especially applies in the case of remorse.

Several critics have objected that, although some slight regret or repentance might be explained by the views I am expressing, it is impossible in this way to account for the soul-shaking feeling of remorse. But I can see little force in this objection. My critics do not define what they mean by remorse and I can find no definition implying more than an overwhelming sense of repentance.

Remorse seems to bear the same relation to repentance as rage does to anger, or agony to pain. For example, take the case of an instinct so strong and so generally admired as maternal love. If disobeyed, this can lead to the deepest misery. Even when an action is opposed to no special instinct, merely to know that our friends and equals despise us is enough to cause great misery.[294]

Where earlier Darwin's thinking led him to anticipate Sigmund Freud's ideas of what conscience is and how it works, now he moves on to anticipate an idea that—still widely familiar—comes from the work of the famous turn-of-the-century sociologist George Herbert Mead. That is, Darwin's observation that conscience "looks backwards and serves as a guide for the future," and the dynamics therein, anticipates Freud's development of the relation between ego, super-ego and ego-ideal.[295] Similarly, in the emphasis he next places on "our deep regard for the good opinion of our fellows," he foreshadows Mead's idea of how our own sense of self is in part formed by the opinion of our "significant others."[296]

It seems further clear to me that these pivotal concepts for both Freud and Mead express more "higher level" facets of the underlying working of organic choice.

Prompted by our conscience, through long habit we can acquire such perfect self-command that our desires and passions will at last yield instantly and without a struggle to our social sympathies and instincts, including our feeling for the judgement of our fellows.[297]

The still hungry person will not think of stealing food, nor will the still revengeful person think of wreaking vengeance. Thus at last we come to feel, through acquired and perhaps inherited, habit that it is best for us to obey our more persistent impulses. The imperious word ought seems merely to imply the consciousness of the existence of a rule of conduct, however it may have originated. Formerly, it must have been often vehemently urged that an insulted gentleman **ought** to fight a duel. We even say a pointer **ought** to point, and a retriever to retrieve game. If they fail to do so, they fail in their duty and act wrongly.

If, when recalled to mind, any desire or instinct that has led to an action opposed to the good of others still appears as strong, or stronger than, the social instinct, we will feel no keen regret at having followed it—but we will be conscious of the fact that if our conduct were known to our friends or fellows it would meet with their disapproval. And few are so destitute of sympathy as not to feel discomfort when this is realized.

Now in the case of someone with no such sympathy, whose desires lead to bad actions that are not over-ruled by the persistent social instincts and the judgement of others, we have the essentially bad person. Dr. Prosper Despine in his Psychologie Naturelle gives many curious cases of the worst criminals, who apparently have been entirely destitute of conscience.[298]

> *The reference is to an ancient source immaterial by now. But the type of person Darwin is referring to here is known today either as the psychopath or the sociopath. In case after case known to the police, courts, and journalists, these social predators, often of charm and intelligence, display either little or absolutely no evidence of a conscience. In seeking a cause for this chilling breakdown in basic humanity, the overwhelming finding is of a lack of love and the prevalence of abuse in childhood. But behind this cause the devastating new findings— which help explain how psychopaths, or the proverbial "bad seed," can emerge in families in which there is ample love and no abuse—are in brain research, where the general finding is of prefrontal lobe deficits, generally right hemispheric.*

> *That is, brain researchers find a failure of the critical brain areas to develop properly through lack of parental caring at the right time in infancy, or brutal child abuse causing brain injury—or other trauma curbing the necessary neuronal development or functioning of these brain areas fundamental to the operation of the moral brain.[299]*

In such a case the sole restraining motive left is the fear of punishment, or the conviction that in the long run it would be best for their own selfish interests to regard the good of others rather than their own.

It is obvious that we may with an easy conscience gratify our own desires if they do not interfere with our social instincts, that is with the good of others. But in order to be quite free from self-reproach, or at least of anxiety, it is almost necessary for us to avoid the disapproval, whether reasonable or not, of our fellow humans. Nor must we break through the fixed habits of life, especially if these habits are supported by reason, for if we do we will assuredly feel dissatisfaction.

We must likewise avoid the disapproval of the one God or gods in whom, according to our knowledge or our superstition, we may believe. And here we may also have the additional fear of divine punishment operating.[300]

As this is the third reference to God in the last several pages, it is time to take a look at what seems to lie behind Darwin's thoughts in these references besides the desire to keep Emma and Henrietta happy (see Chapter 5).

Darwin first noted that an influence in the development of the Golden Rule in our species' early cultural evolution, besides the working of sympathy, reason, and instruction, was—as is the belief in Judaism, Christianity, and Islam— the "love or fear of God." He next observes that in the development of the conscience, especially in the case of remorse, another element, "although not necessary," is "the reverence or fear of the Gods or Spirits believed in by each of us." Here he has told us that another factor in the operation of conscience, "according to our knowledge or our superstition," is our desire to avoid "the disapproval of the one God or Gods," or through fear of divine retribution.

If we read these passages carefully, it is fascinating to see how skillfully he manages to accommodate Emma's and Henrietta's—and many other readers'—need for a place for God in their system of beliefs. But at the same time he remains true to his own need for an open mind on the subject, neither believer nor disbeliever, basically an agnostic rather than an atheist, as he is sometimes portrayed.

If Music be the Food of Love[301]

An interesting question generally unprobed by science is whether there is a connection between moral sensitivity and our sensitivity to beauty, as is so often expressed by religious visionaries, as well as in the traditional interconnection for "the true, the good, and the beautiful" in philosophy. In what follows, Darwin is again the scientific pioneer. The connection also comes up in the "peak experiences" identified by humanistic psychologist Abraham Maslow, as we will see in Chapter 16.

Why was the connection between moral sensitivity and beauty meaningful to Darwin? A good answer to that question would probably take another whole book. All I can do here is note the beginning for his thoughts in this direction that can be seen in how meaningful the beauty of music was to him. Not only did he cherish the sound of his wife Emma, Chopin's student, playing the piano. As I noted in the introduction, he also turned to music in a very funny experiment to probe the operation of "organic choice" far down the developmental scale. Already convinced he could detect sociability and a trial and error form of intelligence at work in earthworms, he organized a family orchestra consisting of Emma on the piano, his son Francis on the bassoon, and his grandson Bernard on the whistle, to gather about a dish of these worms to test their capacity for music appreciation.[302]

Music arouses in us various emotions, but not the more terrible ones of horror, fear, rage, etc. It awakens the gentler feelings of tenderness and love, which readily pass into devotion. In the Chinese annals it is said, "Music hath the power of making heavens descend upon earth." These powerful and mingled feelings may well give rise to the sense of sublimity.[303]

We can concentrate, as Dr. Seemann observes, greater intensity of feeling in a single musical note than in pages of writing. It is probable that nearly the same emotions, but much weaker and far less complex, are felt by birds when the male pours forth his full volume of song in rivalry with other males, to captivate the female. Love is still the commonest theme of our songs.

As Herbert Spencer remarks, "music arouses dormant sentiments of which we had not conceived the possibility, and do not know the meaning; or, as Richter says, tells us of things we have not seen and shall not see."

Conversely, when vivid emotions are felt and expressed by the orator, or even in common speech, musical cadences and rhythm are instinctively used. The negro in Africa when excited often bursts forth in song: "another will reply in song, whilst the company, as if touched by a musical wave, murmur a chorus in perfect unison." Even monkeys express strong feelings in different tones—anger and impatience by low—fear and pain by high notes. The sensations and ideas thus excited in us by music, or expressed by the cadences of oratory, appear from their vagueness, yet depth, like mental reversions to the emotions and thoughts of a long past age.

It appears probable that our progenitors, either the males or females or both sexes, before acquiring the power of expressing their mutual love in articulate language endeavoured to charm each other with musical notes and rhythm.

The Moral Situation of Our Species And Other Life Forms with which We Share this Planet[304]

There can be no doubt that the difference between the mind of the least endowed of our species and the minds of the lower animals is immense.

If able to take a dispassionate view of its own case, an anthropomorphous ape—*that is, an ape let us say with the ability to step out of its own "skin" to easily converse with us as one friend to another*—would probably admit that though it could form an artful plan to plunder a garden, and although it could use stones for fighting or for breaking open nuts, when it came to the idea of fashioning the stone into a tool it would find this was quite beyond its scope.

> *This was of course long before gestalt psychologist Wolfgang Koehler's classic experiments with apes on the island of Tenerife during World War I. There Kohler first discovered the tool-making abilities of apes that more recent studies have expanded with dramatic findings with the famous Washoe and other stars of the ape world.*[305]

Still less, they might admit, could they follow a train of metaphysical reasoning, or solve a mathematical problem, or reflect on God, or admire a grand natural scene. Some apes, however, would probably declare they could and did admire the beauty of the colored skin and fur of their partners in marriage. They would admit, however, that although they could make other apes understand by cries some of their perceptions and simpler wants, the notion of expressing definite ideas by definite sounds had never crossed their minds.[306]

They might insist that they were ready to aid their fellow-apes of the same troop in many ways—to risk their lives for them, to take charge of their orphans. But they would be forced to acknowledge that disinterested love for all living creatures, which must surely be the noblest attribute for our own species,[307] was quite beyond their comprehension.

Nevertheless, the difference in mind between ourselves and the higher animals, great as it is, certainly is one of degree and not of kind.

We have seen that the senses and intuitions, the various emotions and faculties, such as love, memory, attention, curiosity, imitation, reason, etc., of which we boast, may be found in an incipient, or even sometimes in a well-developed condition, in the lower animals.[308]

If it could be proved that certain high mental powers, such as the formation of general concepts, self-consciousness, etc., were absolutely peculiar to our species, which seems extremely doubtful, it likely would also be shown that these qualities are merely the incidental results of other highly-advanced intellectual faculties—and these again mainly the result of the continued use of a perfected language.[309]

At what age does the newborn infant possess the power of abstraction, or become self-conscious and reflect on its own existence? We cannot answer, nor can we answer in regard to the ascending organic scale.[310] The half-art, half-instinct of language still bears the stamp of its gradual evolution.

Pondering the evolution of the moral sense from its earliest appearance among the animals into its rise among us, Darwin sounds the note of continuity moving upward species by species. And in singling out the interaction of love, memory, attention, curiosity, imitation, reason, and language over time we catch for the eighth time overtones of the underlying thrust of organic choice, which in the following passage Darwin connects to the moral Golden Rule.

We have seen how, with the aid of active intellectual powers and the effects of habit, the social instincts—the prime principle of our moral constitution—lead over our evolution to the golden rule "As ye would that others should do unto you, do ye to them likewise."

Here lies the foundation of morality.[311]

CHAPTER FOURTEEN

MORALISM, MORALITY, AND THE MELDING OF THE FIRST AND SECOND HALVES

Basement up through first and now second story, Darwin as architect and builder has done his best to construct the house of moral mind. But after all this, it is not a happy household.

It is, in fact, a house ridden with dissension, occasionally set afire, desecrated by vandals, in continual need of repair. Here we come to one of the most distressing questions that confront us in our consideration of the nature and development of the moral sense: How and why does it fall short? Or—as manifested in the assassinations, massacres, bombings, and other acts of terrorism of our time—how and why does the moral sense go bad?

Darwin opens this chapter with a list of the horrors of moralism. His choice, unfortunately, is exclusively along the savagery versus civilization dimension. Marx and Engels, or Charles Dickens would have countered with the economic savageries of the civilization that Darwin extolled. Soon, also, the world wars of the 20th century were to reveal civilization at its worst. But at the core of Darwin's list of horrors lies the concern that is again ours today.

Today, 100 years later, the problem is the rampant moralism of right-wing Christian preachers and politicians trying to batter down the barrier between church and state so essential to democracy, end the teaching of evolution, and drive women back into subjection. Violence personified, it is the moralism used by rightist Muslim mullahs and others to mask terrorism, spread authoritarianism, and again subjugate women globally.

Of all the threats facing humanity during the 21st century none is so poorly understood or widely ignored as that of an escalation of moralism, as the peoples of this earth, increasingly fearful and unsettled by the consequences of population explosion and the degradation of the environment, turn to the fierce new demagogues who proclaim the salvation of the re-emergent voice of God—their version.

Slippery, self-justifying, elastic as a rubber band and yet also, if needed, as rigid as a doorpost, moralism—or putting a moral face to immoral acts—has encouraged an additionally destructive backlash. Aghast reaction to it led to the 20th century heyday for the cynicism of the deconstructionists and their nonacademic counterparts, who say that morality has no roots, that it is only a façade. It also led to the perspective of the relativists and their nonacademic counterparts, who say there are no fixed standards for morality anywhere, that it's whatever one wants to make of it.

In opening this chapter, Darwin gives the anti-moralism of the anti-moralists all the ammunition for their arguments they could wish for. But intermingled with the horrors, he shows how underlying this façade the foundations for morality not only do exist. They are rooted both within the origin and also—so he intimates—in the destination for our species.

The greatest of these foundations, he reaffirms, is the moral sense, built out of the evolution of social instinct, sympathy, and all else he identified earlier as going into its construction.

The Horror as Well as the Heights of Morality—or Moralism Unmasked[312]

The view that to this point we have presented of the origin and nature of the moral sense, which tells us what we ought to do, and of the conscience that reproves us if we disobey it, accords well with what we may observe of the early and undeveloped condition of this faculty in humankind.

The virtues that must be practiced by humans in an as yet rude or undeveloped state, so that they may live together successfully, are those still recognized as the most important. But they are practiced almost exclusively in relation to people of the same tribe, and their opposites are not regarded as crimes in relation to the people of other tribes.[313]

A paramount consideration is that no tribe could hold together if murder, robbery, treachery, etc., were common.[314] Consequently, such crimes within the limits of the same tribe "are branded with everlasting infamy,"[315] but excite no such sentiment beyond these limits.

A North American Indian warrior is well pleased with himself, and is honored by others, when he scalps a man of another tribe,[316] and a Dyak cuts off the head of an unoffending person and dries it as a trophy. The murder of infants has prevailed on the largest scale throughout the world and has met with no reproach—this because infanticide, especially of females, has been thought to be good for the tribe, or at least not injurious.[317]

Suicide during former times was not generally considered a crime, but rather, from the courage displayed, seen as an honorable act. And so it is still practiced by some semi-civilized and savage nations without reproach, for it does not obviously concern others of the tribe.

It has been recorded that an Indian Thug[318] conscientiously regretted that he had not robbed and strangled as many travelers as did his father before him. In a rude state of civilization the robbery of strangers is, indeed, often considered honorable.[319]

Slavery is a great crime.[320] Yet it was not so regarded until quite recently, even by the most civilized nations. This was especially the case because the slaves belonged in general to a race different from that of their masters.[321]

Among barbarians who do not regard the opinion of their women, wives are commonly treated like slaves.[322] Many savages are utterly indifferent to the sufferings of strangers, or even delight in witnessing them.[323] It is well known, for example, that the women and children of some North American Indians aided in torturing their enemies.

Nevertheless, besides the family affections, kindness is common, especially during sickness, between the members of the same tribe. Moreover, in contrast to the point I am making here regarding the foundations for morality, this kindness is sometimes extended beyond these limits.[324] Mungo Park's[325] touching account of the kindness of the black women of the interior to him is well known.

There also cannot be fidelity without truth, and this fundamental virtue we may commonly find between members of the same tribe, thus Mungo Park heard the black women teaching their young children to love the truth. This, again, is one of the virtues that becomes so deeply rooted in the mind that it is sometimes practiced by savages, even at high cost, toward strangers.[326] But to lie to your enemy has rarely been thought a sin, as the history of modern diplomacy too plainly shows.

As during rude times no one can be useful or faithful to their tribe without courage, this quality has universally been placed in the highest rank.[327] Although in civilized countries a good yet timid man may be far more useful to the community than a brave one, we cannot help instinctively honoring the latter above a coward, however benevolent.

As no one can practice the virtues necessary for the welfare of their tribe without self-sacrifice, self-command, and the power of endurance, these qualities have also been at all times highly and most justly valued. The American savage, for example, voluntarily submits to the most horrid tortures without a groan to prove and strengthen his fortitude and courage. Prudence, on the other hand, though a very useful virtue but which does not concern the welfare of others, has never been highly esteemed.

We have now seen that actions are regarded by savages, and were probably so regarded by the primeval human, as good or bad solely as they obviously affect the welfare of the tribe—not that of the species, nor that of an individual member of the tribe. This conclusion agrees well with the belief that the so-called moral sense is aboriginally derived from the social instincts, for they relate at first exclusively to the community.[328]

In general, we may repeatedly observe how the wishes and opinions of the members of the same community, expressed at first orally but later by writing, serve either to form the sole guides of our conduct or greatly reinforce the social instincts. Such opinions, however, have sometimes a tendency directly opposed to these instincts.

This latter fact is well exemplified by the Law of Honor, that is, the law of the opinion of our equals, and not of all our countrymen. The breach of this law, even when the breach is known to be strictly accordant with true morality, has caused many a man more agony than a real crime.[329]

We recognize the same influence in the burning sense of shame which most of us have felt, even after the interval of years, in recalling to mind some accidental breach of a trifling, though fixed, rule of etiquette. The judgement of the community will generally be guided by some rude experience of what is best in the long run for all its members—but the problem is this judgement will often err from ignorance and weak powers of reasoning. Hence the strangest customs and superstitions, in complete opposition to the true welfare and happiness of humankind, have become all-powerful throughout the world.[330]

We see this in the horror felt by a Hindu who breaks his caste, and in many other such cases. It would be difficult to distinguish between the remorse felt by a Hindu who has yielded to the temptation of eating unclean food and the remorse felt after committing a theft—but the former would probably be the more severe.

How so many absurd rules of conduct, as well as so many absurd religious beliefs, have originated, we do not know. Nor do we know how it is that these absurdities have become, in all quarters of the world, so deeply impressed on the minds of so many of our species.[331] But it is worthy of remark that a belief constantly inculcated during the early years of life, while the brain is impressible, appears to acquire almost the nature of an instinct—and the very essence of an instinct is that it is followed independently of reason.[332]

Neither can we say why certain admirable virtues, such as the love of truth, are much more highly appreciated by some savage tribes than by others, nor again, why similar differences prevail even among highly civilized nations.[333]

Knowing how firmly fixed many strange customs and superstitions have become, we need feel no surprise that the self-regarding virtues, supported as they are by reason, should now appear to us so natural as to be thought innate, although they were not so valued at the outset for our species.[334]

We must acknowledge, it seems to me, that with all our noble qualities, with the sympathy we can feel for the most debased, with benevolence that extends not only to others of our own species but to the humblest living creatures, with our godlike intellect that has penetrated into the movements and constitution of the solar system—with all these exalted powers—we still bear in our bodily frame the indelible stamp of our lowly origin.[335]

For my own part I would as soon be descended from that heroic little monkey who braved his dreaded enemy in order to save the life of his keeper. Or from that old baboon who, descending from the mountains, carried away in triumph his young comrade from a crowd of astonished dogs—as from a savage who delights in torturing his enemies, offers up bloody sacrifices, practices infanticide without remorse, treats his wives like slaves, knows no decency, and is haunted by the grossest superstitions.[336]

Is Morality Driven by Selfishness, or to Attain the Greatest Happiness, or the Greatest Good?[337]

Both prior to and following Darwin, the idea that altruism is basically motivated by selfishness has prevailed among some widely respected authorities. Prior to Darwin this tended to be the view attributed to Adam Smith as economic philosopher (but it was not in fact the view of Adam Smith the moral philosopher) and more rightfully to the leading "scientific" theologian of his time, William Paley. Yet as Darwin's private notebooks reveal, even as a very young man he had already decided this view was wrong, that there was much more to it—namely, the independent thrust of the moral sense as he was to first scientifically substantiate.[338]

In the following passage he also deals with the belief of Utilitarian philosopher Jeremy Bentham, seconded by John Stuart Mill, that we are morally motivated not only by the selfishness of personal pleasure but also primarily by doing whatever will produce the greatest happiness for the greatest number among us.

It has been assumed by philosophers of the derivative school of morals that the foundation of morality lies in a form of selfishness. More recently the "Greatest happiness principle" advocated by Mr. Bentham and the Utilitarians has been brought prominently forward.[339]

It is, however, more correct to speak of the latter principle as the standard, and not as the motive of conduct. In other words, while the greater happiness for the greatest number among us may be a measure of or desirable goal for morality, it is not the motivator for morality

If we turn to consider what is this motivator we find that most of the authors I have consulted think there must be a distinct motive for every action, and that this must be associated with some pleasure or displeasure.[340] Two exceptions are J.S. Mill, who although a Utilitarian and an advocate of the greatest happiness principle, recognizes in his System of Logic in the clearest manner that actions may be performed through habit without the anticipation of pleasure. He is joined in this belief by Henry Sidgwick, who agrees that "our conscious active impulses" are not "always directed towards the production of agreeable sensations in ourselves."

In this regard, I think a dim similar feeling that our impulses do not always arise from anticipated pleasure has been a chief cause of the acceptance of the intuitive theory of morality, for which I am providing a naturalistic or evolutionary explanation. I also think this same feeling must lead us to reject the utilitarian or "Greatest happiness" theory.[341]

For if we simply observe ourselves it is evident we often act impulsively—that is, from instinct or long habit, without any consciousness of pleasure. Moreover, we do this in the same manner as does probably a bee or ant when it blindly follows its instincts.

Under circumstances of extreme peril, as during a fire, when we endeavor to save a fellow-creature without a moment's hesitation, it certainly cannot be said we feel pleasure. Still less, in such circumstances, do we have the time to reflect on the dissatisfaction with ourselves we may experience if we do not make the attempt. Should we afterward reflect on our conduct we would feel there lies within us an impulsive power widely different from the search for pleasure or happiness—an impulsive power that the evidence I present indicates is the result of the deeply planted social instinct.[342]

In the case of the lower animals, it seems much more appropriate to speak of their social instincts as having been developed for the general good rather than for the general happiness of the species. This general good I would define as the rearing of the greatest number of individuals in full vigor and health, with all their faculties perfect.[343] As the social instincts of both ourselves and the lower animals have no doubt been developed by nearly the same steps, I suggest the same definition may be used in both cases.

In short, basing our standard on this heritage of instinct we share with possibly all other creatures, we may take as the standard of morality the general good or welfare of the community, rather than the general happiness, although this definition may require some limitation on account of political ethics.[344]

When we risk our lives to save those of a fellow-creature, it also seems more correct to say that we act for the general good rather than for the general happiness of humankind. No doubt the general welfare and the happiness of the individual usually coincide.[345] Moreover, a contented, happy tribe will certainly flourish better than one that is discontented and unhappy. We have further seen that, even at an early period in the history of our species, the expressed wishes of the community must powerfully influence the conduct of each member. As all wish for happiness, the "greatest happiness principle" will become an important secondary guide and object.

But the social instinct, together with sympathy—which leads to our concerns regarding the approval or disapproval of others—remains the primary impulse and guide.[346]

Thus the reproach is removed of laying the foundation of the noblest part of our nature in the base principle of selfishness—unless indeed the satisfaction which every animal feels when it follows its proper instincts, and the dissatisfaction felt when prevented, be called selfish.[347]

The Higher and the Lower Moral Rules and Where They Seem to Take Us[348]

Notwithstanding many sources of doubt, within evolution we are able to generally and readily distinguish between the higher and the lower moral rules.[349]

The higher are founded on the social instincts, and relate to the welfare of others. They are supported by the approval of our fellow-creatures and by reason.

In terms of the recurring question of what impels us to do good in this world, it could be said this is the morality of altruism.

The lower rules—though some of them when implying self-sacrifice hardly deserve to be called lower—relate chiefly to the self. They arise from public opinion, matured by experience and cultivation.

Though in a far more involved way than is apparent on the surface, it could be said this is the morality of selfishness.

And where are we bit by bit headed?

As our species has advanced in civilization, and small tribes have united into larger communities, reason would first tell each of us that we ought to extend our social instincts and sympathies to all the members of the same nation, though personally unknown to us. This point being once reached, however, there is only an artificial barrier to prevent our sympathies from extending to the people of all nations and races.[350]

That the way is not easy, that we face enormous obstacles, is everywhere evident. As we are separated from others by great differences in appearance or habits, experience unfortunately shows us how long it can be before we look at them as our fellow-creatures. Sympathy beyond the confines of our own species, for example—that is, humanity to the lower animals—seems to be one of the latest moral acquisitions. It is apparently unfelt by savages, except toward their pets. How little the old Romans knew of it is shown by their abhorrent gladiatorial exhibitions. The very idea of humanity, as far as I could observe long ago during the voyage of the Beagle, was new to most of the gauchos of the Pampas.

Nevertheless, this virtue, one of the noblest with which we are endowed, seems to arise incidentally from our sympathies becoming more tender and more widely diffused until they are extended to all sentient beings.

How this change comes upon us and is at present underway can everywhere be observed. As soon as this virtue is honored and practiced by some few of us it spreads through instruction and example to the young and eventually becomes incorporated in public opinion.[351]

As a struggle may sometimes be seen going on between the various instincts of the lower animals, it is not surprising there should be a struggle within us between our social instincts, with their derived virtues, and our lower, though momentarily stronger impulses or desires.[352]

This, as Mr. Galton[353] has remarked, is not surprising, as we have emerged from a state of barbarism within a comparatively recent period. After having yielded to some temptation we feel a sense of dissatisfaction, shame, repentance, or remorse similar to the feelings caused by other powerful instincts or desires when left unsatisfied or baulked.[354] Having yielded, we compare the weakened impression of a past temptation with the ever present social instincts—or with habits gained in early youth and strengthened during our whole lives, until they have become almost as strong as instincts. And we are unhappy, or at least uncomfortable, because we have fallen short of the ideal.[355]

OF SCIENCE AND PROPHECY

And so we near the end of what Darwin has to tell us, short of one last summary of theory. In **The Descent of Man** as originally published, when I came to the Darwin of this and the last chapter a warning bell began to ring. I could glimpse and be stirred by what he was trying to tell us, but in no other area is the probability of the snips and patchwork of Henrietta and possibly other members of the family more evident. For the flow that was Darwin's as a great science writer as well as scientist is continually jolted and diverted in ways that tell one who knows bad editing what must be going on here.

So vehement could Henrietta be in trying to get her own way that later, after Darwin's death, she even threatened to sue her brother Francis to prevent his publishing Darwin's **Autobiography** as he, Francis, thought it should be edited![356]

It is a shame. One can detect in the original for these chapters the tired old man quietly acquiescing to **her** version again and again just to get the damn thing done and out of the way. On his as well as our behalf, I have done my best to restore what might have been closer to the original, or to what he might have written. Still these chapters (14 and 15) must come off as more than a bit choppy, so it may be helpful to summarize the case he is trying to make here.

To begin with, Darwin is taking a careful look at how we experience the drive of moral sensitivity, and the regulation of morality, and the impact of action as a moral agent on our everyday lives in terms of the "virtues" that, for a long time now, we have tended to look upon as the old-fashioned stuff of embroidered wall hangings. In the previous chapter and this one, he compels us to look with new eyes at the virtues of courage, fidelity, freedom, kindness, truthfulness, self-sacrifice, self-command, fortitude, prudence, sympathy, and true honor.

In the last chapter, he moved on to give us his ultimate view of selfishness. As we saw, he specifically lambastes it as a "base principle" for "laying the foundation of the noblest part of our nature." In keeping with the similarly lost or ignored findings of practically all of his great predecessors and successors in the scientific study of morality, he tells us there are two very different kinds of morality—one driven by the moral sense and concern for the welfare of others, the other by concern for the needs of ourselves.[357]

Gradually his vision rises. The point will come in civilization, he told us in Chapter 14, where "there is only an artificial barrier to prevent our sympathies from extending to the people of all nations and races." In Chapter 16, he sets forth the case for his belief that over the long run "virtue will be triumphant" and "a still higher destiny" lies ahead for our species.

How are we to achieve this? He points specifically to the agency of education—and to that great surprise considering how Darwin has been painted by Creationists and others as both Satan and Anti-Christ. For now he steps forth from the chamber in which he has been locked away for over 100 years as an advocate of the moral agency of progressive spirituality and progressive religion!

Reading these and earlier passages, it is evident that not only in his emphasis on the nurturing force of love rising out of nature are Darwin's views surprisingly akin to those of the late 20th century emergence of the women's spirituality movement. They also resonate with more widely established religion. Among Christians, denominations such as the Unitarians, Quakers, Episcopalians, Christian Scientists, Churches of Religious Science, and progressive Catholics, most Jews, in Islam the

Bahais, Sufis, and moderate Islamics, and most Buddhists and progressive Hindus and Confucians will find him to be not only a congenial companion but also the surprising advocate for many of their own most passionate beliefs.

Of great interest to many will be his fascinating assessment of the belief in a God or other deity—on one hand arising only with a maturing of reason in our species and of great service in the advancement of our moral evolution, on the other hand all too often used to imprison us in ignorance, delusion, and vicious superstitions.

Above all, in this chapter, in keeping with the tradition for both progressive religion and progressive science, he extols the transcendent responsibility and impact of the conscience of each of us as "supreme judge and monitor."

Carrying us forward in its wake, despite as well as because of ourselves, all this is caught up within and driven ahead by the sweep of his superstructural vision of second-half Darwinism rising out of its foundation in the first half.

Where before there was nothing but selfishness, now the movement is toward altruism. Where before violence seemed everywhere to prevail, now the movement is toward peace. Where before there was brutality, now the movement is toward greater love. Where before there was no meaning, now there is meaning.

In other words, where before there was no direction other than what the impartial processes of natural selection and random variation might chance upon, now—shaped by organic choice and driven by the moral sense—there is the direction that Darwin's emergent vision of the destiny of our species provides.

The Direction for Human Evolution

With the question of where the cumulative acquisition of the moral sense is taking us in mind, let us review some of the ground we have earlier covered. How did the primeval human, or our apelike progenitors, acquire our social and moral faculties?

As we have seen, to become social they must have acquired the same instinctive feelings that impel other animals to live in a body, and they no doubt exhibited the same general disposition.

They would have felt uneasy when separated from their comrades, for whom they would have felt some degree of love. They would have warned each other of danger, and have given mutual aid in attack or defense. All this implies some degree of sympathy, fidelity, and courage. Such social qualities, the paramount importance of which to the lower animals is disputed by no one, were no doubt acquired by our progenitors in a similar manner, namely, through natural selection aided by inherited habit.[358]

Important as the struggle for existence has been and even still is, yet as far as the highest part of our nature is concerned there are other agencies more important.

For the moral qualities are advanced either directly or indirectly much more through the effects of habit, by our reasoning powers, by instruction, by religion, etc., than through natural selection—though to this latter agency, as we have seen, may be safely attributed the social instincts, which provided a foundation for the development of the moral sense.[359]

> *Here in his own words, where they have been in plain sight, not once out of print, for over 100 years, surely nothing could be clearer as to Darwin's differentiation between the levels, the territories, and the primary processes of the Origin and the Descent theory of evolution.*

Is it possible to continue to ignore what is by now so abundantly obvious? Is it possible to deny that here in Darwin's own words, we are looking at the difference between the two halves of—and the challenge for completing—his theory of evolution?

We may be excused for feeling some pride at having risen, though not through our own personal exertions, to the very summit of the organic scale. It is this fact of our having thus risen, instead of having been aboriginally placed in perfection here, that gives us hope for a still higher destiny in the distant future.[360]

On Moral Intelligence, and the Agency of Education, Spirituality, and Conscience[361]

The moral faculties are generally and justly esteemed as of higher value than the intellectual powers. We should bear in mind that the activity of the mind in vividly recalling past impressions is one of the fundamental though secondary bases of conscience.[362]

This affords the strongest argument for educating and stimulating in all possible ways the intellectual faculties of every human being.

No doubt even the torpid among us, if our social affections and sympathies are well developed, will be led to good actions, and may develop a fairly sensitive conscience. **But whatever renders the imagination more vivid and strengthens the habit of recalling and comparing past impressions, will make the conscience more sensitive.** It may even somewhat compensate for weak social affections and sympathies.

Our moral nature has reached its present standard, partly through the advancement of our reasoning powers and consequently of a just public opinion. But especially this advancement has come through our sympathies having been rendered more tender and widely diffused through the effects of habit, instruction, and reflection.

In the above passages, returning to this insight for the tenth time, Darwin defines the relationship of reasoning and feeling, or of cognition and affection, as well as learning and education to organic choice.

As for religion and spirituality, the conviction of the existence of an all-seeing Deity has had a potent influence on the advance of morality.

The belief in God has often been advanced as not only the greatest, but the most complete of all the distinctions between ourselves and the lower animals. It is however impossible, as we have seen, to maintain that this belief is innate or instinctive in ourselves.

The assumed instinctive belief in God has also been used by many persons as an argument for His existence. But this is a rash argument, as we should thus be compelled to believe in the existence of many cruel and malignant spirits, only a little more powerful than ourselves, for the belief in them is far more general than in a beneficent Deity. The idea of a universal and beneficent Creator does not seem to arise in the mind of our species until we have been elevated by long-continued culture.

More generally, a belief in all-pervading spiritual agencies seems to be universal, and apparently follows from a considerable advance in our reason, and from a still greater advance in our faculties of imagination, curiosity and wonder.[363]

And where does this advance in our capacities for reason, imagination, curiosity and wonder lead us? In the following passages I must twice put in a line of my own in italics to provide the kind of transitions that seem to have been chopped out in the original editing, but which are needed to provide both flow and intelligibility to what Darwin is saying.[364]

It will also be helpful to know that what Darwin is wrestling with here is the pivotal nature of the evolution of the norms that guide our moral behavior and evolution. In other words, all the rules we live by—all the customs, expectations, laws, commandments and so on—are defined as "norms" in social science. These norms are established in our lives by general agreement that they seem to be the best way for us to live and interact with one another at a particular time in our history. In the horse and buggy days, for example, the norm was that you didn't steal your neighbor's horse or your neighbor's horse feed. But time moves on and things change. So what works for an earlier stage of evolution often must be transcended for our species to evolve.

What Darwin is saying here is that what drives this transcendence, thus driving evolution ahead, is both the thrust of organic choice—touched on, just ahead, for the eleventh time—and the vision and the conscience of the creative individual serving as an evolutionary outrider.[365]

It is an exceptionally important thought, rising here from Darwin for the first time in science. Thus it is a landmark in the evolution of the human mind. Beyond education, religion, and spirituality—all of which can be and generally are limited by the constraints of the customs and beliefs of a particular society, community, family, or other social group—lies the ultimate call and judgment of the individual conscience.

Thus we move ahead as a species—both morally and generally.

As we have seen, the first foundation or origin of the moral sense lies in the social instincts, including sympathy, and these instincts no doubt were primarily gained, as in the case of the animals, through natural selection.[366]

Any instinct, permanently stronger or more enduring than another, gives rise to the feeling that we express by saying that it ought to be obeyed.[367] **This fact, as regards the development of the moral sense out** of the foundational drive of the social instincts and the derived virtue of sympathy, becomes of special importance at our level of brain and development, where special capacities become available to the mind.

As we have seen, owing to one of the most important of the special capacities of our minds, we cannot avoid looking both backwards and forwards, and comparing past impressions. Hence after some temporary desire or passion has mastered our social instincts, we reflect and compare the now weakened impression of such past impulses with the ever-present social instincts. As then we feel that sense of dissatisfaction that all unsatisfied instincts leave behind them, we resolve to act differently in the future—and this becomes *the dynamo of* conscience.[368]

This conscience of ours, we have seen, is fundamentally shaped by our sensitivity to the approval or disapproval of our fellows. Ultimately, however, we do not accept the praise or blame of our fellows as our sole guide.

Our habitual convictions, controlled by reason, afford us the safest rule. Our individual conscience becomes the supreme judge and monitor.[369]

Of the Transcendent Conscience of the Individual, Freedom, Slavery, and Blind Chance

Throughout these chapters, we have had the thoughts of Darwin as an old man nearing the end of his life, reflecting on the past and future. With only a burst here and there of discernibly deep feeling, it is important to realize that throughout the writing of Descent he was held back by the fear, as he was to openly express it, that he might get "too evangelical."[370] He was a man naturally given to the honest expression of love, delight, and great enthusiasms. But here he felt he must sit on himself in order to remain as objectively scientific as was possible.

Here, by contrast, is the Darwin as the young man I write of in Darwin in Love, more overtly passionate and less scientific on the subject of the conscience—in this case his own, as tormented by his experiences in Brazil while on the voyage of the Beagle.

I thank God I shall never again visit a slave-country. To this day, if I hear a distant scream, it recalls with painful vividness my feelings, when passing a house near Pernambuco, I heard the most pitiable moans, and could not but suspect that some poor slave was being tortured, yet knew that I was as powerless as a child even to remonstrate.[371]

Near Rio de Janeiro I lived opposite to an old lady, who kept screws to crush the fingers of her female slaves. I have stayed in a house where a young household mulatto, daily and hourly, was reviled, beaten, and persecuted enough to break the spirit of the whip (before I could interfere) on his naked head, for having handed me a glass of water not quite clean; I saw his father tremble at a mere glance from his master's eye.

It is often attempted to palliate slavery by comparing the state of slaves with our poorer countrymen. If the misery of our poor be caused not by the laws of nature, but by our institution, great is our sin; but how this bears on slavery, I cannot see. As well might the use of the thumb-screw be defended in one land, by showing that people in another land suffered from some dreadful disease.

Those who look tenderly at the slaveowner, and with a cold heart at the slave, never seem to put themselves into the position of the latter—what a cheerless prospect, with not even a hope of change! Picture to yourself the chance, ever hanging over you, of your wife and your little children—those objects which nature urges even slaves to call their own—being torn from you and sold like beasts to the first bidder! And these deeds are done and palliated by men who profess to love their neighbors as themselves, who believe in God, and pray that His will be done on earth!

It makes one's blood boil, yet heart tremble, to think that we Englishmen and our American descendants, with their boastful cry of liberty, have been and are so guilty.

> *Though lessened by age, the passion remained. Also remaining unchanged from the year following his return from the voyage of the Beagle was his conviction of the central thrust into the unknown of both the moral sense and what I have identified as organic choice.*

> *In this regard, as earlier noted, in* **Descent** *a striking passage has for over 100 years fundamentally contradicted what his successors were to call Darwinian theory. Twice Darwin further repeats this observation in his autobiography, also continuously in print over 100 years, and then again for the fourth time, in the same language, in a letter to a friend.[372] If we now juxtapose the young Darwin on conscience and the old Darwin on the idea that this is a world governed solely by "blind chance," in which such things as the moral sense and conscience matter for nothing—as became dogma for first half theory—we see Darwin's affirmation of the opposite in one last angry flash of the old fire.*

I am aware that the conclusions arrived at in this work will be denounced by some as highly irreligious. But those who denounce them are bound to show why it is more irreligious to explain the origin of ourselves as a distinct species by descent from some lower form, through the laws of variation and natural selection, than to explain the birth of the individual through the laws of ordinary reproduction.[373]

The birth both of the species and of the individual are equally parts of that grand sequence of events that our minds refuse to accept as the result of blind chance.

The understanding revolts at such a conclusion.[374]

Still again Darwin has returned—for the ninth time—to a key portion of the underlying dynamics involved in the operation within us of the pivotal thrust into the future for second-half Darwinian theory of what I have identified as organic choice.

CHAPTER SIXTEEN
THE DRIVE TOWARD TRANSFORMATION

The foundation—and first level for Darwin's theory of the moral agent—was the biology we share with all other species on this planet. Through a journey into the sex life of the very deep past, in Chapters 6 and 7 we saw how he grounded his vision in biological evolution, with a leap ahead in mind into cultural and moral evolution.

In Chapters 8 through 11, we pursued his construction of the super-structure and second level for his theory. Through his wealth of stories and the quirks of animal life, we were taken on a trip through the inner and outer workings of prehuman cultural and moral evolution.

Over the past four chapters, moving ever upward developmentally, Darwin has now roughed out the rest of the house of moral mind—a third level for his theory primarily involving the psychology specifically of ourselves, we human beings of such incredible potential yet such dev-astating disappointments. It is a diverse sprawl of systems within systems given direction and meaning by the thrust of moral sensitivity and the reasoning, learning, and accumulation of moral intelligence and action into the future.

Now, with a foreshadowing of the concern with *personal* evolution increasingly ours as we enter the 21st century—and with the evolution of consciousness as well as moral evolution—come a few last touches to bring both vision and theory better into focus.

Before we move on to what he has to tell us, again a few observations and something of the setting for his thoughts at this point will be helpful.

As a psychologist wondering how to capture what Darwin, by training and profession the non-psychologist, has to tell us about ourselves in this last fragment of his theory I was suddenly struck by how little we know of ourselves after all these years.

The problem is not lack of information, but lack of perspective—which I think Darwin begins to again provide. Life for most of us today is the story of informational overload and piecemeal education for the piecemeal mind—of being unable, as the old saw has it, to see the forest for the trees.

What Darwin did in *Descent* that has also been mainly overlooked for over 100 years was to provide, along with a new vision of the glory of the human mind, a grounding for that other part of ourselves we so take for granted we seldom realize its wonder. Only with death, as we are about to leave it, do many of us realize the glory of the *body* of the human that is the mind's housing or evocation.

So that we may clearly see who and what we are, in the pages leading to his exploration of the moral sense and moral agency, Darwin grounds the ever greater scatter of our minds in the bedrock physicality of the body that over thousands of years of evolution has also shaped our mind.

In contrast to the hoofed and flippered species prior to ourselves and our fellow simians, he holds up before us the power of our hands, "which are so admirably adapted to act in obedience to our will."[375]

He points to the difference that, by giving us the advantage of feet "rendered flat" with "the great toe that has been peculiarly modified," allows us to walk upright and stand firmly erect.[376]

He notes the difference of a unique set of "vocal organs," which give us the advantage of the power for "the utterance of articulate language."[377]

But most important of all, there is the difference of our brain that Darwin—in a remarkable foreshadowing of modern brain research that is as yet, even now, only minimally known—connects to the peculiarly human expansion of frontal brain: "the seat," he remarks, "of intellectual faculties."[378]

Out of the upward ascendancy of multi-billions of creatures driven to discover and fulfill their organic destiny, Darwin helps us see at last clearly, with scientific rigor, what many humanist visionaries have perceived and tried to tell us about ourselves. Constrained by old paradigms for science as well as religion, throughout the 20th century most of us were unable to believe this of ourselves. But the picture Darwin vividly paints is of how, in our species, evolution arrives at a creature built not just to adapt to what is—or to what presently exists, as first half Darwinism has been so diligent in telling us.

> *The central point for the findings and vision of the Darwinian second half is of how out of evolution there has been given to us the capacity to drive the whole of this special planetary venture toward what can be, or our possibilities for the future, and what should be, or the course that moral sensitivity urges upon us.*

Evolution in our species, he shows us, arrives at what the greatest among us can become, but which *all* of us bear within ourselves in potential—the capacity for being the scouts or venturers in new directions, or the evolutionary outriders for our species.

In the excerpts that follow, here is the portrait he gives us. He reaffirms his basic discovery of the mid-1800s, which in affirming evolution as fact split the past from the present. He reaffirms his vision of how morality has developed as a system through the chain linking of action from a long ago beginning toward an unknown end. He restates the high points of the first and second levels of his theory. Then to make clear the thrust that carries us beyond the barriers of instinct and group that constrict us, a brief final vision takes us to the searching edge of our venture through space and time.

The Third Level
of the Theory of the Moral Agent

The main conclusion here arrived at, and now held by many naturalists who are well competent to form a sound judgement, is that we are descended from some less highly organized form. The grounds upon which this conclusion rests will never be shaken, for the close similarity between ourselves and the lower animals in embryonic development, as well as in innumerable points of structure and constitution, both of high and of the most trifling importance—the rudiments we retain, the abnormal reversions to which we are occasionally liable—are facts that cannot be disputed.

They have been long known, but until recently they told us nothing with respect to the origin of our species. Now, when viewed by the light of our knowledge of the whole organic world, their meaning is unmistakable. The great principle of evolution stands up clear and firm when these groups of facts are considered in connection with others, such as the mutual affinities of the members of the same group, their geographical distribution in past and present times, and their geological succession.[379]

As we have seen, the foundation for the moral sense lies in the social instincts, including under this term the family ties. These instincts are highly complex, and in the case of the lower animals give special tendencies toward certain definite actions. But the more important elements for us are love, and the distinct emotion of sympathy. Animals endowed with the social instincts take pleasure in each other's company, warn each other of danger, defend and aid each other in many ways.[380]

These instincts do not extend to all the individuals of the species, but only to those of the same community. As they are highly beneficial to the species, they have in all probability been acquired through natural selection.[381]

A moral being is one who is capable of reflecting on past actions and motives, comparing them with contemplated future actions, and approving of some and disapproving of others. The fact that we are the one being who with certainty can be thus designated makes the greatest of all distinctions between ourselves and the lower animals.[382]

As we have seen, the moral sense as it operates within ourselves follows, first, from the enduring and ever present nature of the social instincts we share with a wide range of organisms and animals prior to us on the evolutionary developmental scale; second, from our appreciation of the approval and disapproval of our fellows; and third, from the high activity of our mental faculties, with past impressions extremely vivid—and in this capacity we differ importantly in degree from the lower animals.[383]

Social animals are impelled partly by a wish to aid the members of their community in a general manner, but more commonly to perform certain definite actions. We are impelled by the same general wish to aid our fellows, but with few or no special instincts.[384]

We also differ from the lower animals in the power of expressing our desires by words, which thus become a guide to the aid required and bestowed. The motive to give aid is likewise much modified in our species: it no longer consists solely of a blind instinctive impulse, but is much influenced by the praise or blame of our fellow humans. The appreciation and bestowal of praise and blame, in turn, both rest on sympathy. Sympathy, in turn, though gained as an instinct, is then much strengthened by exercise or habit.[385]

As the reasoning powers advance and experience is gained, the remoter effects of certain lines of conduct on the character of the individual and on the general good, are perceived. As all of us desire our own happiness, and as the self-regarding virtues come within the scope of public opinion, praise or blame is bestowed on actions and motives to this end. And as happiness is an essential part of the general good, the greatest happiness principle indirectly serves as a nearly safe standard of right and wrong.[386]

The social instincts acquired by us as by the lower animals for the good of the community from the first have given us the wish to aid our fellows, feelings of sympathy, and the desire to seek the approval and fear of the disapproval of others. These impulses served in the early development of our species to provide a rude rule of right and wrong. But as our species has gradually advanced in intellectual power,

and thus has been enabled to trace the remote consequences of our actions;

and has thereby acquired sufficient knowledge to reject baneful customs and superstitions;

and as we have regarded more and more not only the welfare but also the happiness of our fellow beings;

and as then from habit, following on beneficial experience, instruction and example, our sympathies have become more tender and widely diffused—extending to people of all races, to the imbecile, to the maimed, to other seemingly useless members of society, and finally to the lower animals[387]

—so has the standard of our morality risen higher and higher.[388]

Looking to future generations, there is no cause to fear that our social instincts will grow weaker, and we may expect that virtuous habits will grow stronger, the struggle between our higher and our lower impulses will be less severe, and virtue will be triumphant.[389]

A Restatement in Terms of Modern Social and Systems Science

As is evident in these last touches to the house of moral mind, Darwin could leave us with only the shell, open to the winds, to the skies. It is a theory very much needing the work of many others to make of it the solid habitation that Darwin could glimpse beyond his own time as well as beyond ours.

In my rediscovery of what had actually been buried in Darwin's original all these years, when I came to these passages—particularly the last two excerpts—I was thunderstruck.

I realize that what Darwin has said in these final selections will not seem particularly remarkable. Indeed, to some what he is saying may seem rather humdrum, while others may find the idea of the triumph of virtue suspect as no more than shallow Victorian optimism. But again we are looking at Darwin the seer—for in feeling and in overtones what I have quoted leaps ahead over seventy years to the development of both social science and moral science that his successors were not to reach until the devastation of the Nazis and World War II.

Sick, rapidly aging, very much aware that his own death could come at any time, Darwin foreshadows the reaction to the giant backward step in evolution the Nazis represented. For in its revelation of the dark prospects for the death of our culture and all that humanity had strived toward for over thousands of years, this blow jolted 20th century social science—for an all-too-brief time—into the reaffirming search that earlier drove Darwin to seek the origin and nature of what was the best rather than the worst in us.

The stuff of life and of science is endless and it is overwhelming. But what Darwin saw—and what, sparked by the horror of being forced to face the fact of the Holocaust, the social science of the 1940s, 50s, and 60s briefly focused on—is the matter of humanistic priorities, or of what is unquestionably fundamental and what is of so very much less importance in our lives.[390]

This third level to Darwin's lost theory foreshadows the much later thrust for social science and society perhaps best expressed by the well-known work of one psychologist, Abraham Maslow, the much less well-known work of two psychiatrists, Roberto Assagioli and Kazimierz Dabrowski, and some findings of modern brain research that have yet to sift into comprehension beyond the circle of their discoverers.[391]

This work—foundational to the development of humanistic psychology, with relevant core concepts shown here in Table 16.1—more than any other begins to fill out the shell of Darwin's last fragments.

Table 16.1

Humanistic Psychology's
Directions for Moral Evolution

Maslow	defense motivation	growth and meta-motivation
Assagioli	unconscious	superconscious
Dabrowski	inauthenticity	authenticity

Evolutionary time line is from left to right

Maslow, Assagioli, and Dabrowski

Humanistic psychology, as we enter the 21st century, is under the cloud of the same paradigm, both scientifically and socially, that first obscured then buried the Darwin who re-emerges in these pages. For thousands of us, along with the launching of what became the human potentials movement, it was the great liberating discovery of the 1960s. But with the fearful shift toward conservatism for both science and society during the 1970s, 80s, and 90s, humanistic psychology has come to be generally perceived as somehow naive, specious, shallowly optimistic, "unscientific," "far out"—as, in short, "New Age," with all the negatives that have been loaded by rampant and regressive conservatism onto this once hopeful phrase.

Today, however, it lies at the center of the great split or schizophrenia in modern mind as we move into the 21st century—on one hand, an enormous skepticism, cynicism, an immense pull backward; on the other hand, increasing optimism, a new rise of vision, and ever more fiercely, the determination to move ahead.

However inadequately humanistic psychology, or its "child," transpersonal psychology, has yet realized the vision we can now see was Darwin's as well as Maslow's, it bears within its heart the great question of our time. Rising out of every context of doubt and evasion, this question is what is to become of the widespread new perception of the urgency of *personal* evolution, with its concomitant requirement of the evolution of consciousness and moral evolution.

What lies ahead for both humanistic psychology and Darwin as its surprising precursor is a time of a vast and vital reappraisal

First, let us be clear about where we are here. Why does the psychology of Darwin so uncannily anticipate Maslow?

I did not see this at first. Why did I "feel it in my bones," as we say? I called the Darwin side of it "The Third Level," yet found myself wondering if I could scientifically justify calling my hunch that. It was not until a year later that I suddenly remembered that the grounding place and take-off point for Maslow was what he called "the third force in psychology." The first great psychology to gain widespread adherents in the 20th century, Maslow explained, was Freudian—a brilliant psychology of sickness. The second psychology to gain not only a widespread but even greater impact was Watsonian behaviorism—a psychology in which literally everything about us, through conditioning and learning, was imposed on from us *outside* ourselves. By the 1940s, however, a new "third force" was emerging. This was a psychology different from Freud in being a psychology of *health*, and differing from behaviorism in being a psychology of the evolutionary rise *from within ourselves* of a basic goodness.[392]

And here is precisely what we find in Darwin seventy years earlier.

Practically everyone who has ever taken a psychology course is aware of Maslow's two-part breakdown of our motivational system, or what drives us to do everything we do. There is a basic level of "defense" motivations, Maslow tells us. At this level we are concerned with "needs for safety, belongingness, love and respect."[393] These needs can be called basic, "or biological, and likened to the need for salt, or calcium or Vitamin D because" the "deprived person yearns for their gratification persistently."[394]

This is not merely "pop psych," into which the effort has been made to stuff humanistic psychology. Maslow may have bathed naked and danced in the moonlight at Esalen and reveled in playing the jive-talker, but he was also one of the best-grounded and most knowledgeable psychologists of his time.[395] It can now be seen how at the human level his psychology offers a bridge between advanced biology and psychology—that is, how his defense and growth structure for motivation mirrors the central interest in the relation of natural selection to self-organizing processes in advanced biology.[396]

It can now also be seen that Maslow's theory of defense and growth motivational structures, extensively studied and confirmed by modern research, both closely mirrors and confirms the earlier pattern for Darwin's theory of the development of the moral sense, moral intelligence, and moral agency.

In Chapter 6 we examined our inheritance from the multi-million year evolutionary sequence of the rise first of sexual, then parental, and social instincts, capped by the first touches of the capacities that are to become emotion and reason. In terms of modern brain research, these are needs and motivations that derive from the structure and requirements of the brains for both ourselves and precursor animals up through the early stages of development for the limbic system.[397]

In other words, up to this point the emergence of organisms leading to the arrival of our own species is primarily shaped by biology as well as often (but by no means *always*) by natural selection and random variation. In terms of the simple differentiation proposed here for understanding both Darwin and ourselves today, we are looking at the human needs and drives that are *foundational.*

But atop this foundation rises the superstructure. We have the second level for Darwin's theory that we examined in Chapters 8 through 10. We have the superstructural situation for ours and other higher species. Step by step, now primarily (but not exclusively) driven by organic choice, we have the sequence that Darwin outlines of

the rise of sympathy,

the cognitive capacity for comparing past with present and foreseeing future consequences,

the acquisition of language and a growing sensitivity to the opinions of others,

the social implantation of this increasing sensitivity through the power of habit,

which drives us to a higher level and a higher capacity for moral sensitivity and moral agency.

In terms of modern brain research—as indicated in Table 16.2—we are looking at capacities dependent on the existence and adequate functioning of a number of brain areas. Most relevant to where we are headed is the linking of the most advanced developmental level of the limbic system to the prefrontal cortex of the frontal brain. From here we go to the motor areas that cross right and left brain halves horizontally. Out of this linking of advanced limbic system, to frontal brain, to motor areas then comes the governance of every aspect of our behavior—from the movement of the lungs and tongue and larynx to speak, to eyes to see, to ears to hear, to our hands that move in the caress or in writing, or our hands and legs to move in defense of ourselves or others.[398]

Table 16.2

Brain Science Directions for Moral Evolution

MacLean	reptile level	mammal level
	lower limbic brain	higher limbic plus frontal brain

Evolutionary time line is from left to right

In terms of Maslow's theory—which not only psychologists but also sociologists, economists, anthropologists, and political scientists have found useful—we are looking at what he called the "growth" needs. Later, he more finely tuned this idea of growth motivations into his idea of a third, or even higher level, system of "metamotivations."[399]

It is at the growth level that the famous drive of "self-actualization" begins to take over. We have a "clearer, more efficient perception of reality." We have "more openness to experience."[400] We display an increased spontaneity, aliveness, a more firm identity, a greater ability to love.

The "peak experiences" that come to the self-actualizer far more often than to others are also characterized by the sense of the unity of the "true, the good, and the beautiful" that Darwin—as we saw in Chapter 13— intuited and sought a scientific explanation for. The world in the peak experience, Maslow tells us, "is seen only as beautiful, good, desirable, worthwhile, etc., and is never experienced as evil or undesirable."[401]

Above all, at the transcendent and transformational level of metamotivation, we transition into the stage of self-actualization that—if we now read again what Darwin had to say—he was over 100 years ago describing in the evolutionary progression for the three levels of his theory.

We reach this stage where, as Maslow describes it, "they have a feeling of belongingness and rootedness, they are satisfied in their love needs, have friends and feel loved and loveworthy, they have status and place in life and respect from other people, and they have a reasonable feeling of worth and self-respect."[402]

And what happens at this stage is ***precisely in alignment with Darwin's theory of the moral sense, moral intelligence and moral agency***.

Emerging within us and among us, hardly ever to "make the news," but providing both the inspiration and the bonding that is to hold together all healthy and life-affirming and life-advancing social life—from the family, to the nation, to our world as a whole—is the following revealing set of behaviors.

Removing the quote marks in the original, here I provide a handful of characteristics out of Maslow's long list.[403]

At this stage people delight in bringing about justice. Delight in stopping cruelty and exploitation. Love virtue to be rewarded. Try to set things right, to clean up bad situations. Enjoy doing good. They do not do mean things, and they respond with anger when other people do mean things. They enjoy watching and helping the self-actualizing of others, especially of the young. They enjoy bringing about law and order in the chaotic situation, or the messy or confused situation, or in the dirty and unclean situation. They hate (and fight) corruption, cruelty, malice, dishonesty, pompousness, phoniness and faking.

Throughout all this, they also "manage somehow simultaneously to love the world as it is and to try to improve it."[404]

Is this not what Darwin has been telling us? Isn't this what runs through all his stories of how, as with the growth over time of a vine or the unfolding of a flower, this liberating consciousness moves up stage by stage through all the precursor animals he writes of, to reach its widest and most sustained and persistent expression in ourselves?

Is this not what, through Darwin's eyes, we see in the rabbits who stamp loudly on the ground to warn others, the horses who are miserable when separated from their companions, the pelicans who fish in concert, the baboon rescuers, the courageous dogs who defend their owners, the considerate elephants? Is this not also the metamotivational stage of growth that Darwin himself—this scientific grandfather to us all, so different from what we have been told—often personally reflects?

Of the social scientists later to emerge, Maslow is probably most expressively Darwin's heir in relation to the lost second half of his theory of evolution. Two others I mentioned earlier, the psychiatrists Assagioli and Dabrowski, are also forcefully second-half Darwinians. This can be seen, first, in the firm place of evolution theory in their own thinking and therapies, and secondly, in their similar grounding, as both psychiatrists, in the perspective of the relation of the biological foundation to the psychological superstructure.

Standing out from their peers—and neglected both in their own time and today because of this—they, along with others I identify in the notes,[405] were also Darwin's heirs in their insistence on the centrality of moral sensitivity, moral intelligence, and moral agency in both the motivational foundation and the motivational superstructure for our species.

Both came by this conviction not through books, but rather through the searing experience in common of the Nazi devastation of Europe.[406] Assagioli was thrown into prison at one point by the fascists, Dabrowski was forced to witness the killing of Jews and the march to the death camps in Poland.

Out of this experience, so much in line with what Darwin is expressing earlier—in contrast to Freud's focus on the unconscious—came Assagioli's articulation of the action within us of the morally driven "superconscious," and the drive of "the will" in moral agency.

"When danger threatens to paralyze us," he writes of the moral agency that ranges from Darwin's monkey who rescues his keeper to his own confrontation with the fascists, "suddenly, from the mysterious depths of our being, surges an unsuspected strength which enables us to place a firm foot on the edge of the precipice or confront an aggressor calmly and resolutely.

"Before the threatening attitude of an unfair superior or when facing an excited mob, when personal reasons would induce us to yield," he continues, "the will gives us the power to say resolutely: 'No! At all costs I stand by my convictions; I will perform what I take to be right.'"[407]

Out of this same experience, but to the north of Italy, in Poland during its occupation by the Nazis, came the moral vision of Dabrowski—who as the administrator of a hospital for the mentally ill was forced to witness the evil of the Nazis at its worst.

"Superficiality, vulgarity, absence of inner conflict, quick forgetting of grave experiences, became something repugnant to me," he writes of the Nazis—as well as those of his as well as our own time who can shrug and accept the worst in us as only to be expected, about which nothing can be done. "I searched for people and attitudes of a different kind, those that were authentically ideal, saturated with immutable values, those who represented 'what ought to be' against 'what is.'"[408]

The Task for the 21st Century

So there it is, Darwin's theoretical house of moral mind. We have this foundation and superstructure for what he fervently hoped might be of some use to us in the shaping of our future—and indeed possibly in determining whether for our species there is to be a future at all.

We have this theory that in its fragments is like the unexpected arrival of some bright leaves blown into our so often sad and troubled dimension out of another time. We have this theory that seems as though it has arrived, in terms of physicist David Bohm's perspective, out of the mystery of the "implicate order" into the hurly-burly of the all too familiar "explicate order" of our lives—these long-lost but now suddenly new and relevant scraps out of the arbitrary and seemingly uncaring whirlwind of time.[409]

And we have all this work, besides that of Maslow, Assagioli, and Dabrowski, that we may now see bears on the wedding of the first half to the second half in the completion of Darwin's theory of evolution.

What does all this tell us of ourselves and the prospects for our future? This we will explore in the single brief chapter for Part III.

PART III
The Vision

CHAPTER SEVENTEEN

A VISION FOR THE 21ST CENTURY

The word "revolution" has been overworked. With *The Origin of Species*, however, Darwin undoubtedly seeded the 19th century's major revolution in science. But his impact went far beyond this. Because of science's increasing impact on the shaping of our minds—which in turn shape everything we feel or do—*Origin* also seeded a major revolution in society.

If we now consider what we have uncovered in the lost world of the private notebooks and *The Descent of Man*, it is evident that here are the seeds of revolution for the 21st century.

It is not that this revolution is new with the recovery of the "new" Darwin. All of it is already underway—every last positive and hopeful thing he thought and felt and wrote about not only the origin but also the future course and possible destination of our species has been said again, and spawned hope and action throughout the 20th century. But throughout science, society, and within the intimacy of every aspect of our lives, this vision—which actually has been the central vision of humanity over thousands of years—has been blunted and blocked by the age-old difficulty for our species of shedding the shells of old paradigms for the new.

The problem is compounded for us today by the fact that, contrary to what many of us think, the revolution of *Origin* is not behind us and only the other now lies ahead. Worldwide we are caught in the maelstrom of *both* Darwinian revolutions simultaneously.

Within the more educated and modernized segment of humanity—that is, those of us in countries and socioeconomic classes wealthy enough to provide us with schools and computers and the like—rapidly increasing numbers of us are not only ready for, but everywhere strain to move on through the second Darwinian revolution, which this book articulates. A survey by sociologist Paul Ray becoming widely known identifies those of us who feel this way as not some tiny minority, but *one out of every four Americans*. This is Ray's projection for the segment of the American population he identifies as "the Cultural Creatives." Working in Europe, he finds a similar configuration. But as this is the only direction into the future that makes any sense, I believe those ready for the second Darwinian revolution may also include a large number of those identified by Ray as "the Modernists," as well as a surprising number of those among Ray's "Traditionalists," or "Heartlanders."[410]

But the greater part of our species—still globally locked into ignorance, poverty, and lacking freedom and equality in both the less developed world, as with the Islamic Taliban, and in the so-called developed world, as with the Christian Creationists—has yet to work through the first Darwinian revolution's liberation of mind and aspiration.

Moreover, everywhere the electronic juxtaposition of the two Darwinian revolutions further unsettles our species. Via television, I can see the starving peasant with a child in rags. Through my resonation to the higher call and caring of the second revolution I can feel the guilt and frustration of one whose privileged position was gained by the first Darwinian liberation. Via the same medium the starving peasant sees someone like me in a sumptuous living room filled with well-fed children. Is it so surprising that he or she is overwhelmed with rage and ready to support terrorism because the liberation of her or his world is yet to come?[411]

What can the "new" Darwin offer us at this difficult and painful juncture? Many things, I believe, but these two above all.

He can, first, in the grandeur and hope of this lost theory, offer us a grounding for science and society in a completion for the humanistic theory and story of evolution in which each of us is again meaningful, with an active part in building the destiny for our species.

Secondly, he offers us a vision of ourselves and our future grounded in the truths rather than the fictions of morality.

The "Old" Theory and the "New" Theory

A first essential point is that the "old" theory is not "bad." This may seem overly simplistic, but unfortunately at this stage of our own evolution, advance in either science or society seems to usually require the kind of fierce fighting among ourselves that forces us into thinking that either this or that is true. It is often the case, however—as here—that both perspectives are "true." The difficulties rise from ignoring differences of scale, or level, or mistaking a part for the whole.[412]

Scientifically, the general feeling is that the theory of *Origin* is not fundamentally in error. It is in error in details and emphasis and scope, as Darwin tried to tell us himself. Technically speaking, we can never know the whole truth about anything. We can only more closely approximate the truth as a step-by-step matter itself of evolution over time. But for this stage of the knowledge of our evolving, within their proper limits, the theory of *Origin* is not in error as far as the ideas of natural selection and random variation that Darwin helped establish are concerned.

As again and again the story of Darwin's lost theory makes evident, the problem is mainly with what the ruling economic, political, religious, and educational forces for society do with science. The problem is paradigmatic hang-up—or the consequences of belief solely in the theory of *Origin* and its biological elaboration as the be-all and end-all of wisdom regarding evolution. The critical difference, all too often blurred in the minds of scientist and non-scientist alike, is between the fiercely "truncated" Darwinian first half and an alternative that has been unable to dislodge the "old" Darwin from either the textbooks or the minds of most of us.

It is the difference between the neat, tight, and rather simplistic clockwork theories in the biology of E.O. Wilson, Robert Trivers, W.D. Hamilton, and Richard Dawkins, and the more loose and shaggy theories of Stuart Kauffman, Richard Lewontin, Brian Goodwin, Vilmos Csanyi, Stanley Salthe, Mae-Wan Ho, Lynn Margulis, Humberto Maturana and Francisco Varela that provide the vital biological first step into the larger social and systems scientific territory we have only barely entered in this book.[413]

Though the theories of first-half or *Origin* Darwinism vary in detail, what they tend to share is a view of evolution as a great machine whereby all life—human as well as prehuman—is shaped in only the two basic ways. We are constructed either by forces largely external to us and blind to our will or wishes—specifically the ruthless and inexorable force of Natural Selection and Random Variation—or by the conflict, bloody or otherwise, of organism against organism in an eternal struggle for Survival of the Fittest.[414]

Up to a certain point, this is true, the Darwin of the "lost theory" tells us in *Descent. But what he repeatedly stresses is that this is not the whole truth and nothing but the truth.* It is only half of the truth. Moreover, it is only half of that half! For out of the seed already planted and anticipated in the Darwin of Descent, his successors as we move into the 21st century are revealing the counterpart power at the Origins level of cooperation, the "biology of love," and all else—for example, the drive of dialectical and self-organizing processes—contained within Darwin's invisible rediscovery of "organic choice."

In other words, we have been told that the Darwinian theory of *Origin* tells us that we are inherently, predominantly, and indeed overwhelmingly selfish and aggressive. But the theory that emerges in *Descent* tells us that both over the short term and the long term we can be—and generally are— more powerfully driven by concern for the regard of others and by love.

The old theory tells us that we are driven mainly by the need to perpetuate our own genes or the genes of our closest kin. The new theory tells us that we are also driven by the need to transcend ourselves, resonating to the whole of humanity and to the whole of life.

The old theory tells us that we are alone in the universe. The new theory tells us, in the phrase picked up in simultaneous book titles by both biologist Stuart Kauffman and physicist John Wheeler, that we are "at home in the universe." It tells us that we are linked to one another and to the universe by something that is just "out there," whether we call it spirituality, God, the cosmic connection, the Akashic Record, or the quantum vacuum.[415]

The old theory tells us that our destiny is whatever chance and forces larger than ourselves select for us. The new theory offers something immeasurably more difficult to understand, but immeasurably hopeful once we understand it. It tells us that although we are massively constrained by all that really is larger and more powerful than ourselves, we are also driven by self-organizing and self-regulating processes that open up within the constraints a surprisingly large leeway, or "window of opportunity." Given then our capacity for the *will* to shape it, the choice of destiny *to a vital degree is ours.*

The old theory tells us there is nothing inherent within us to help tell good from bad or right from wrong—that throughout our lives from birth to death "moral sense" must always be hammered into us by self-appointed authorities who know better. The new theory tells us that moral sensitivity has been embedded within us over at least one billion years. It tells us that, by providing an inner voice of basic guidance, it has escalated upward level by evolutionary level to reach the culmination of choice within ourselves.

The old theory encourages us to just sit back and enjoy the medium, for supposedly the message is settled. Having been scientifically worked out and certified by people much smarter than we are, who are we to question what we have been and will again and again be told? Oh sure, the message may not be what we want to hear, but the old theory affirms that this is the grim reality we must each—as best we can—*adapt* to.

The new theory tells us that the message is open-ended and eternal, stretching out of the dim past into the mists of the future for our species.

It tells us that we have a voice in the shaping of the message—but that this message needs a great deal more nurturing, and understanding, and the assignment of much more of the power of the media to its spreading. Above all, it tells us that we are not just what we more or less dutifully adapt to. Much more importantly, *we are what we refuse to adapt to.*

The old theory tells us with scientific precision why we are driven by what used to be called our vices. The new theory scientifically accounts for, and offers hope and encouragement for, expansion of the kind of values that used to be called our *virtues.*

For example, Darwin's lost theory, as expanded by a powerful component for the science of the 21st century, accounts for and offers hope and encouragement for our gaining more of such virtues as the *courage* of a Gandhi, the *compassion* of an Eleanor Roosevelt, the *perseverance* and *self-discipline* of a Helen Keller or a Stephen Hawking in the face of inconceivably debilitating handicaps.

It celebrates the *cheerfulness and friendliness* that lighten the life of others, which distinguished Franklin Roosevelt, Will Rogers, Darwin himself, or the Dalai Lama today. It further explains the *helpfulness* that psychiatrist Robert Coles points to in Dorothy Day's leadership of the Catholic Workers Union, or the all-too-often unappreciated *responsibility* that countless political leaders take on in giving of themselves to look after the rights, livelihoods, and betterment of others throughout the world.

These "virtues" are not just "nice" things for embroidery on Victorian walls or the Boy Scout or Girl Scout Manual. As I will probe in depth in *Darwin for the 21st Century*, in terms of their evolutionary function, all the virtues I identify within these paragraphs are among those either experientially defined by Darwin in the development of the theory of *Descent*, or empirically defined by psychologists Milton Rokeach, Abraham Maslow, and Darwin's other modern successors in psychology.[416]

Most of all, the theory of *Descent* accounts for the majesty of mind—for the virtues of the *intellect, of logic, of imagination, of "broadmindedness"* and of wisdom embodied in an Einstein, Freud, Marx, in Darwin himself, in the legendary Hypatia, or a Marie Curie, or a Maria Montessori.

The theory of *Descent* also begins to account for the *love of beauty* of a Mozart, Chagall, Schubert, the *passion* of a Van Gogh, or how Isadora Duncan could throw herself into dance or Sarah Bernhardt into drama.[417]

It certainly accounts for the virtue of *self-transcendence* that Darwin writes of in the human rescuers of others from fires and from drowning. It is also clearly what he has in mind in the third level for his theory of the moral agent. It is this virtue of self-transcendence he also sees emerging among prehumans: the rabbits who stamp their feet, the sheep that whistle, and the monkeys that cry out to warn others.[418]

In short, what Darwin gives us is what everybody who hungers for intelligence, decency, stability and hope in our world today is seeking. In this second half for his theory, he gives us the most extensively grounded and carefully reasoned vision of the wonder of what is within all of life—including, most of all, what is within ourselves, as well as where this force can take us.

He gives us this vision of a completed theory of evolution, where out of the truncated first part—in which the educated mind of the 20th century was embedded—rises the thrust of what used to be called heart and soul as well as mind into the vast hopeful expansion of a higher level for evolution.

He gives us the challenge for 21st century science that I will further pursue in the sequel that all that has been uncovered here calls for. In other words, here we can go just so far, and then one needs to stop for a breather. We will pick up again from where I must leave off here in *Darwin for the 21st Century*.

In terms of the scientists and science I could only barely touch on here, we will look at prospects for a reconciliation of natural science and social science in joining the parts together to build the *completed* theory of evolution we so urgently need. There, too, we will examine the prospect that Darwin's agonizing over the relationship between science and religion raises—of the possibility for their reconciliation, or more generally speaking, of the prospects for a new working partnership of science with spirituality on the behalf of a better future for all of us.

The Centrality of Darwin's Moral Vision

On the subject of evolution, our minds have been not only fixed but indeed at times ferociously hammered in place for over a century, so it is hard to change them. Thus, to many of us it may still seem impossible that someone who died in 1882 could have much to say of relevance to the problems and prospects for the science and society of the 21st century.

Could Darwin really have anticipated the Butterfly Effect of chaos theory? Come now, let's be realistic here. Or could he really have rediscovered "organic choice" by tapping into the islands of self-organizing processes that lie at the heart of what is today called complexity theory? Or could he have foreseen the need for what we know today as humanistic psychology, the human potentials movement, or the resurgence of interest in the power of love?

Rising above one's own age to look far forward as well as backward into time is the hallmark of a particular kind of genius.[419] But I am also convinced that the reason why Darwin's capacity for scientific prophecy is so striking is, most of all, a matter of moral positioning.

It may be hard for the stereotypically anti-religious and hard-headed scientific mindset to accept, but Darwin could speak to the ages beyond him for the same reason that Jesus and Buddha and other great religious figures spoke to the future as well as to their own time. Moral vision seems to be a matter of anchoring oneself in a perception of—in Darwin's terms—the dynamics of the moral sense. What could this mean? It is the idea that to some degree Darwin was able to foreshadow the future through his perception of, or feeling for, what the evolutionary thrust of moral sensitivity will favor as well as what works against it, and where this is likely to lead us over time. In this sense, by so doing and looking out upon the world, we stand on rock, instead of sand, in the midst of the whirlwind of time.

We have seen how Darwin's central driving interest in the origin and evolution of the moral sense drove him to consider everything else that goes into the building of the human mind. Most importantly and meaningfully, he was driven to integrally relate to the moral sense—as providing both the core drive and structure for mind—everything else involved in the development of our minds. Go the next step then, and we see that beyond ourselves, he is writing of the moral impact of the evolving mind of humanity as a whole upon the shaping of ourselves, and upon all else that constitutes the human world.

Alas, that it should be so difficult for us to see this! But having for so long lost the language or the social encouragement to know ourselves and the meaning of life in this way, it is asking for mind to step out into the unknown. But we must try, for the future hangs on the effort.

However ignored, however discounted, however misperceived, distorted and degraded—or laughed at and dismissed as merely quaint and outdated—in Darwin's vision the moral sense remains in the background shaping our personal, social, economic, political, educational, and religious world. That is, it is the hidden driver of our cultural world emerging out of the wider environmental world affecting all other species along with ourselves.

Thus, his interest in intelligence, creativity, love, et cetera—and how habit and language work to cement together all of this—emerges from an evolutionary perspective in which all else that constitutes our mind is shaped by moral sensitivity as the central integrating force in whole systems terms.

This is to say that everything else, like players on a stage, can seize the foreground. But the stage itself was constructed over time at two levels. And it is the higher level of this stage, built upon and now transcending the lower level, which shapes the course of evolution. All else is dependent on, or constrained by moral sensitivity—if only to provide the systems requirement that as we journey into the future, seeking to achieve our potential and again and again failing, we make up moralistic cover stories, or moralistic excuses, for all that the ancient voice from within ourselves tells us is wrong or immoral.

"The moral faculties are generally and justly esteemed as of higher value than the intellectual powers," Darwin told us in expressing his conviction of the centrality of moral vision to the functioning of *true* intelligence—as opposed to the often empty overload of our highly touted Information Age.

Defining the Good and the Bad

Given this beginning for the upward flowering of moral sensitivity over the ages according to Darwin, how might we define the good and the bad for the 21st century?

An increasingly critical problem that Darwin can help with is defining what good is **not**. It is clear, for example, that it is **not** the use of "morality" by rightist and authoritarian religious and political interests as a club for beating—or killing—all who might disagree with them.

Large buildings, even hundreds of people, are blown up; people trying to check a potentially disastrous population explosion globally and save rape victims are machine-gunned; being "poor" is relabeled "evil"; our right to bear assault rifles is defended as a holy cause; whole villages are slaughtered down to the last woman and child; and, via the booming persuasion of the media in all its forms, political character assassination and actual assassination is becoming an advanced art—all in the name of Jesus, Allah, or some other supposedly unquestionable source of "moral" law.

This is *moralism*, not morality. And how may the difference be defined? If we examine closely both what Darwin in his own time and we in ours find appalling, we see that *moralism* can be defined as a false, fake, or hypocritically self-promotional "morality," generally designed to put down, intimidate, or terrorize rather than be helpful to others. But what then is morality?[420]

As we have seen, building on the earlier groundwork of Hume, Adam Smith, and the Darwin family friend and in-law Sir James Mackintosh, Darwin's central concept of the *moral sense* is what today would be called *moral sensitivity*. As he makes evident in the warm wonder and all the ins and outs of his tales of goodness at work in the so-called animal world, but also more abstractly at our level, this is the ability to empathize, to feel sympathy for, to care for, to resonate to, to want to nurture, or heal, or help—in short, to be morally sensitive to others. But what his exploration makes clear is that he is writing about considerably more than *moral sensitivity*.

If we are morally sensitive to another we may resonate to their needs or plight with mind and heart—or cognition and affection. This, however, doesn't necessarily mean we are going to get up from our easy chair with book or watching television to do anything to help them. This depends on courage and all the other components of what we call the *will*, or in psychological terms, conation.

Throughout Darwin's explanation of how the moral sense developed and operates in both animals and humans, we can see that what holds everything together—advancing the individual over its lifetime and the species over aeons—is this more active involvement in the fate of one another. It is the drive of *moral agency*.[421]

An agent *acts on the behalf of another*. Moral agency is then the force of action on the behalf of moral sensitivity and of another. A *moral agent* is the person who acts in such a way.

This is why Darwin's is actually a theory of moral agency rather than of the moral sense, which carries only the more passive meaning of the old philosophical term.

And what is *moral intelligence*? Out of the grand sweep of the second and third levels for his theory of the moral agent, the evolutionary picture Darwin provides is the drive of moral *sensitivity*. Through inspiration and education, this drive is given the edge of moral *agency*. Then comes what builds true wisdom for our species. For out of the thrust of moral agency comes the *learning experience* that builds within us the core to higher mind of *moral intelligence*.

And what is *morality*? The codes, the programming, the human software of whatever evolutionarily prevails at any point or place in time. It is the huge built-in user's manual that provides the guidelines for human-to-human and human-to-prehuman behavior.

It is everything that, based on the experience of the past, we have collectively agreed to be ruled by. It is the norms, rules, customs, laws, and commandments whereby out of the power of caring, the power of reflection, the power of language, and the power of habit, we establish social expectancies for moral sensitivity, moral intelligence, and moral agency.

Ethics is then all the sub-booklets in mind, the sub-routines or more finely-tuned differentiations of how these codes are to be applied in specific situations.

The "moral sense" for Darwin is all this. *But still it is more.* Yearning for comfort and reassurance, sensing a transcendent reality and source of meaning, for the sake of a word that might bring this concept to earth, for thousands of years most of us have called this "more" God, or earlier and again increasing in our time, Goddess.

For many of us the idea of some hidden transcendental or immanent deity—including at least four of the greatest Asian spiritual visionaries, Gautama, Lao Tsu, Confucius, and Mencius, as well as Darwin historically—this has posed difficulties.[422] However this may be, more important than what now or in the future this Greater Force may be called, it is something that is more surely *felt* than named, and seems to me undeniable— and here, too, a groping in this direction can be detected in Darwin.[423]

Out of something that is timeless and larger than ourselves, embracing the future as well as the present and the past, there works within us something else that additional to our experience of the past also seems to speaks to us in the shaping of all moral codes. It is simply there. Out of the evolution of the cosmic mystery that is both within ourselves and surrounds us, unknowable by that part of our self we think of as our conscious mind, yet at times most surely felt within all our being, there seems to be this voice that quietly but persistently urges everything emergent on this earth, including ourselves, to be the *best* that is in us.

Let It Be

In the end, then, beyond improving things within this person we see in the mirror and are to live with throughout our lives—or improvement within our own families, towns, cities, nation, the world as it today—where does consideration of all this take us?

Though Darwin seems to have glimpsed other vistas ahead, the overriding question before our species today is one he could in no way have foreseen. Who could have predicted 100 years ago what has happened in so short a span of time to our species?

Emerging four billion years ago out of a sequence of nebular explosion and then cellular eruption, eventually a small reptile becomes a form of ape, becomes a Neanderthal, then modern homo sapiens sapiens. The first digging tool or sewing needle becomes a wheel, and in succession thereafter, a stirrup for the horse, a boat, a bridge, a whole city, a whole nation, a train, a car, an airplane, movies, radio, television, computers and the wondrous new worldwide web linking of mind to mind. So we survive and miraculously grow in capacity and ingenuity for over 100,000 years. But who could have guessed that within the eyeblink of a single century our species would reach the brink of self-extinction?

Living before the devastation of two world wars, nuclear bombs, population explosion, the hole in the ozone layer, global warming, the rise of the new terrorism, and so on and on, Darwin could look with confidence to a long future for our species.

We, however, are forced to ask ourselves what does the 21st century—as the all-too-short span of time that can make or break us—hold for us, and for our children and grandchildren?

Of the things that are said of us at this junction, perhaps the most frightening is not that we lack the capacity to save ourselves, but that increasing numbers of us lack the vision of why this is even important any more—that is, of who we really are, who we can become, and where to go from here.

And yet, out of its hiding during the rise of a century of inhumanity, there is this vision that the re-emergent Darwin now provides us. In an age awash in either a mindless consumerism or the agony of deprivation, this lost top half to his theory shows us not only what is hopeful but also what is of the highest and of less and least priority.

If he were alive today, what would Darwin himself say was most hopeful about us? I think that he might just point to the courage and the heroism he found in the animals, which he writes of in Chapters 6 and 7 of this book.

"If courage and response to some kind of higher calling can be found here with such consistency and frequency," he might say, "why not more consistently among ourselves? Can't we see past the doubts, fears, and distrust of one another now entrenched in the worst of both religious and scientific dogmas, which have been robbing us of our rightful future? Can't we believe in and work to strengthen what is so much more widely prevalent among ourselves?"

The media focus on the killing, the murders, rapes, the frauds and scandals now considered the big news of our time. But isn't the greater news that the vast majority of people who worldwide at present make up our species are *not* on any one day making the news in this way? Isn't the big news instead that, on any one day, they are going about the business of life with courage, kindliness, and confidence?

If we stop to think about it, we see this all about us every day. The woman at the counter in the drug store leaves off chatting with the customer ahead of us, obviously an old friend, and in turning to us has the same smile for us, the stranger. The boy along the railroad track waves for no reason other than to establish recognition, being to being. Working ourselves at a counter, we know we can always depend on a certain old man for a joke. Or suddenly out of nowhere there appears on the computer screen the email lines from an old friend, long forgotten, who has just rediscovered us, or our work or our company, on the Web.

And there are the gatherings—the masses of us who knowing nothing of each other except our humanity in common gather to celebrate the unusual accomplishment of some member of our species, or to protest injustice, or to mount social and political action.

And more and more, there is the global sharing of these moments of both a higher reality and a higher destiny that the media provides in the interstices between the twisted fictions as well as the grim realities of the other side. Indeed, isn't what Darwin has both shown us and foreshadows the progressive globalization of *moral* mind?

It has been said we are entering the age of global mind, with the point-to-point hook-up of electronic linkings acting as a global brain.[424] But is this to be the globalization of the lower kinds of mind that Darwin tried to free us from—but that in subtle turnabout seized and buried him? Or is it to be the globalization of the moral mind the awakened Darwin reveals?

There are these moments of a global sharing, of a neighborhood intimacy across thousands of miles that we may now experience through the new electronic liberation. And isn't *this* the shape of our future—if those who ferociously cling to the past, who are so determined to undermine and delude and fight us every step of the way, will just step aside and let us go there?

Isn't this the larger and warmer and more comfortable vision of the future for our species—if they will just let it be? Or rather if those of us who believe in the vision will work, and if need be, *fight* for it—and if those who don't believe in it, but could believe in it if it were already here, will just let it be?

While our formally classical composers mainly focused on the zeitgeist of fragmentation and alienation during the 20th century, we can see now how in sharp contrast an unlikely group of rock musicians from Liverpool focused on the themes of longing, love, and renewal foretold by the lost Darwin.

As the Beatles sang, and as our hearts have called out to the best in ourselves and in others over the ages—but now more than ever before, with the fierce new longing for the vision born of the fear that it may be denied us:

Let it be. Let it be. Let it be.

APPENDIX

DARWIN'S LOST HEIRS AND HEIRESSES AND THE REDISCOVERY OF THEIR HERITAGE:

ISSS, SCTPLS, WESS, SFI, AND THE GENERAL EVOLUTION RESEARCH GROUP

In **Darwin's Lost Theory** we have seen how throughout the 20th century one body of scientists, tending to claim they were Darwin's sole legitimate heirs, pretty much took over evolution theory and ran the store, one might say. Meanwhile, another body of scientists tried for a bit to have a voice in the matter, but as they were in various ways boxed out of the process by the purported Darwinians, they soon gave up and turned to other matters. They found, for example, that they could get along very well without evolution theory, and when they needed to refer to it they simply dropped the product of the company store into the bag, so to speak, along with whatever they were offering. Now, however, the situation has changed. For it is now apparent that **both** bodies of scientists were Darwin's legitimate scientific heirs and heiresses. It also becomes apparent that, for humanity's sake, a dramatic update for the product—that is, the evolution theory and the evolution story—is needed; and this will take the best efforts of both working together.

Fortunately, for both parties to the venture still a third body of scientists has been at work during recent years laying the needed groundwork.

Though at present they represent only a comparative handful of people in relation to science as a whole, their training—that is, their fields, their disciplines, their expertise—span the territories of both the first half and the second half for Darwin's theory. They also have had the advantage of a period of working together—which is not easy considering differences in concepts and languages across fields.

What they offer at this time, it seems to me, is the good fortune of a head start in the needed direction. This, it further seems to me, can be very useful to science as a whole in re-aligning itself to the full spectrum not just of Darwin's theory, but of the much larger underlying reality of which his theory provides the most useful glimpse presently available to us.

Here is a brief report on Darwin's lost heirs and heiresses who—with no awareness of their direct kinship—have recognized and, on the behalf of science and humanity, have been working to respond to the same challenges that originally engaged him on the Isle of Wight and at Down house during the long winter of 1868-69.

The HoloDarwinian Venture

In the sequel to this book, *Darwin for the 21st Century*, I will cover some of the story of this venture. Orienting to the whole of Darwin's theory without realizing it, they tend to be social and systems scientifically as well as biologically aligned, hence might be called *holoDarwinians*. Embodying this perspective, they gather today in small groups and other clusters, transcending the old barriers of disciplines, languages, nations, and traditional institutions, to explore the possibilities for pooling the power of a more open, free-ranging mind than, in most places, was scientifically allowed during the 20th century.

Their wide-ranging interests and concerns are reflected today in a number of organizations. Not specifically focused on the development of evolution theory, but still indicating what an adequate evolution theory for the 21st century must embrace, are the probes of consciousness funded by the Institute for Noetic Sciences, the pioneering studies of the Wellesley College Center for Research on Women, the gender-balanced and multiculturally sensitive new partnership education being advanced globally by the Center for Partnership Studies in Tucson, Arizona, or the practical dimensions of Deep Ecology explored by the Institute for Ecoliteracy in Berkeley. HoloDarwinian concerns about the issues of global warming, environmental devastation, and our continuing capacity for nuclear disaster are notably reflected by organizations such as the Union of Concerned Scientists and the World Future Society. The holoDarwinian concern can also be seen in the global monitoring of our life support systems and human advancement by the Worldwatch Institute, the Human Development Reports team of the United Nations, Ruth Sivard's monitoring of military expenditures for World Priorities, in proposals by futurist Hazel Henderson for the financing and reform of the United Nations and economic and quality of life indicators, and in the rich further mix of hundreds of other action-oriented research groups.

Focusing specifically on the exploration of new evolutionary theory that was Darwin's central passion are the efforts of many independent scholars throughout our world today and at least four research organizations with which I am acquainted. I will briefly sketch their nature and situation and then explore in somewhat greater depth the General Evolution Research Group, as this is the one with which I am best acquainted as a co-founder, and as a member of the editorial board and the first book review editor for its journal.

International Society for the Systems Sciences

One of the oldest groups of this nature, of great historical importance, is the International Society for the Systems Sciences (ISSS). Originally inspired by the general systems theory of Ludwig von Bertalanffy, formed by economist Kenneth Boulding, anthropologist Margaret Mead, psychologist James Miller and others, this was the society of those who, by providing a way for bridging the boundaries and re-integrating the sciences, opened the way for the development of the humanistic, ethically-sensitive, and action-oriented *general* theory of evolution that Darwin's completed vision foreshadows.

In *Darwin for the 21st Century*, I will explore the remarkable similarity between Darwin's sequential, step by step development for the second half completion for his theory and the brief theory of human evolution that ISSS pioneer James Miller—naturally knowing nothing of Darwin's prior venture—outlines in one of the great works for modern systems scientists, his *Living Systems*, published in 1978. Evolution theory remains an active interest for many ISSS members—for example, former ISSS president Bela H. Banathy who is also a member of the General Evolution Research Group. Recently headed by Banathy's son, computer scientist Bela A. Banathy, and currently by synergistic evolution theorist Peter Corning, the group is aligned to active journals in systems research. It sponsors annual and regional meetings and is gathering together many other organizations for a World Congress of the Systems Sciences in Toronto, July 5-12, in the year 2000. Its journal is one of the best in this field, *Systems Research and Behavioral Science*.

Its Web site, an experimental use of the video streaming technique for "live action" broadcasts via computer that includes the speech I gave to the group initiating the Evolution Project.

The Society for Chaos Theory in Psychology and Life Sciences

The Society for Chaos Theory in Psychology and the Life Sciences (SCTPLS), with a small international membership, is newer and more typical of what is going on. This is a free floating organization that got underway, as is typical for anything labeled "new thought," by shifting its locational base around the U.S. according to who happened to be a faculty member at a university willing to provide a phone line for a web site, some free copying and printing, and a receptive department chair. Since then SCTPLS has become considerably more solidly based and financed. But still, despite the size and importance of our evolutionary challenge, it's quite possible that even now the study of basket weaving or mid-Victorian crochet skills may still be provided with more foundation funding and social emphasis. SCTPLS's focus is on the multidisciplinary advanced probe of ramifications for science and society of chaos and complexity theory. It is an active membership organization, with members already in 30 countries, one third of them outside North America. It has affiliated organizations in Italy, Germany, and Russia. It has annual conferences, with meetings in between around the U.S., a newsletter, and a journal *Nonlinear Dynamics, Psychology, and Life Sciences* published by Human Sciences Press.

Although I have not been active in recent years, I was a member of the original founding council. For good collections of early basic and pioneering papers by their members, see in my references Abraham and Gilgen, *Chaos Theory in Psychology*, and Robertson and Combs, *Chaos Theory in Psychology and the Life Sciences*, in which I have an important paper. Although rather involved to punch out without a mistake, here is another excellent web site for more information: AnS/psychology/cogsci/chaos.

Washington Evolution Studies Society

The most active society with the largest membership in the world currently exclusively exploring advanced evolution theory is the Washington Evolution Studies Society (WESS). Based in Washington, D.C., WESS' members are primarily from around the Washington area, although many fly or drive in from the surrounding states for special attractions, say a particularly noted lecturer or "hot topic" at the time. With members from over 100 different disciplines ranging throughout science and philosophy into the humanities, WESS not only has annual conferences and regular dinner meetings, but also organizes luncheons, walks, and has a regular newsletter.

As with the Chaos Society, they are also actively linked with many other groups exploring evolution theory. See their lively Web site (www.wess.org) for full information.

The Santa Fe Institute

Of the four, the non-profit Santa Fe Institute (SFI) in Santa Fe, New Mexico, is a horse of another color, as they say, in being much more narrowly restricted in focus and one of only perhaps two or three at most sufficiently well funded entities to maintain a fully functioning research institute, in this case with a twenty-seven member staff. Along with the Institutes in Belgium and Texas that Ilya Prigogine heads, this is one of few in the world devoted to probing the kind of advanced evolution theory needed to move beyond the truncation of neo-Darwinian, sociobiological, or first half Darwinian theory.

Further reflecting the gap between the need and the reality is the fact that, while the overwhelming need is for a new involvement of the social and systems sciences with evolution theory, the Santa Fe Institute is almost exclusively focused on the physics and biology of complexity theory. *But at least it is a place that begins to indicate what is needed to meet the challenge of building a more adequate theory of evolution.* Up to 150 scientists from around the world visit the Institute for short stays and they have many seminars during a year. They also maintain an active publications program with a book series published by Perseus Books. Biologist Stuart Kauffman (*At Home in the Universe*)—chief exponent of the view that self-organizing processes constitute a third major principle for evolution—is one of the best known scientists associated with SFI. See their web site (www.santafe.edu) for an idea of the scale of scientific effort that urgently needs to be widely established for scientists orienting to the *full* or holoDarwinian perspective throughout the world.

General Evolution Research Group

This brings us to The General Evolution Research Group, or GERG as it is known—of which I have written a history elsewhere.[425] This excerpt from that history will, I believe, provide a sense of a place in time, a historic meaning, and the sense of both the excitement of an adventure and of an important mission that occasionally grips everybody involved in all five of these groups and in small clusters elsewhere. The people vary from group to group, but this look behind-scenes into the formation and present nature of GERG shows what is happening more generally during the shift into the 21st century for evolutionary science.

The seed that became GERG was planted during the early 1980s when systems philosopher Ervin Laszlo began to look for a way to update evolution theory and make it more generally useful. At the time, Laszlo—a world-circling concert pianist who left that life to scale the walls of academia at many universities—was Director of Research for the United Nations. After helping to establish the general systems theory perspective through some key books, he became aroused by the vision of a *general* evolution theory—that is, an evolution theory that, in keeping with what we can now see was Darwin's original vision, might go considerably beyond the limits of biology to find concepts in common across the boundaries of all the scientific fields.

Out of this background, and encouragement by the Nobel medalists Ilya Prigogine and Jonas Salk, emerged Laszlo's idea for a research group that might bring together evolutionary theorists from a wide range of disciplines and countries throughout the world. I was, at its inception, the Group's social psychologist and a budding moral evolution theorist. Meeting in La Jolla, California, in 1986, Laszlo and a small band of us formed the General Evolution Research Group for the purpose he had envisioned.

Going It On Our Own

At the beginning we hoped some way might be found at Salk's Institute to bring a core group of us together for the sustained evolutionary research program such as apparently only the Santa Fe Institute and Ilya Prigogine's Institutes (in Brussels, Belgium, and in Texas) can carry on in the world as it is today. But as this didn't materialize, as we sat there demoralized in our hotel suite casting about for what to do next, I suggested we take a leaf from the experience of the "mom and pop think tanks"—that is, the founding of small "centers" and "institutes" in their homes by progressive scientists fed up with the repression of "new thought" in academia at large—and just go ahead on our own. Springing up to call the publishers in England, within five minutes—converting his journal *World Futures to World Futures: The Journal of General Evolution*—Laszlo had set us up with the single most vital component for this outrageous exercise of chutzpah, our own journal.

Thereafter, over the years we have met in Vienna, Florence, Bologna, Turku, Finland, Sardinia, and other exotic places whenever Laszlo could find a sponsor sufficiently inspired by our mission to provide the funding necessary to pull us together from around the world for a conference of anywhere from three days to a full week.

The Grim Facts and the Will to Prevail

Considering what our species faces in the way of challenges during the 21st century, that this area of study so crucial to both the advance of science and the well-being of our society could at this juncture in our evolution be so little recognized and poorly funded as these vignettes for ISSS, SCTPLS, WESS, SFI, and GERG reveal, is both a wonderment and a telling example of how unbalanced and skewed are global priorities for both science and society. As for the scientific study of the core for Darwin's completion of theory—our *moral* evolution—one sees an occasional book or paper on the subject, but other than my own work in this direction, second-half-grounded and almost wholly unpublished as yet, I know of no other sustained and active study elsewhere. We are at least a full century behind where we could have and should have been.

Meanwhile, with heads bloodied but unbowed, as W.H. Henley might have put it, the holoDarwinians persist. With GERG, for example, speaking a variety of languages, we come from countries scattered throughout Europe, Asia, and North America—as of the last tally, from England, Germany, Italy, France, Sweden, Belgium, Chile, China, Hungary, Russia, Sri Lanka, Switzerland, and the United States. Among us there are biologists, physicists, astrophysicists, mathematicians, systems, brain, social and computer scientists, psychologists, historians, philosophers, and chaos, feminist, and management theorists.

Because of the difficulties of the old paradigms for the sciences and nations out of which each of us comes, sometimes it seems that we gather together from around the world only to read papers born of separate disciplines, in separate scientific languages as well as national languages, each immersed only in our own pet study or theory. But informally, behind scenes, in the chats over breakfast, luncheons, during and after dinners, and afterwards in e-mail and other communications internationally, at times there has flowed among us the very special creative excitement that here and there has globally seized up the wider scientific community.

Some Hopeful Impact

Within this larger scientific community, already independent work by General Evolution Research Group members reveals a new meaningfulness in relation to the prospects for both the second half and the interlinked completion of Darwinian theory. This is true of the dissipative structures theory of Belgian thermodynamicist Ilya Prigogine, the autopoesis theory of Chilean (now French resident) biologist Francisco Varela, and the autogenetic evolutionary theory of Hungarian biologist Vilmos Csanyi and Hungarian computer scientist Gyorgy Kampis.

It is further true of the search for an ultimate grounding for evolution in Hungarian (now Italian resident) Ervin Laszlo's QVI-field theory; the work of U.S. brain scientist Karl Pribram (also a WESS member) in holonomic and active brain theory; and the action and partnership versus dominator model perspective of Vienna-born U.S. theorist Riane Eisler's cultural transformation theory. Also: Italian evolutionary philosophers Mauro Ceruti and Gianlucca Bocchi's probe of our historical understanding of evolution; the exploration of evolution in terms of levels of emergence by U.S. biologist Stanley Salthe (also a WESS member); and of U.S. mathematician Ralph Abraham's exploration of chaos theory and the humanizing potentials for computer modeling.[426]

Other GERG members are at work applying evolution theory to a wide range of areas: in the U.S., astrophysicist Eric Chaisson to the sweep of life from origin to morality, systems scientist Alfonso Montuori to creativity, psychologist Allan Combs to consciousness, historian Robert Artigiani (also a WESS member, currently Vice President) to historical patterning, systems scientist Bela Banathy to education, and biologist John Corliss (also a WESS member) to the deep sea origins of life.

Also: systems scientist Sally Goerner (who was the third president for SCTPLS) to a humanizing of systems theory; futurist Duane Elgin to the patterns for our probable future; in China, philosopher Min Jiayin to the dynamics of history in terms of gender relations; in Finland, management scientists Pennti Malaska and Mika Pantzer, and in

Switzerland, Thomas Bernold, to organizational systems management; in England, biologist Peter Saunders to advanced theoretical biology and systems scientist Peter Allen to dynamical systems; in Italy, historian Ignazio Masulli to evolutionary history, political scientist Miriam Campanello to politics, and psychologist Maria Sagi to energy healing; in Sweden, psychologist Singa Sandelin Benko to individual psychology; in Germany, physicists Jurgen Kurths and Rudolph Treumann to physics and educator Gerlind Rurik to education; from Sri Lanka, now U.S. systems scientist Susantha Goontilake to information theory; and in Russia, philosopher Edward Markarian to ecology.

World Futures and the GERG Books

Generally initiated by Laszlo, a rather amazing outpouring of scientific creativity almost wholly unknown outside the small circle of evolution theorists has been generated during recent years. For those with an interest in exploring the fascinating new world of advanced evolutionary theory, the Group's Journal, *World Futures: The Journal of General Evolution*—a quarterly with now forty volumes covering every conceivable aspect of evolution theory—provides a usually demanding but often lively forum for thinking about evolution theory.

The Group is also the sponsoring organization for the World Futures General Evolution series of books in this area. A representative example is the keynote volume for the General Evolution Research Group, *The New Evolutionary Paradigm*. Edited by Ervin Laszlo, this book contains papers by those of us who were among the Group's founders outlining evolutionary prospects for our various fields. Other notable books in the series include *The Age of Bifurcation: Understanding the Changing World*, by Laszlo; Cooperation: *Beyond the Age of Competition*, edited by Allan Combs; *The Evolution of Cognitive Maps: New Paradigms for the 21st*

Century, edited by Laszlo, Ignazio Masulli, Robert Artigiani, and Vilmos Csanyi; and *Chaos and the Evolving Ecological Universe,* by Sally Goerner.

The publisher of both the journal and the GERG book series is the international science publisher Gordon and Breach (for information and addresses, see web site www.gbhap-us.com). So prolific has been the Group's output that two other publishers are now involved. The 21st Century Studies series for Adamantine Press in England (and Praeger books in the U.S. (www.greenwood.com) is the publisher of *The Evolutionary Outrider: The Impact of the Human Agent on Evolution,* a book honoring Laszlo, of which I am the editor, with contributions by Fritjof Capra, Hazel Henderson, Karl Pribram, Riane Eisler, Ralph Abraham, Mae-Wan Ho, Ray Bradley, Maria Sagi, Paul Ray, Alfonso Montuori, Mauro Ceruti and Tiemo Piavani, and *Changing Visions: Cognitive Maps Past, Present, and Future,* by Ervin Laszlo, Robert Artigiani, Allan Combs, and Vilmos Csanyi. U.S. publisher Hampton Press is also publisher of a series on systems science, of which Alfonso Montuori is the editor, which includes new editions of Laszlo's key books *Evolution and An Introduction to Systems Philosophy,* and new books by Mauro Ceruti, Edgar Morin, and myself (*Making It in the Dream Factory*).

Information for interested subscribers to the Journal or the book series may be obtained through the above web site for Gordon and Breach or by writing to *World Futures: The Journal of General Evolution,* Uri-u.49, 1014 Budapest, Hungary.

Among books by GERG members more generally available in book stores are Laszlo's *Macroshift* and *The Whispering Pond*—a *Choice* selection for one of the outstanding scholarly books of 1997; Prigogine, *Order and Chaos* and *The End of Certainty;* Eisler, *The Chalice and the Blade, Sacred Pleasure, Tomorrow's Children;* Min Jiayin, *The Chalice and the Blade in Chinese Culture;* Chaisson, *Cosmic Dawn, The Life Era;* Combs, *The Radiance of Being, The Enchanted Loom;* Goerner, *After the Clockwork Universe;* Abraham, *Chaos, Gaia, and Eros;* Montuori, *Evolutionary Competence, From Power to Partnership;* Pribram, *Brain and Perception;* Salthe, *Development and Evolution;* Csanyi, *Evolutionary Systems and*

Society; Varela, *The Tree of Knowledge; Ceruti, Constraints and Possibilities*; Bocchi and Ceruti, *The Origin of the Story;* Saunders, *Beyond Neo-Darwinism*; and Elgin, *Awakening Earth.* All of my own out of print books (*The Healing of a Nation, The Leadership Passion, The Knowable Future, and The Sphinx and the Rainbow*) are available, as is presently *Darwin's Lost Theory,* through the Internet publisher iUniverse.com (Soon also to be published are *Arrow Through Chaos: How We See into the Future and Making It in the Dream Factory: Creativity and Survival in Hollywood and the Global Marketplace.*

What Might Have Been, What Now Must Be

Looking back over this list, it is amazing how much has come from such small investments here and there in funding. All told—for at the core the stories are similar for all of these groups—it is really a sort of loaves and fishes tale for science. Yet how much more there could have been with adequate funding.

And how much more is needed if—for the sake of our children and their children and all else we hold dear—we are to achieve what we must during the 21st century.

NOTES

1. See Meg Sommerfeld, "Lawmakers Put Theory of Evolution on Trial," *Education Week*, June 5, 1996; Robert Johnston, "70 Years After Scopes, Evolution Hot Topic Again," *Teacher Magazine*, March 13, 1996; and Kate Beem, "Debates Over Evolution in the Classroom Rage Counry-wide," *Kansas City Star*, June 13, 1999.

2. For good summaries of the varieties of evolution theory, see references for Ervin Laszlo's Evolution, and particularly for biologically-oriented questioning of the gross social "footprint," Peter Corning's "Holistic Darwinism," Stanley Salthe's *Development and Evolution*, or David Depew and Bruce Weber's *Darwinism Evolving*.

3. A fascinating new resource for the researcher is *Darwin 2nd Edition*, a CD-ROM produced by Pete Goldie for Lightbinders, Inc., 2325 Third Street, Suite 324, San Francisco, CA 94107. Not only are the texts beautifully accessible but the reproductions of the original engravings and color plates in Darwinian works are amazing. Besides *The Descent of Man*, this CD-ROM offers *The Origin of Species, The Voyage of the Beagle, The Expression of Emotions in Man and Animals,* and many other useful items.

4. Desmond and Moore, *Darwin*, p.558.

5. Darwin, Princeton edition *The Descent of Man*, p.2. [Unless specified otherwise, the Princeton University Press edition of the 1871 first edition is the edition referred to hereafter].

6.Portrayed in this book and its sequel and commentary, *Darwin for the 21st Century*, the evidence for these connections is as follows. Roots for Freud's construction of conscience in terms of the superego, ego ideal, and ego can be found in Darwin's multi-level development of the moral sense, Chapters 6-16 in this book. In Chapter 14 can be found Darwin's perception of the "two worlds" of morality that figure in Jean Piaget's analysis of moral development. In Chapter 6 we examine his anticipation of the developmental pattern for Paul MacLean's exploration of the evolution of the moral brain, his anticipation of the evolutionary connection between the origin of sex and the development of cooperation and caring in the work of Lynn Margulis. In Darwin's surprising focus on love—specifically expressed by his use of the word 95 times in *The Descent of Man* alone—we see the anticipation of the late 20th century revival of interest in the biology of love in the work of Mae-Wan Ho and Humberto Maturana noted in Chapter 2. Darwin's broadening of evolutionary perspective from the prehuman into the human level, including the evolution of language, caring, and consciousness, focused on here in Chapter 10, anticipates the interest of Ervin Laszlo and others in the development of a general (as contrasted with strictly biological) theory of evolution. In Chapters 8 and 9 we examine his anticipation of Franz de Waal's focus on the study of morality in primates. The sophistication of Darwin's social scientific perspective, specifically of the capacity for multiple variable analysis evident here in Chapter 10 and elsewhere, at times seems to anticipate the fluidity that entered the field of psychology fifty years later with Kurt Lewin's field theory. Darwin's development throughout of the nature and impact of the moral sense anticipates Pitirim Sorokin's later emphasis on the power of altruism. His focus on the influence of praise and blame on the development of the conscience, here expressed in Chapter 12, anticipates George Herbert Mead's view of the impact of "the significant other." And Darwin's development of the concept of "organic choice," with observations in other chapters summarized here in Chapter 11, anticipates William James' later involvement in the development of the concept of organic selection, Norbert Weiner's cybernetic theory, and the more recent interest of Richard Lewontin, Stanley Salthe, Francisco Varela, Ilya Prigogine, Ralph Abraham, Stuart Kauffman, and Vilmos Csanyi in various aspects of self-organizing processes.

7.This may seem exaggerated or unnecessarily harsh, and I wish I could be kinder to everybody concerned. But the size of what happened to Darwin—and its consequences for us—cannot be comprehended unless reported without compromise or the usual scholarly shading.

8.See Desmond and Moore, *Darwin*, for a fascinating account of Babbage's possible influence on Darwin's early theorizing.

9.Hofstader, *Social Darwinism in American Thought*.

10. See Montagu, *Man's Most Dangerous Myth: The Fallacy of Race*, and Loye, *The Healing of a Nation*, for critiques of Jensen and Shockley, and Gould, Curveball, for a critique of *The Bell Curve*. See Hofstader, *Social Darwinism in American Thought*, for the classic study, as well as the chapter on Herbert Spencer in my book *The River and the Star*.

11. Darwin, *Descent*, p.100.

12. Ibid, p.101.

13. Soros, *The Capitalist Threat*; Korten, *When Corporations Rule the World*.

14. Darwin, *Descent*, p.162, for "mutual aid." From Darwin's phrase, which characterizes so much of what he presents as motivational for both prehumans and humans in *Descent* Peter Kropotkin developed his classic compilation of observational science to this effect in *Mutual Aid*. Elsewhere in *Descent*, as can be seen in what lies ahead, the text is fairly peppered with "sympathy" and "love."

15. Monod, 1971.

16.*Descent*, p.152.

17. Ibid, p.404.

18. Ibid, p.396.

19. See references for Dart, Ardrey, Morris, Goulding.

20. Montagu, *The Nature of Human Aggression*.

21. For seven years, while on the faculty of the UCLA School of Medicine, I was the Research Director of the then largest field study of the impact of movie and television violence on adults. See details in Chapter 2 here, as well as Loye,

Gorney, and Steele, 1977; Loye, 1978; and *Making It in the Dream Factory*, 2000. See also Gerbner and Signorelli, *Violence and Terror in the Media.*

22.*Descent*, p.405.

23. Emphasis added. Ibid, p.402.

24. Ibid, pp.403, 404.

25. Dawkins, *The Blind Watchmaker.*

26. Dawkins, *The Selfish Gene.*

27. Hamilton, *The Evolution of Altruistic Behavior.*

28. Trivers, *Social Evolution.*

29. Wilson, *Sociobiology.*

30. The goals for morality Wilson states well in *Sociobiology.* The problem is his fixation, as for the other sociobiologists, on selfishness as the sole prime motivation.

31. See Allott, "Objective Morality," and "Evolutionary Aspects of Love and Empathy" for examples of the unusual scope for studies in part inspired by the sociobiological initiative.

32. Wilson, *Human Nature*, p.157.

33. Ibid, p.167.

34. Darwin, *Descent*, p.98. See Richards, *Darwin and the Emergence of Evolutionary Theories of Mind and Behavior*, pp.114-119, and Desmond and Moore, *Darwin*, p.283, for the pivotal influence on the young Darwin of the theological philosopher James Mackintosh personally and of Mackintosh's theory of the moral sense as specifically *not* based on selfishness. Typically, few Darwinian biographers make anything of the Mackintosh connection.

35. The Freudian view of altruism as selfishly motivated is, typically, rather complex, variously involving the concepts of rationalization, libido, narcissism, and egoism. See Fromm, *Man for Himself*, p.132; Freud, *A General Introduction to Psychoanalysis*, p.362.

36. The concern of media researchers, which can be documented now in hundreds of books and studies, is perhaps best exemplified by the work of sociologist George Gerbner, former Dean of the Annenburg School of Communication at the University of Pennsylvania and founder of the Cultural Environment Movement. See Gerbner and Signorelli, *Violence and Terror in the Media*. See also Loye, *Making It in the Dream Factory* for my fully detailed critique.

37. See Loye, D., Gorney, R., and Steele, G. 1977. *Effects of Television: An Experimental Field Study, and Loye, Television Effects: It's Not All Bad News*. See also Gorney, R., Loye, D., and Steele, G. 1977. *Impact on Adult Males of Dramatized Television Entertainment*.

38. See Loye, *Making It in the Dream Factory*.

39. So what, the skeptic will say. Why not when he was writing mainly of sexual selection throughout most of the book? Ah, but it is not so easy as that—as both the skeptic and the open-minded will discover by reading *Darwin in Love*.

40. Ho, "Organism and Psyche in a Participatory Universe." In Loye, *The Evolutionary Outrider: The Impact of the Human Agent on Evolution*.

42. Ibid.

42. Darwin, *Descent*, p.2.

43. Ibid, p.152.

44. Ibid, p.155.

45. Ibid, p.156.

46. Ibid, p.157.

47. Darwin, *Descent*, p.70.

48. Ibid, Part II, p. 404.

49. Essentially written at this point but for the final polish, the title will be *Darwin's Invisible Book: A Requiem for the Prisoners of Paradigm*.

50. In *Darwin's Invisible Book* I will go into the remarkable distortions of, for example, Daniel Dennett and Robert Wright in their skip-reading of small portions of this material.

51. See Loye, *The River and the Star, The Glacier and the Flame.*

52. As I did not extensively survey either moral philosophy or theology, both my training and interest being in science, here it is possible I have overlooked someone, although if they didn't appear in Rawls or Niebuhr, with whose work I was familiar, it seemed unlikely. See Chapter 5 for the one work of moral philosophy I came on late in my research to deal with the new Darwin.

53. The spelling here is a running source of minor confusion in Darwin. He lived in Down House, in the community of Downe, which at some point changed its name from Down to Downe.

54. Curiously, as I go into in *Darwin's Invisible Book*, one of the few who did see this need was the leading sociobiologist Edward O. Wilson.

55. Romanes, *Darwin and After Darwin*, p. 2.

56. Ibid, pp. 9-10.

57. Ibid.

58. Numerous examples can be found in Loye, *The Evolutionary Outrider*, or in many other books in the World Futures General Evolution series, as well as in the nearly fifty volumes to date of *World Futures: The Journal of General Evolution* (see Appendix A for more information on the World Futures book series and journal).

59. In terms of psychological, sociological, and systems scientific studies, I analyze how and why this happens in depth in "Evolutionary Action Theory: A Brief Outline" and *The Glacier and the Flame.*

60. The Princeton University Press edition of *Descent* I refer to, in most widespread use by American scholars, tells us that "*Descent* runs around forty entries annually in the Science Citation Index in recent years." (p.xxxiv). But these are overwhelmingly solely citations relating to Darwin's preponderant attention to sexual selection in *Descent*. The general pictures remains as earlier pictured here.

61. Of a seemingly endless stack of books to this effect, the works of Lewis Mumford, Habermas, Adorno, the Frankfurt School, most post-modernists, post-structuralists, Ervin Laszlo's *Evolution*, Fritjof Capra's *The Turning Point* and *The Web of Life*, as well as von Bertalanffy, Lewin, Maslow, Pribram, Einstein, Bohm, and many other physicists come to mind.

62. See Lerner, *The Politics of Meaning*; West, *Race Matters*; Kung, *A Global Ethic or Global Politics and Economics*; Bellah, *The Good Society*; Eisler, *The Chalice and the Blade*, *Sacred Pleasure*; as well as Loye, *The Glacier and the Flame*.

63. In *The Glacier and the Flame* I explore the nature of this trance, what it has done to us, and how we may wake from it in terms of what I call Ice Age Mind.

64. That is, they perceive the diversion away from morality but not the fact they themselves are, of all of us, most deeply so entranced.

65. *The Evolutionary Outrider, The Glacier and the Flame, The River and the Star*, indeed practically everything I've written.

66. Clark, *The Survival of Charles Darwin*, p. 221.

67. See Depew and Weber, *Darwinism Evolving*, and Clark, *The Survival of Charles Darwin: A Biography of a Man and an Idea*, for absorbing accounts of what happened from the natural scientific viewpoint.

68. Desmond and Moore, *Darwin*.

69. Though he labored for eighteen years on what became *Origin*, this was an immense manuscript out of which Darwin lifted and rewrote what is now *Origin* in only thirteen months. This same original manuscript then furnished parts not only of *Descent* but other later publications.

70. Desmond and Moore, *Darwin*, p. 556.

71. Gruber and Barrett, p. 398.

72. Ibid, p. 577.

73. This is particularly well developed in Desmond and Moore in terms of the political as well as religious pressures.

74. It was to express this unusual capacity and central difference for Darwin that I wrote *Darwin in Love*.

75. Ibid, p. 1.

76. Ibid, p. 3.

77. Desmond and Moore provide a particularly vivid picture of the Powers-That-Be in all their complexity at work against Darwin in his time.

78. Desmond and Moore, *Darwin*, p. 573.

79. Ibid, p.575.

80. Ibid, p.577.

81. These chapter designations are for the 1871 edition only. See General Guide to Selection, preamble to note 1, Chapter 5, for differences between the 1871 and 1874 and 1879 editions.

82. See *Darwin in Love* for this aspect of his work and how it specifically relates to both the foundation of *Origin* and the superstructure of *Descent*.

83. In *Darwin in Love* I tell the fascinating story of how in Darwin's theory of sexual selection he plays up the role and power of the woman in evolution, and why this led to suppression of this aspect of his theory by an overwhelmingly male scientific establishment. Elsewhere, Niles Eldredge and Marjorie Gren, for example, make the case for considering sexual selection as important as natural selection in evolution theory, offering a new perspective based on sexual selection as the basis for "reproductive evolution" and natural selection as the basis for "economic evolution." See *Interactions: The Biological Context of Social Systems*. See also Bonner and May's introduction to the Princeton University Press edition of *Descent*.

84. See Chapter 1 here for the quote from Chapter 21 of *Descent*, as well as two more comparable passages in his *Autobiography*, one of which follows here. In other words, not just once did he rail against the idea of blind chance in *Descent*, but in fact three times for his readers to see how radically Darwin differed from his successors on this point! From his *Autobiography*: "Another source of conviction in the existence of God… follows from the extreme difficulty or rather impossibility of conceiving this immense and wonderful universe, including our species with its capacity for looking far backwards and far into futurity, as a result of blind chance or necessity. When thus reflecting, I feel compelled to look to a First Cause having an intelligent mind in some degree analogous to that of ours; and I deserve to be called a Theist." *The Autobiography*, pp.92-93. Earlier, however—demonstrating the ambivalence and conflict that takes over whenever he deals with religion—we find this: "There seems to be no more design in the variability of organic beings and in the action of natural selection, than in the course which the wind blows." (*Autobiography*, p. 87). If we put the two statements together, he seems to be saying—contrary to his neo-Darwinian interpreters—that one simply cannot account for all that one sees of apparent design through the operation of natural selection and variability alone, but neither is the idea of God as the designer satisfactory. Clearly, regarding the idea of God, Darwin is of a multiple mind, being variously atheist, agnostic, or, as above, a theist. What in the end comes through is that he feels intensely that something else is going on out there beyond us. But what it is he concedes is ultimately beyond him or any other scientist to know. In other words, natural selection and random variation simply cannot account for everything.

85.See Gruber and Barrett, *Darwin on Man*; Richards, *Darwin and the Emergence of Evolutionary Theories of Mind and Behavior*.

86.See the Great Invisibility, Chapter 3.

87.Kropotkin, *Mutual Aid, Ethics*.

88.Montagu, *Darwin: Competition and Cooperation*. As I will write of in a later book at present titled in mind as *Up Against the Paradigm*, Montagu had twice played a pivotal role in advancing my career as a social scientist and we were good friends. But when I turned to him for advice and aid with this one he did everything but hit me with a club to get me to quit it! I will also write further there, or in *Darwin for the 21st Century*, about this important book of his.

89.See Wilson, *The Moral Sense*; Wright, *The Moral Animal*.

90.Because of what it reveals of the dangerous "pop" zeitgeist of sociobiology and ostensibly evolutionary psychology, I will deal further with Wright's book in *Darwin's Invisible Book*.

91.Desmond and Moore, *Darwin*.

92.Desmond and Moore, *Darwin*, p.579.

93.The importance of Richards' pioneering cannot be overstressed. It is a masterpiece of scholarship. At some length, however, he makes it clear that Darwin was convinced that our desire to help others, or altruism, could *not* be attributed solely to selfishness. But then he joins the sociobiologists in attributing their selfishness *über alles* view to Darwin as its pioneer!

94.Rachels, *Created From Animals*, p. 223. This book has the best short biographical sketch both of Darwin's life and the development of the primary theory of *Origin* that I know of.

95.*Darwin's Lost Theory, Darwin in Love, Darwin for the 21st Century.*

96.The New School for Social Research, from which I received my M.A. in the psychology of personality and my Ph.D. in social psychology.

97.The multinational, multidisciplinary General Evolution Research Group. See Appendix A as well as Laszlo, *The New Evolutionary Paradigm*; Loye, "A Brief History of the General Evolution Research Group"; Loye, *The Evolutionary Outrider.*

98.See Loye, "Scientific Foundations for a Global Ethic at a Time of Evolutionary Crisis," "Moral Sensitivity and the Evolution of Higher Mind," "Evolutionary Action Theory: A Brief Outline," "Can Science Help Construct a Global Ethic?" As for the "series" of books I refer to, alas, as of this writing they are all still unpublished. *The River and the Star* and *The Glacier and the Flame* completed, *Freedom and Equality, Love and the Guidance System of Higher Mind*, and *Moral Sensitizing* in fragments of several hundred pages each—a commentary on the monumental lack of interest in this subject that I hope *Darwin's Lost Theory of Love* may end.

99.An experience well known to most of us either as students or editors is the hair tingling, if not at times sky rocketing, sensation that can seize one by being forced to really *read* rather than simply scan something with the intensity of the student facing an exam tomorrow or the editor facing a deadline. Suddenly there begins to leap out at you meanings that would be impossible to gain otherwise.

100.See Loye, *Darwin in Love.*

101.See Bowlby, *Darwin*. Of the many theories advanced, including Darwin's being bitten by the bug producing Chagas disease while on the voyage of the Beagle, Bowlby centers on the impact of the early death of Darwin's mother and the subsequent complex rise of the physical symptomology of hyperventilation syndrome and the psychiatric symptomology of anxiety and panic attacks.

102.As Desmond and Morris note in *Darwin*, Emma—in contrast to Charles— spoke several foreign languages and had been taught to play the piano by no less than Chopin. Bowlby, however, whose portrait of Emma is outstanding and much more warmly detailed, reports nothing of Chopin.

103.Desmond and Moore, *Darwin*, p.573. Bowlby's *Darwin* reports Darwin's high praise of Henrietta's editing as well as Emma's direct involvement in the editing. All in all, a situation calculated to generate both massive inhibitions and a devil-may-care, let-the-chips-fall-where-they-may attitude on Darwin's part toward the sensitive parts of *Descent*.

104.See Barlow, *The Autobiography of Charles Darwin*.

105.Desmond and Moore, *Darwin*, p. 573. Bowlby says Emma even became directly involved in the editing of galley proofs.

106.Some invaluable concordances are: Weinshank, D.J., Osminski, S., Ruhlen, P., and Barrett, W. *A Concordance to Charles Darwin's Notebooks, 1836-1844.* Ithaca: Cornell University Press, 1989. Barrett, P., Weinshank, D.J., Ruhlen, P., and Ozminski, S. *A Concordance to Darwin's The Descent of Man.* Ithaca: Cornell University Press, 1987. I am much indebted to Donald Weinshank for relevant pages on morality as well as pointing me toward the invaluable source of the Pete Goldie-Lightbinders CD-ROM for *The Descent of Man, The Origin of Species,* and many other choice items.

107.Darwin, *Descent*, Preface to the revised edition of 1874, p. v, published by Appleton and Company, 1879.

108.Darwin, *Descent*, Preface to second edition, 1879 edition, pp. v-vi.

109.See Lorenz, "Irregularity: A Fundamental Property of the Atmosphere." See also Loye, "Darwin's Lost Theory: The Case for a Chaos Revolution," as well as the sequel to this book, *Darwin for the 21st Century*, for a more extensive exploration of Darwin's prefiguring of chaos theory. Chaos theory is more generally covered in Glieck, *Chaos Theory*; Loye, Chaos and Transformation; or in applications to psychology, Robertson and Combs, *Chaos Theory in Psychology and the Life Sciences*, and Abraham and Gilgen, *Chaos Theory in Psychology*. See Depew and Weber, *Darwinism Evolving* and Wesson, *Beyond Natural Selection*, for explorations of the relation of chaos, dynamics, and nonlinear theories to biology.

110. Without this preface to call attention to what otherwise is so buried in other matters as to escape notice, not only does the Princeton edition makes access to the chaos connection highly improbable, but this goes on and on in the world of the scholarly mangling of Darwin. For neither does the University of Chicago-Encyclopedia Britannica Great Books printing of the 1874 revised edition contain this preface—although Darwin originally specifically attached this key preface to it. But also here—bearing the seemingly unquestionable reliability and authority of both the University of Chicago and the Encyclopedia Britannica—we find an edition that not only drops this preface but also nowhere even bothers to tell the reader that this is the 1874 revised edition! Is there a good edition available? So far the New York University Press edition in Darwin's Collected Works seems one's best bet, and I am told by James Moore that he and Adrian Desmond are completing a new edition of *Descent* for Penguin books. It will be interesting to see if they have anything positive to say about the moral sense this time.

111. This was a strange experience. I was aware of the old book for years and had it close by for comfort as I tackled Darwin. But rather than stress the brittle old pages and binding, I did not open it, working rather with clean modern editions. Late in my research, baffled by being unable to find an original publication year for the Great Books edition of *Descent*, I picked up the old book and there discovered that it was the 1879 edition, that this was the same edition as the Great Books edition, that it contained the important Preface I have noted—and that the signature inside was of my great-grandfather, with beneath it the signature of my father, to whom it had passed. Who knows what these things mean, but I must admit that it seemed to me a most welcome form of blessing and encouragement at a time this book was being more often damned than praised in early manuscript.

112. All will be told in *Up Against the Paradigm*.

113. Gruber and Barrett, *Darwin on Man*.

114.Though this has been the popular view for a long time, Spencer is currently enjoying a revival among systems scientists and others who are discovering much merit in his microtheories.

115.von Bertalanffy, *General System Theory*.

116.Laszlo, *Evolution: The General Theory*, *The New Evolutionary Paradigm*.

117.Loye, *The Glacier and the Flame* and *The River and the Star*.

118.Pribram, *Brain and Perception*; Luria, *The Working Brain*; MacLean, *The Triune Brain in Evolution*. Loye, "The Moral Brain," provides a quick guide to all three.

119.E.g., the pioneering of Lynn Margulis in the symbiotic emergence of sex and, more generally, of Kauffman, Goodwin, Csanyi, Maturana, Varela, Ho, Saunders (see references). See Margulis, *Symbiosis in Cell Evolution*, and Margulis and Sagan, *Origins of Sex*.

120.Gruber and Barrett, *Darwin on Man*. p.295.

121.Ibid.

122.Ibid, p. 330.

123.Einstein's theory, I feel compelled to note, brought us the threat to our survival of the nuclear bomb, but Darwin's opens to us the prospect not just for survival but also for the fulfillment of our species.

124.The estimate of one billion years ago for the emergence of sex depends on how one defines sex. The leading authority in this area, biologist Lynn Margulis, portrays sex as a symbiotic development over a period of about three billion years, with the process of meiotic sex, or the mating of two separate organisms, coming about one billion years ago. See Margulis and Sagan, *Origins of Sex: Three Billion Years of Genetic Recombination*.

125.Margulis, *Symbiosis in Cell Evolution*.

126.Margulis makes the point that it is impossible to conclude that this was the "purpose" of how the multitude of things came together that wound up being classified as sex. But the discernible benefit thereafter is evident.

127.Margulis, "Early Life," in Thompson, *Gaia: A Way of Knowing*, p. 109.

128.Ibid, p. 243. See Margulis, *Symbiosis in Cell Evolution*.

129.See *Darwin in Love* for a chapter exploring the love life of the barnacle in detail.

130.See Desmond and Moore for an exceptionally meaningful reading of the story and significance of Darwin's barnacle research, e.g., p. 408 for the summary of description over several chapters.

131.Quotes by Desmond and Moore, *Darwin*, pp. 355 and 367.

132.See Margulis, *Symbiosis in Cell Evolution*. See Capra, *The Web of Life* or "Evolution: The Old View and the New View" for a lucid explanation of the nature and importance of symbiogenesis. See Swimme, *The Universe Story*, for a particulary readable and evocative account of what otherwise can at times become hard to follow in Margulis.

133.The idea of a step upward is my view rather than, unequivocally, Margulis's. Varying from the views of other biologists in this regard, in a way I find hard to understand, at least in some writings she views meiotic sex as neither adding to the genetic variety of life nor a logical step "upward," referring to it as no more than an accident and a "detour."

134.Based on Margulis, Swimme's expression of what he characterizes as a "cooperative...system of intimate interrelationships" is particularly evocative. See *The Universe Story*, p. 102.

135.See MacLean, *The Triune Brain in Evolution*. Or Loye, "The Moral Brain," *The Glacier and the Flame*.

136.Biologist Lynn Margulis's arresting phrase for one part of this process. See Margulis and Sagan, *The Mystery Dance*.

137.See Swimme, *The Universe Story*; Chaisson, *Cosmic Dawn* and *The Life Era*; Laszlo, *Evolution*.

138.Three excellent books in this regard are *Beyond Natural Selection* by Robert Wesson, *Beyond Neo-Darwinism: The New Evolutionary Paradigm* by Ho and Saunders, and *The New Evolutionary Paradigm* edited by Laszlo.

139. See Richards, *Darwin*, pp. 214-219. More recently, see Sober and Wilson, *Unto Others*.

140. See Eisler, *The Chalice and the Blade, Tomorrow's Children*, and other writings. See Loye, *The Glacier and the Flame* and many other writings regarding partnership moral sensitivity and morality versus dominator moral insensitivity and dominator moralities.

141. MacLean, *The Triune Brain in Evolution*, p. 265.

142. Ibid, p. 536.

143. Ibid, p. 388.

144. Ibid, p. 353.

145. Ibid, p. 397 ff.

146. Ibid.

147. Ibid, p. 380.

148. Ibid, p. 520.

149. In the *Mahabharata* 5:1517. See *Bible of the World* for this and other selections.

150. In the *Udanaraga*.

151.*The Dartmouth Bible*, p. 967.

152. Leviticus 19:18.

153.*The Dartmouth Bible*, p. 967.

154. Matthew 7:12.

155. In Sunan.

156. Loye, *The River and the Star*.

157. Quoted by Will Durant, *The Story of Philosophy*, p. 263.

158. Kant, *Foundations of the Metaphysics of Morals*, pp.166, 230, 253. Page references are to commentaries with varying translations.

159. Ibid, pp. 167, 179, 231.

160. Ibid, pp. 195, 292.

161. Having lost my note on this point, I gave up trying to find the passage after many a fruitless trek through the bramble patch of his notebooks. A similar passage occurs on page 74 of the Princeton edition of *The Descent of Man*.

162. See Chapter 2 as well as elsewhere throughout the Princeton *Descent* for what still remains one of the most perceptive analyses of all aspects of intelligence in the so-called lower animals. In Chapter 2 alone, Darwin details and analyzes evidence of intelligence, i.e., reasoning powers, in chimpanzees, baboons, orang utans, Rhesus monkeys, elephants, bears, rats, and even fish—a pike who learned to stop smashing his head against a plate of glass. As is true of much else, the pike is an addition by Darwin to the later and better Great Books edition of *Descent*, p.292, in which Darwin shifted Chapter 2 to become Chapter 3.

163. See MacLean, *The Triune Brain in Evolution*, or a diagram specifically showing this relationship in Loye, "The Moral Brain."

164. Darwin, *The Expression of Emotion in Man and Animals*. Still today, over 100 years later, in psychology this is considered an important beginning point for the study of emotions. It is also an impressive demonstration of Darwin's capacity for social as well as natural science in his use of questionnaires and other methodologies of social science.

165. See Loye, "The Moral Brain," as well as Fuster, *The Prefrontal Cortex*; Halstead, *Brains and Intelligence*; Freeman, *Psychosurgery*; Luria, *The Working Brain*, and Shore, *Affect Regulation and the Origin of Self*.

166. MacLean, *The Triune Brain*, p. 58.

167. Ibid, p. 60. Is this sequence just an isolated finding by a single researcher? For some idea of the scores of studies by other brain researchers finding connections between the same limbic and prefrontal cortex regions, especially right hemispheric prefrontal cortex, and the development of all aspects of moral sensitivity, see A.N.Shore, *Affect Regulation*. Chapter 27 alone cites a dozen confirming studies.

168.Luria, *The Working Brain*; Pribram, "On Brain, Conscious Experience, and Human Agency."

169.See Hume, *An Enquiry Concerning the Principles of Morals*; Smith, *The Theory of Moral Sentiments*. Most formatively, for Darwin, was the exceptionally well-grounded theory of the moral sense of Sir James Mackintosh, of which we may catch revealing glimpses in Richards' *Darwin* and Gruber and Barrett's *Darwin on Man*. See also my portrait of the Mackintosh relation to young Darwin in *Darwin in Love*.

170.Darwin, *Descent*, p. 70.

171.Darwin's citation of Mackintosh at this point is highly significant. Sir James Mackintosh was a leading theological philosopher whose own theory of the moral sense was the best developed for his time. As I develop in *Darwin in Love*, he was also a close family friend and relative by marriage of enormous influence on the young Darwin. A key point of Mackintosh's theory was his disagreement with the famous contemporary theologian and philosopher, William Paley, who believed that our basic motivation for altruism is selfishness. Mackintosh strongly disagreed, stating the position that became Darwin's from youth on, for which Darwin was to develop the scientific rationale. For details, see Gruber and Barrett and Richards' indexes.

172.This placement of Kant at the outset is also highly significant. Here Darwin refers to the pivotal point of Kant's theory of the moral agent: that we are driven by his Categorical Imperative, a restatement of the Golden Rule, to do good in this world, that indeed this is our *duty*. In effect Darwin is telling us, "This is what I believe and I am going to prove it to you by, for the first time, showing specifically how the moral sense emerges in animals and humans."

173.Following the above opening passage in the original, Darwin summarizes what I identify in this book as the second level of his theory of the moral agent. These passages I have moved ahead to Chapter 5 in order to focus on and adequately explore them.

174.*Descent*, p. 73. As explained in the Guide to Selections, note 1 for Chapter 5, the passages under this heading *begin* on page 73 of the Princeton edition.

175.The nature and dynamics of this concept will be tracked with each re-emergence of Darwin's observation, which I explore in depth in Chapter 11.

176.*Descent*, p. 74.

177.This was an interest of Darwin's that the entomologist and sociobiologist E.O.Wilson pursued with distinction.

178.See references for de Waal, Masson, and Kropotkin.

179.*Descent*, p.75.

180.Ibid, p.76.

181."Captain Stansbury also gives...old birds": This is a line moved up from a footnote in the original on page 77.

182.Sources identified in the next two notes.

183.*Descent*, p.77. This curious passage seems to contradict the contentions of Darwin's early notebooks and *Descent*: that the moral sense develops out of basic sexual, parental, and social instincts. I have left it in to give a sense of how Darwin goes back and forth on key matters. I have also found such contradictions typical of the great moral theorists in feeling their way through to their conclusions—Kant especially striking in this regard, as I develop in *The River and the Star*. It is easy for us to see the clear path now—that is, to impose the consistency that emerges within the context of their thought as a whole. But it was not so easy for them in their pioneering.

184.Darwin's contemporary, the psychologist Alexander Bain, earlier referred to. This reference to Bain and the rest of this section comes from a footnote at the bottom of p. 71 which seemed to me merits returning to the text as placed here.

185.In the British Isles alone, twenty-six authors "whose names are familiar to every reader" could be found for whom the question of the existence of the moral sense was of great importance. This stands in rather sharp contrast to what prevails today—not a single such author could be found.

186.For Mill and the other Utilitarians the purpose of morality was the attainment of the greatest happiness for the greatest number of humans. Darwin will return to this issue when he takes up the moral sense in humans in Chapter 12 of this book.

187."The ignoring of serious blemish Mr. Mill": This last line is a later addition by Darwin. See Great Books *Descent*, p.301.

188.Ibid, p. 77.

189.Ibid, p. 40.

190."As an old writer…luvs himself.": A later addition by Darwin, Great Books *Descent* p. 289.

191."For the purpose of…weeks old": I have included this later addition by Darwin both because of the humorous picture it presents and how it reveals his bent for simple, direct experiments. It comes from a footnote to the Great Books *Descent*, page 290. I have dropped the rest of the paragraph here as not adding much of importance. This section resumes at the bottom of p. 41, Princeton *Descent*.

192."Dogs shows…practical joke": Added later by Darwin, Great Books *Descent*, p. 290. The rest of this chapter in the original deals with other animals' qualities and matters not relevant to this excerpt.

193.Ibid, p. 78.

194.Louis Agassiz, one of the foremost naturalists of the time, abominated Darwin's evolution theory. "I hope you will at least give me credit…for having earnestly endeavored to arrive at the truth," Darwin wrote in sending Agazziz a copy of *Origin*. "This is truly monstrous!" Agassiz wrote in the margin of the copy. (Clark, *Darwin*, p.173).

195."But the elephant…noble fidelity": This vignette was added by Darwin, Great Books *Descent*, p.307.

196.Princeton *Descent*, p. 79.

197.See Lewin, *Field Theory in Social Science*.

198.Today the *American Heritage Dictionary of Science*, with more than 16,000 entries, omits the word "instinct" entirely. In editing Darwin, I puzzled for a while over whether to replace his use of this troublesome word with more accept-able modern scientific language—"drive," or "urge." But in the end, it seemed best to leave Darwin's use of "instinct" in place rather than further add to a sci-entific comedy or tragedy of errors. After Darwin, psychology went wild with the word "instinct." William James soon produced a list of no less than forty-six "instincts" to account for our behavior. According to James, we had "instincts" for everything from sucking and biting to hunting and hoarding and modesty. This overreaching use of the word forced the realization that rather than explain-ing motivation, psychologists were simply plastering it with a set of essentially meaningless labels. In the reaction that set in, the term was relegated to the past, to the 19th century, or to biology—where in turn it was also rejected as seeming to suggest a specific direction or goal for behavior, which, according to the neo-Darwinian paradigm, could have neither direction nor goal. Cutting itself off from use of the word, however, intensified modern psychology's isolation from our vital biological roots.

199. Princeton *Descent*, p. 82.

200. "We can perceive…paramount force": This paragraph comes slightly later. I have shifted it to precede rather than blunt the effect of the touching para-graphs that follow here.

201. Regarding Blackwell's observations, this moves a footnote at the bottom of p. 84 in the original into the text.

202. Ibid, p. 80.

203. "…the young remaining for a long time": later addition by Darwin, Great Books *Descent*, p.308.

204. "In contrast…earwigs": added later by Darwin, Great Books *Descent*, p. 308.

205. "With strictly…community": Princeton *Descent*, p.155.

206. Ibid, p. 166.

207. Ibid.

208. See Elliot Sober and David Sloan Wilson's classic contribution to the bookshelf for those who care, *Unto Others: The Evolution and Psychology of Unselfish Behavior.*

209. See Eisler, *The Chalice and the Blade*, and Marija Gimbutas, *The Civilization of the Goddess*, as well as the work of Chinese archeologists and anthropologists at the University of Beijing in probing the full span for Chinese history reported in *The Chalice and the Blade in Chinese Culture*, Min Jiayin, editor.

210. See Loye, Evolutionary Action Theory: A Brief Outline, in Loye, *The Evolutionary Outrider*. Using Cultural Selection as a more general term for Community Selection, I explore the vast differences between dominator paradigm expansion and defense and comparable processes for partnership-oriented people and groups.

211. Princeton *Descent*, p. 81.

212. Adam Smith is a pivotal earlier social scientist, credited with being the "father" of economics for *The Wealth of Nations*, whose views often have been not only grossly misinterpreted, but who has been used as another icon for selfishness as basic personal, economic and social policy. His earlier book was *The Theory of Moral Sentiments*. "The man of the most perfect virtue, the man whom we naturally love and revere the most, is he who joins, to the most perfect command of his own original and selfish feelings, the most exquisite sensibility both to the original and sympathetic feelings of others," he there observed (p. 152).

213.I'm not sure quite how one should read this. The pattern for Darwin's thought is to identify the social instinct as an instinct and sympathy as a higher order motivator, or in my terms sympathy is superstructural, a derivation from the social instinct. Yet here he calls sympathy an instinct. This may be an instance of something he would have clarified had it been called to his attention before publication.

214."This is a point...other instinct": These two brief paragraphs are an insertion into text of a footnote in the original at the bottom of p. 81.

215. This paragraph resumes the text in the original after my insertion of the footnote in text.

216."See Trivers, *Social Evolution*, or Stephen Jay Gould, *Ever Since Darwin* and *The Panda's Thumb* for easy accounts of the sociobiological complexities of Hamilton and Trivers.

217. In this chapter, I would note, I have done more than the usual amount of editing in order to straighten out what Darwin seems to be saying, which at times can be hard to follow in the original.

218. See Margulis and Sagan, *Origins of Sex*. See Swimme and Berry, *The Universe Story*, also for an evocative picture of the emergence of sex.

219. The following statement of Darwin's second level theory is the result of some rather difficult problems of scholarship in contention with the need for clarity for the modern reader. The basic problem for scholarship is that the versions in the standard Princeton edition of *Descent* (pp. 72-73) and the later version of the Great Books edition of *Descent* (p. 304) vary considerably in certain places. He is saying roughly the same thing both times, but the later edition is distinctly superior in grace and clarity of thought and expression. I have, accordingly, based my editing on the later edition. The first statement is the same for both. The second contains the addition of "or even misery" in the later edition. The third statement differs in both a discrete cutting of needless words and a strengthened clarity for the remainder. The last statement is again somewhat strengthened and clarified by working the concept of "sympathy" where before, in the Princeton edition, he only speaks vaguely of "impulses."

220.I have added the phrase "Out of a comparison of past, present, and future" to make explicit the implicit or "missing link" between these two lines. This, as we will see, touches on the dynamics of the concept of "organic choice." Darwin also adds to this line some rather involved wording that I have cut in order to provide a more forceful and clean-cut statement. For those who would like to have the rest: After "would arise," the original (in the Great Books *Descent*, p. 305) continues: "as often as it was perceived that the enduring and always present social instinct had yielded to some other instinct, at the time stronger, but neither enduring in its nature, nor leaving behind it a very vivid impression. It is clear that many instinctive desires, such as that of hunger, are in their nature of short duration; and after being satisfied, are not readily or vividly recalled."

221. Regarding acquisition of language, brain scientist Paul MacLean—whose work corroborates Darwin's theory of the biological development of the moral sense—has a fascinating and relevant theory of how language arose from sounds the child makes in nursing at its mother's breast. See MacLean, *The Triune Brain in Evolution*, or Loye, *The Glacier and the Flame.*

222. The idea associated with W.D. Hamilton's kinship selection theory.

223. The position for sociobiologists generally, notably articulated by Robert Trivers and E.O. Wilson.

224. Freud, primary process, secondary process, sublimation; Durkheim, social facts, social phenomenological surfaces; Pareto, residues, derivations; Pavlov, first and second signal system.

225. See references for Sorokin, Montagu, Gilligan. See Engels, *Dialectics of Nature*, pp. 209, 279ff, for a remarkable paralleling and expansion of both the data and perspective Darwin is beginning to lay out here. For example: "Let us accept for a moment the phrase 'struggle for life' for argument's sake. The most that the animal can achieve is to *collect*; man *produces*... Production soon brings it about that the so-called struggle for existence no longer turns on pure means of existence, but on means for enjoyment and development. Here—where the means of development are socially produced—the categories taken from the animal kingdom are already totally inapplicable." This is from p.209. The development of this theme in Engels in Chapter 9, "The Part Played by Labour in the Transition from Ape to Man," pp. 279-296, is another lost masterwork that actually goes beyond Darwin in insight along the line Darwin pursues in the development of the second level of his theory of the moral agent.

226. Freud, *New Introductory Lectures*; Jung, *Psychological Reflections*; Adler, *Understanding Human Nature*.

227. Lewin, *A Dynamic Theory of Personality*; Cantril, "The Human Design"; Allport, *Becoming*; Dabrowski, *Positive Disintegration*; Berne, *Games People Play*.

228. See Loye, *Darwin in Love*, "Lovers Wiles and Ways."

229. See Carroll, *Language and Thought*, re Chomsky and Whorf; Korzybski, *Science and Sanity*; re relation of semiotics to evolution theory, see Ceruti, *Constraints and Possibilities*.

230. Csanyi, *Evolutionary Systems and Society*; Dawkins, *The Blind Watchmaker*.

231. The sequence here has been more generally identified as thesis, antithesis, and synthesis.

232.There is some dispute over whether this ever actually happened or was a story made up by Marx's rather shady son-in-law, Charles Aveling. Some also say it was Aveling who made the offer.

233.This is spelled out at length in "Darwinian" terms by Engels in *Dialectics of Nature*. See note 8 for details.

234.See Marx, *Capital I*, p.197.

235.See Sorokin, *Sociological Theories of Today*, which has a particularly good section on dialectical theories both ancient and modern.

236.Ibid.

237.See Loye, "Chaos and Transformation: Implications of Nonequilibrium Theory for Social Science and Society," and other papers by Abraham, Bocchi, Csanyi, Malaska, and Eisler in Laszlo, *The New Evolutionary Paradigm*. For the advanced biological theory, see Depew and Weber, Chapters 16, 17, and 18, *Darwinism Evolving*, as well as sections in Salthe, *Development and Evolution*.

238.As I found Darwin's prefiguring of chaos theory getting too involved for this text, I lopped the paragraphs for placement in this book's sequel, *Darwin for the 21st Century*.

239.See references for Ralph and Fred Abraham, particularly Abraham's book *A Visual Introduction to Dynamical Systems Theory for Psychology*, a classic contribution to the psychology of the 21st century.

240.See Capra, *The Web of Life*, for a particularly good account of Wiener and cybernetic theory.

241.I use the concepts of feedback and feedforward with very broad strokes here. The main point is that Darwin was already seventy years ahead of the development of this approach in systems science, correctly visualizing and applying feedback and feedforward in his own analysis of evolution. For background on positive and negative feedback, see excellent explanations by Fritjof Capra relating these concepts to the pioneering work of Norbert Weiner in cybernetics in *The Web of Life*. For comprehensive background on the operation of feedback at all levels of living systems—including their involvement in evolution in considerable detail—see Miller, *Living Systems*. For feedforward, a good explanation of the goal-seeking aspect of this process is in Kent, *The Brains of Men and Machines*. For the classic statement relating these concepts to cognitive psychology, see Miller, Gallanter, and Pribram, *Plans and the Structure of Behavior*. For the dynamics of their interaction in cycling forward through time, see Capra, Miller, Gallanter, and Pribram, and especially Jantsch, *The Self-Organizing Universe*.

242.Ibid, p. 85.

243.Kauffman, *At Home in the Universe*, p. 71.

244.See, e.g., Yogananda, *The Autobiography of a Yogi*.

245. Bowlby, *Darwin*, p.393.

246.E.g., Lewontin, Kaufman, Goodwin, Csanyi, Salthe, Margulis, Ho, Saunders, Maturana, Varela, etc.

247.De Waal, *Good Natured*; Masson, *When Elephants Weep*.

248."The chief distinction in the intellectual powers of the two sexes is shown by man's attainment to a higher eminence in whatever he takes up than can woman—whether requiring deep thought, reason, or imagination, or merely the use of the senses and hands," he tells us in one of the parts of *Descent* that also after long neglect now gets some attention. (*Descent*, p. 327). He was also, however, in a time in which this was considered a radical view, forthrightly for education for women. It is also interesting that in *Descent* (p.326) Darwin also anticipates psychologist Carol Gilligan's well-known findings over 100 years later of stereotypical moral differences between males and females. "Woman seems to differ from man in mental disposition, chiefly in her greater tenderness and less selfishness, and this holds good even with savages." See Loye, *Darwin in Love*, for an extensive probe of what, beneath the stereotypes pro and con, was the reality of Darwin's position on gender differences.

249.As a general rule, the only exceptions were the experimentalists known as the Social Utopians, the stellar example of John Stuart Mill, Marx and Engels—as I bring out in my portrait of the pair in *The River and the Star*—and the amazing Frederick Douglass, whom I write of in *The Healing of a Nation*.

250. For background, see Richards, *Darwin and the Emergence of Evolutionary Theories of Mind and Behavior*.

251.I would urge those who wish to pursue this further to read Romanes, *Darwin and After Darwin*. In this book by Darwin's treasured protégé, Romanes shows how already by 1897 Darwin's views on the inheritance of characteristics were inaccurately lumped in with Lamarck. I strongly suspect that as biological psychologists and psychologically oriented brain researchers become more involved in the development of evolution theory they will find the Darwin long discredited by biologists had some valid observations here.

252. Loye, "Darwin's Lost Theory: The Grounding for a Scientific Revolution," p. 3. Paper presented to the annual meeting of the International Society for Systems Study, Asilomar, June 19, 1999.

253. As I bring out in *The River and the Star*, this belief in moral universality was the chief passion driving the research of Lawrence Kohlberg. It is also the passion of the world ecumenical movement, as most strikingly exemplified in expressions deriving from the work of Hans Küng, e.g., *A Global Ethic, Yes to a Global Ethic*, and *A Global Ethic for Global Politics and Economics*.

254. See text under the subhead "The horror as well as the heights of morality, or moralism versus morality," in Chapter 14.

255. See Loye, *The River and the Star*.

256. See Darwin, *The Voyage of the Beagle*, pp.219-220, as well as the famous quote ending *Descent*, p.405.

257. See text under the subhead "On the transcendent conscience of the individual, freedom, slavery, and blind chance" in Chapter 14 of this book. This is an excerpt from *The Voyage of the Beagle*, pp. 502-503.

258.*Descent*, p. 84.

259. Here, to show how I am occasionally changing a Darwinian line to eliminate the exclusively male referents customary for his time, is the Darwinian original: "Most persons admit that man is a social being." (*Descent*, p.84).

260. This is a difficult but important line. How, if he is building the case for a moral agency in humans driven by the developmental succession of sexual, parental, and social instincts, can Darwin now say that we have lost any instincts our predecessors had? Here he recognizes the pivotal point of the transition from prehuman to human of a motivational superstructure that to some degree is now freed of the instinctual foundation, a perception that with the rise of sociology and psychology was to liberate thinking for social science.

261.Ibid, p.85.

262.See Eisler, *The Chalice and the Blade* and *Sacred Pleasure*, which report a wide range of studies by anthropologists and others bearing on this vital difference for which Darwin had no adequate differentiating model in mind. Another useful perspective is that of anthropologist Ruth Benedict on the difference between high synergy and low synergy tribal as well as more advanced societies. See Loye, *The Glacier and the Flame* for accounts of both works in this regard.

263.Benedict, "The Synergy Lectures."

264.British philosopher David Hume, an important moral theorist who, in contrast to psychologist Lawrence Kohlberg, who focused on moral reasoning as paramount, held that emotion, specifically sympathy, was the great moral motivator.

265."In his Enquiry...imagination": This is my insert into text of a footnote at the bottom of page 85. The copy following this insert resumes in the text above.

266.This line is an insert from the Great Books *Descent*, p. 310, as the change Darwin later makes is significant. The qualifier in the line in the earlier version of the Princeton *Descent* is "also probable." This Darwin changes to "almost certain" in the later version.

267.We are now on page 86 in the Princeton *Descent*. This paragraph in the original is hard to follow because of Darwin's contradictory and confusing use of the word instinct. This derives in part from the difficulties he faced as a natural scientist lacking the vocabulary to express his insights into social science— a vocabulary that by and large did not yet exist. In this he seems to foreshadow all the problems social scientists were to face well into the early part of the 20th century in trying to either shed or modify the idea of instincts, as discussed here in Chapter 10. But also his problem is that, in contrast to many natural and social scientists today as then, he was able to perceive life as *multi-motivational,* as well as involving other subtleties we are only now, at the beginning of the 21st century, exploring with sophistication through chaos theory.

268. "This is an interesting passage in what it reveals of the range of Darwin's reading of the moral philosophers. It seems to relate both to Kant's categorical imperative for morality and to a touching account by one of Kant's students of his last visit with this key moral philosopher, who by then had lost his great mind to senility or possibly Alzheimer's disease. I use it to conclude my two chapters on Kant in *The River and the Star*, but this is not the sort of thing one comes by without an extensive knowledge of Kant.

269. *Descent*, p.163.

270. Here sympathy is identified as an "instinct," while elsewhere Darwin identifies it as a "derived virtue."

271. "meanwhile loving...ourselves": This is a paraphrase of a later insert by Darwin, Great Books *Descent*, p.322.

272. This is the ending of this passage on page 165.

273. *Descent*, p.87.

274. To this paragraph Darwin makes two critically important additions bearing on the central difference between his position and that of modern sociobiologists. To make clear the differentiation he makes in both levels and kinds of altruistic motivation, he first inserts the line: "A savage will risk his own life to save that of a member of the same community, but will be wholly indifferent about a stranger." This a sociobiologist would likely leap on as support of both Trivers' reciprocal altruism and Hamilton's kinship selection. To the last line about the human at the higher level of civilization we assume for ourselves, however, he makes the following significant addition. To this picture of the person who will plunge "at once into a torrent to save a drowning person," which is where the earlier edition ends, Darwin adds the phrase to make clear his position on a motivation for altruism *transcending* selfishness or blood ties, "though a stranger."

275. "Moreover, if...may be felt": A paraphrase of a line added by Darwin to the later edition to emphasize the *strength* of selfishness-transcendent altruistic motivation, Great Books *Descent*, p.311.

276. *Descent*, p.87.

277. "They make...morality": Added by Darwin, Great Books *Descent*, p. 311.

278.Thomas Huxley, Aldous and Julian's grandfather, was famous as "Darwin's bulldog," or his theory's most ferocious and formidable champion. Leslie Stephen was a magazine editor, famous essayist, and social theorist of the time.

279."—and I am delighted...such distinctions": A combination of text and footnote added by Darwin, Great Books *Descent*, p.311.

280.This ability to reflect and compare past with present actions is notably a capacity of prefrontal brain areas, the site of what I identify as the guidance system of higher mind. See Loye, "Moral Sensitivity and the Evolution of Higher Mind." Here we are looking at a "higher" or more advanced development of the more fundamental thrust of "organic choice."

281.Given the fact Darwin has spent so much time giving us instances of what he identifies as moral behavior among animals, this seems an inconsistency—and on one level it is. However, here he seems to be trying to have his cake and eat it too by recognizing the gulf between the degree of imprisonment of prior species in their environment and the degree of freedom that enters evolution with the emergence of the human.

282.See MacLean, *The Triune Brain in Evolution*. Loye, "The Moral Brain" relates the higher limbic and frontal brain work of MacLean, Pribram, Luria and others to Darwin's theory point for point.

283.Princeton *Descent*, p. 89.

284.The words "superstructural" and "foundation" inserted for clarity. The reference to "love of praise and fear of blame" is a later Darwin insert, Great Books *Descent*, p. 311.

285.Princeton *Descent*, p. 89.

286."Even when we are...social instincts": A significant addition by Darwin, Great Books *Descent*, p. 311.

287.The passage in the earlier Princeton *Descent* ends at this point, on p. 90, and goes on to something else. In the later edition, however, Darwin adds the significant material given in six paragraphs here, again on the *transcendent* motivational processes at the human level beyond the operation of natural selection, ending "...is esteemed of great moment." See note 39 for specifics.

288. Here is an instance where the differences of tribal societies governed by the partnership model from those governed by the dominator model of evolutionary theorist Riane Eisler become striking. Darwin generally draws on examples of dominator model tribal societies. In sharp contrast is, for example, the tribal society of the Teduray studied by anthropologist Stuart Schlegel. His account of the morality of the Teduray in *Wisdom of the Rain Forest* is a contribution of considerable importance in what it reveals of the potential for the "natural" tendency toward goodness that is the point of the second half of Darwin's theory.

289. The greater part of the above passages Darwin added later, "If we look for...love or fear of God," is from a footnote, with the concluding two paragraphs, "We will thus... of great moment," from the text, Great Books, *Descent*, p.312.

290. *Descent*, p.91.

291. At this point Darwin later made the large insert that follows.

292. What seem Freudian overtones here are not coincidental. Soon Freud, influenced by Darwin, was to advance this level of insight with his development of the formation of the conscience in terms of his powerful concepts of the super ego and the ego ideal—both of which can be found in embryonic form in these lost writings of Darwin.

293. Here, crisply, is the relationship that can become hard to follow elsewhere. Sympathy is both something long ago implanted within us through evolution, or what Darwin calls innate, and also something that each of us learns through the experiences of our own lifetime, or acquired.

294. The above passages, in six paragraphs here, are one of the best demonstrations of both the substance and the nuances of what is being lost through scholarship based solely on the standard Princeton *Descent*. See Great Books *Descent*, p. 313.

295. I provide a detailed analysis of this relationship in *The River and the Star*. See Freud, *Introductory Lectures on Psychoanalysis*, and *New Introductory Lectures on Psychoanalysis*.

296. Mead, *George Herbert Mead on Social Psychology*.

297. Great Books *Descent*, p.313. Thereafter both editions resume with "The still hungry person..." See following note for commentary.

298. The above passages are in both editions, but with slight changes throughout that smooth the rough spots in the later edition. The final paragraph is pulled up from the footnote in both editions. Princeton *Descent*, pp. 91-92; Great Books *Descent*, pp. 313-314.

299. See references for Allan Shore and Adrian Raine. See also Loye, "The Concept of Evil," in *The Encyclopedia of Violence, Peace, and Conflict*, and Loye, "The Moral Brain."

300. "In such a case...punishment operating": Essentially the same for both editions. Princeton *Descent*, pp. 92-93; Great Books *Descent*, p. 314.

301. Same for both editions: Princeton *Descent*, pp. 335-337; Great Books *Descent*, pp. 570-571. For more on Darwin's own intense love of music, see Loye, *Darwin in Love*, where I use the same subhead.

302. See Sims, *Darwin's Orchestra*; Desmond and Moore, *Darwin*, pp. 649-650.

303. This and the following passages are from the Princeton *Descent*, pp. 335-336. The sentence about the Chinese annals was inserted later by Darwin in the revised edition of 1874.

304. Princeton *Descent*, p.104; Great Books *Descent*, p. 319—both essentially the same.

305. Kohler, *The Mentality of Apes*.

306. Again, research since Darwin finds a wide range of species expressing what must be considered ideas—e.g., "run for your lives," "I've discovered a good dinner for us all," or "I'm ready for love"—with a range of sounds. See MacLean, *The Triune Brain in Evolution*, regarding the universality of the separation cry.

307 Again a critical place where Darwin makes clear the difference between the sociobiologists' idea of selfishness as the sole or even prime motivator of goodness in us and his own massively substantiated scientific conviction. See Loye, *The Glacier and the Flame*.

308.Here Darwin is referring not only to Chapter 4, which deals with the moral capacities of animals—which I solely draw on here—but also to Chapter 3 of *The Descent of Man*, which deals with the intellectual capacities of animals, and deserves, I might observe, the same kind of rescue operation as this for the modern reader.

309.Above phrase "which seems extremely doubtful" added by Darwin to later edition. Great Books *Descent*, p. 319.

310.Such questions have, of course, been amply answered by child psychologists and psychiatrists since Darwin's time. See, for example, the work of Jean Piaget who, inspired by Darwin, pioneered psychologically in precisely these directions, or more recently, the work of Stern, *The Interpersonal World of the Infant*, or Shore, *Affect Regulation*, or the work of this nature I write of in *The Glacier and the Flame*.

311.A key use of the word "foundation," to which Darwin recurs in making his fundamental differentiation between the biological, or first half, and the cultural, anthropological, sociological, and psychological second half for his theory.

312.*Descent*, p. 93.

313.Here, limited both by an access to a far more limited database than we are today as well as by the "survival of the fittest" or "dominator" paradigm, Darwin is led to overgeneralize. Since his time, works by anthropologists and others find evidence of both the brutal ethnocentricity he focuses on and a peaceful and welcoming attitude toward others beyond the margin for each group or tribe. In general, drawing upon hundreds of references in many fields, this is the difference characterized by evolutionary theorist Riane Eisler in her identification of the difference between societies and social groups orienting to the "partnership" versus the "dominator" models of social organization, or by anthropologist Ruth Benedict in her differentiation of high- and low-synergy cultures. See Eisler, *The Chalice and the Blade*, *Sacred Pleasure*; Benedict, "The Synergy Lectures"; Loye, *The Glacier and the Flame*.

314.This is a critical point I develop at length in Chapter 7 of *The Glacier and the Flame*.

315.An attribution to Walter Bagehot, banker, editor of the London *Economist*, and a well known essayist of the time.

316.While certainly prevalent, this was of course hardly true of all tribes.

317.Even today as we enter the 21st century, with female deaths still in the millions by this means, female infanticide remains the scandal of China, India, and other primarily Asian areas. See Amartya Sen, "More Than a Million Women are Missing," or regular reports in Fran Hosken's *Women's International Network News*.

318.Not a thug in our sense today, though this is the historical derivation of the term. Darwin is here referring to the Thugee, a sect in India that seized the imagination of the Victorians—including A. Conan Doyle, who uses this in one of the Sherlock Holmes stories. The original Thugs specialized in a particularly quick and gruesome method of strangling their victims to death with a cord.

319.Again, while prevalent, this is by no means as universal as Darwin implies.

320.From this line I have removed this very strange and inexplicable phrase inserted in the original between "Slavery" and "is a great crime": "although in some ways beneficial during ancient times." This makes no sense in view of Darwin's passionate hatred of slavery, nor is any explanation offered for it other than a footnote referring to an essay by Walter Bagehot, which no doubt would take ages to track down to little purpose. This paragraph comes from the Great Books *Descent*, see next note for special relevance.

321.Here again, in this dig at racism unique to the later edition, is another refutation of Social Darwinism. The paragraph comes from the Great Book *Descent*, p.315.

322.The original here (Princeton *Descent*, p. 94) is a sweeping and inaccurate statement, which I have modified both to fit the facts and reader sensitivities.

323.Ibid.

324.This is one of the main points where Darwin departs so markedly from those of his heirs who find altruism exclusively motivated either by selfishness or kinship.

325.A famous African explorer who died by drowning when attacked by natives and his canoe was overturned. This was a type of episode then prevailing that provided the base in reality, which we tend to forget, for the Darwinian view of savagery.

326.Another notable departure from what the advocates of an altruism limited to selfishness and kinship believe.

327.This passage could make some uncomfortable as it refers to courage in war-fare—but also courage generally. Darwin's frequent admiring references to the virtue of courage are of special interest in two regards. One is that it reminds us of this very special quality in himself—the courage to go against not only the weight of the Church and the mass mind governed by the Church, including his own wife and some close friends, but also a significant part of prior scientific opinion. It is also a reminder of what seems one of the saddest facts of our time. This is our increasing lack of courage at all levels of society. Most of us—and this is perhaps most distressing of all in academia, which was supposed be the bastion of the free mind—are afraid to speak up and say what we see or think or feel without first finding out what others believe, or what the latest polls show, or finding the proper authority to cite. Out of a long lifetime as both a journalist and a social scientist, I feel compelled to say that beneath our postures of inde-pendence, most of us are still sheep seeking the leader who will tell us precisely how and when to bleat.

328.At this point in my excerpting, I skip from p. 97 to 99 in the Princeton *Descent*.

329.This is a fascinating observation revealing, all at once, the connection between the "code of honor" prevailing among the courtly gentlemen of Darwin's social and scientific circles, the same code again invoked in macho society globally to justify the stoning or the killing of the wife, lover, sister or mother found to stray from being the property of the particular possessing male, and the Mafia in determining which transgressor is to be buried at sea with feet embedded in con-crete or merely to lose a finger.

330.This again touches on the problem of dominator versus partnership moral-ity I address in *The Glacier and the Flame*, as well as the dominator versus the partnership model of social organization Eisler analyzes in *The Chalice and the Blade* and *Sacred Pleasure*.

331.Here Darwin speaks to a question and a concern becoming ever more critical in our time. In other words, in a world threatened with environmental degradation and disaster and mounting political instability through over-population, one wonders how long humanity can afford the position of the Roman Catholic Church against birth control and abortion. Similarly, in a world threatened with mounting terrorism, including the terrorism of a renegade state or group with nuclear arms, one wonders how long humanity can afford the fomenting of hatred and the condoning of killing by the extremist mullahs of Islam.

332. Here Darwin is both anticipating, and looking for an answer, to the field of psychology then emerging—which soon was to provide dramatic answers to his question by Freud and countless psychologists thereafter.

333. Here again Darwin anticipates the fields of anthropology, sociology and political science then emerging, soon to provide answers to the questions he raises through the works of Peter Kropotkin, Franz Boas, Max Weber, Emile Durkheim, Ruth Benedict, Hortense Powdermaker, and hundreds of others, as well as most recently through the application of systems science to this matter by Eisler.

334. Excerpting ends here on page 100 in the Princeton *Descent*. The final excerpt for this section skips ahead to Chapter 21, with locations indicated as follows.

335.*Descent*, p. 405.

336. Ibid, p. 404.

337. The following section is primarily from the Great Books *Descent*, as indicated below.

338. See Richards re Paley, *Darwin*, pp. 114, 115. Adam Smith was not, as Richards implies, also exclusively of the selfishness school. His actual position was extremely close to Darwin's in that he felt we are motivated by selfishness, stressed in *The Wealth of Nation*, as well as by altruism, stressed in his earlier *The Theory of Moral Sentiments*. "The man of the most perfect virtue, the man whom we naturally love and revere the most, is he who joins, to the most perfect command of his original and selfish feelings, the most exquisite sensibility both to the original and sympathetic feelings of others." (Smith, *The Theory of Moral Sentiments*, p. 152). The best analysis of Smith I've come by, albeit brief, is by Daniel J. Campbell in Galtung and Inayatullah, *Macrohistory and Macrohistorians*.

339. Princeton *Descent*, p. 97; Great Books *Descent*, p. 316.

340. Great Books *Descent*, p. 316.

341."Two exceptions are..."Greatest happiness theory": This passage involving Mill and Sidgwick is one I have pulled up from the footnotes in the original to give it its proper place in the text. Henry Sidgwick was a fascinating figure. A leading scholar of his time, he helped found the Society for Psychical Research in 1882 and became a leading psychic researcher along with William James in the U.S. Though the co-discoverer of the principle of natural selection, Alfred Wallace, also became an ardent psychic researcher, all this was bosh to Darwin.

342."For if we simply observe...deeply planted social instinct": Again emphasizing the power of an altruistic moral sense in contrast to selfishness, this is another example of the advantage of working with the later edition. These two paragraphs come from the Great Books *Descent*, p.316. Material following can then be found in both editions, e.g., page 98 in the Princeton *Descent*.

343. Writing over 100 years ago, here Darwin not only anticipates the self-regarding morality of the revolutionary health movement of recent years but also the closely linked vision of the healthy mind and body of modern human potentials movement. What I mean by self-regarding morality is the valuing of the self, and of oneself, as in a sense a sacred entitlement in this context. In other words, having been given this body and this opportunity to live, it is our duty to do well and not ill by it.

344. This line takes on considerable meaning in view of the drive in late 20th century America to cut welfare and social services as part of a general pattern for the rise of racist, classist, and sexist policies as against concern for society as whole.

345. Here, from the security and comfort of his own situation and theory, Darwin assumes something that generally is not true from the perspective of a wide range of other theorists—for example, Marx and Engels in his own time, or more recently anthropologist Ruth Benedict. What he describes is the social state that Benedict defined as that of synergy—the coinciding of the purposes or goals of the group with the individual. But what Benedict, as well as many others, Eisler and myself for example, have found is the problem of a vast disjunction between the system requirements of what Eisler calls dominator systems, which globally prevail, and the more partnership system oriented ethos of the most enlightened and progressive individuals within these systems. In terms of the differences between partnership moral sensitivity and morality and dominator moral *in*sensitivity and morality, I develop this difference at length in *The Glacier and the Flame.*

346.The reminder regarding the impact of approval or disapproval of others is Darwin's insert into the later edition, p. 317. Otherwise, the last five paragraphs can be found in both editions, e.g., Princeton *Descent,* pp. 98-99.

347.Here Darwin boxes himself into a logical dilemma with this qualification. He is, on the one hand, saying that we are in effect driven by billions of years of biological development of the social instinct comprising one of the main components of the "altruistic" other-regarding moral sense. But now he seemingly contradicts himself by opening the way to find this social instinct and moral sense is also selfish.

348.*Descent,* p.100.

349.Showing the continuity for this perception and classification in terms of the works of Kant, Marx and Engels, Spencer, Durkheim, Freud, Piaget, Kohlberg and Gilligan, these are the "two worlds" I explore in *The Glacier and the Flame* and *The River and the Star.*

350.Here Darwin speaks directly to our time—as also Immanuel Kant, in his historically pivotal essay on Perpetual Peace, did still much of a century earlier in his call for what has in our time become the United Nations.

351.At this point, excerpting skips from Princeton *Descent,* p. 101 to pp. 103-104.

352.Toward the end of Chapter 4, *Descent,* immediately above the subhead *Summary of the last two chapters.*

353.A reference to Darwin's cousin Francis Galton—a genius of the more readily recognizable type, obviously both to Darwin and to others Darwin's more traditionally intellectual superior. Historically, Galton was one of the most important influences in the development of modern psychology, a brilliant experimentalist, a pioneer in the study of individual differences, and the "father" of modern statistics.

354.In addition to the relation of this observation to the later discovery of the Zeigarnik effect by a student of Lewin, as noted earlier, this also touches on the phenomenon investigated in the study of frustration-aggression by Dollard and Miller and others of the "Yale School" and of frustration-regression by Lewin.

355.Italicized final line added here for logical completion of thought and transition to next copy block.

356.The episode did not make it into most accounts either by Darwin's descendants or many biographers. But brother Leonard spilled the beans in 1942. "She felt that on religious questions it was crude and but half thought-out," he wrote of Henrietta's crusade against publication. (Clark, *The Survival of Charles Darwin*, p.205). As a consequence, Francis was forced to lop some fifty passages from the autobiography. A letter from his mother, Emma, to Francis also provides further insight into the pressure Darwin was under in writing *Descent*. What she objects to here was the main point for his whole theory! "There is one sentence in the Autobiography which I very much wish to omit, no doubt partly because your father's opinion that *all* morality has grown up by evolution is painful to me." (The later version of the autobiography in which Granddaughter Nora Barlow restored the cuts, published 1958, p.93).

357.In *The Glacier and the Flame* and *The River and the Star*, I identify this persisting perception of the "two worlds" of morality in terms of the works of Kant, Marx and Engels, Spencer, Durkheim, Freud, Piaget, Fromm, Frenkel-Brunswick, Kohlberg, Gilligan, and others.

358.*Descent*, page 161. Naturalist Peter Kropotkin expanded Darwin's observation and original use of the phrase "mutual aid" into his enduring classic *Mutual Aid*, which continues the Darwinian tradition of observations of an ethical drive among a wide range of animals.

359.*Descent*, pp. 403-404.

360.Ibid, p. 405.

361.Ibid, pp. 393-395.

362.In these passages, Darwin defines the connection of education and the learning process to organic choice.

363.The above four paragraphs come from various places on pp. 394-395 of the Princeton *Descent* (they are also found, as is true of everything else besides modifications noted, in the Great Books *Descent*). As the sentences are scrambled about and do not track well as published, my re-ordering attempts to unscramble and make them more meaningful. As indicated in the introduction to this book and in the Desmond and Moore biography, this scrambling seems to derive in part from Henrietta's editing and Darwin's concern about Emma's feelings. Certainly we can visualize Darwin's strong statement about the positive impact of the conviction of the existence of an all-seeing deity on morality being in part an observation for Emma's benefit. But note then how he enters his own conviction of the fictional nature and other problems with the idea of deity— which remained in the text, indicating Emma and Henrietta's respect for the integrity of his beliefs. Behind the scrambling also lie the difficulties of Darwin's understandably conflicted view of religion. On one hand, having considered the ministry himself, greatly admiring theological scholars such as Mackintosh, and resonating to a naturalist's dimension of spirituality transcending formal religion, he recognized the importance of religion and, as he clearly notes, spirituality. On the other hand, there were the superstitions and the absurdities, as he put it, as well as the ferocity of the diatribe mounted against him by the religion of his time—and even still, among the persistent Creationists, in our own. See the fascinating, more extended discussion of God, religion, and spirituality concluding Chapter 2 of the Princeton *Descent* or chapter three of the Great Books *Descent*, as well as in Darwin's autobiography.

364. The sentences for the brief section that follows, again as re-arranged, come from pp. 593-594 of the Great Books *Descent*. Comparable but somewhat less well-developed passages for the same material can be found in the Princeton *Descent*, pp. 391-392.

365. Loye, *The Glacier and the Flame, The Evolutionary Outrider.*

366. Great Books *Descent*, p. 593.

367. Ibid, p. 592.

368. Ibid, p. 592.

369. Ibid, p. 593.

370. Desmond and Moore, *Darwin*, p. 573.

371.This and the next four paragraphs come from *The Voyage of the Beagle*, pp. 502, 503—for which I am indebted to Howard Gruber for calling to my attention.

372.See Desmond and Moore, p. 653.

373.Princeton *Descent*, p. 395.

374.This passage, which so wholly contradicts Darwin as he has been presented to us—also foreshadowing the heresy of Einstein within physics that "God does not play dice with the universe" as well as Ervin Laszlo's QVI field theory—can be found where it has always been: on page 396 of the Princeton *Descent* and page 593 of the Great Books *Descent*.

375.*Descent*, p. 141.

376.Ibid.

377.Ibid, p. 139.

378.Great Books *Descent*, 281. This observation appears only in the later edition. Earlier Darwin had noted the measurement of differences in sizes of skulls of ancient and modern humans by "Professor Broca," who is the famous Pierre Paul Broca who identified the area for language processing in our left brain hemisphere. In the later edition Darwin specifically notes that "the increased size...was exclusively in the frontal part of the skull—the seat of intellectual faculties," which accords with a confirmation by the brain research of Luria, Pribram, MacLean and others seventy years later.

379.Ibid, pp. 385-386.

380.Princeton *Descent*, p. 391.

381.Ibid.

382.This is a composite of the differing versions in the earlier and later editions. Curiously, the earlier version is the better of the two here. It is more spontaneous, warmer in its use of "each other" rather than the later, more distant "one another," and it includes the vital dimension of the future in the key matter of the comparison of past, present, and future in organic choice. The later version, however, adds the vital phrase "reflecting on" to this key definition. From Princeton *Descent*, p. 391, and Great Books *Descent*, p. 592.

383. Great Books *Descent*, p.592. The Princeton edition is the same except for the addition of the "approval and disapproval" phrase here.

384. Ibid. This paragraph picks up later on the page after a cut shifted elsewhere.

385. Ibid. The same passage is on p. 393 in the Princeton *Descent*.

386. Ibid. This is a slight re-ordering of passages also found in the Princeton *Descent*.

387. Rather than let stand unmodified something that doesn't fit the rise of compassion that Darwin is expressing here, I have added the word "seemingly" to this line, which otherwise is in striking contrast to the callous so-called Social Darwinist or unalloyed "survival of the fittest" position of Herbert Spencer, the other major evolutionary theorist of Darwin's time. (See Hofstader, *Social Darwinism in American Thought* for details on Spencer as social barbarian).

388."The social instincts... risen higher and higher": This passage—which I have separated into phrases to emphasize both its prophetic character and cadence—comes from the Princeton *Descent*, p.103, and the Great Books *Descent*, p. 318. It subtly differs from other summaries in giving the sense of a statement going both ways, into past and future, as a statement of vision. To emphasize this thrust, I have changed the tense to make explicit what I find implicit in Darwin: a final statement in keeping with his deep feeling for the welfare of all species displayed in this as well as his more familiar writings.

389. Great Books *Descent*, p. 319. I have removed a confusing instance of Darwin's complicated and tentative belief that the build-up of virtuous habits over time might affect evolution by becoming an inherited trait, a belief that was also Spencer's, but about which Darwin expressed both pro and con feelings.

390. As a veteran of World War II, resonating to the work of Kurt Lewin, the great authoritarian personality study of Adorno, Frenkel-Brunswick, Levinson, and Sanford, Milton Rokeach's and Silvan Tomkins' work, and so much else that came in response to the shock of what the Nazis represented—which I write of in *The River and the Star*—I have been greatly disappointed as a social scientist with the decline in comparable vision since then. Fortunately, we have had the jolts of the civil rights, peace, environmental, and—above all—the women's movement to focus us on fundamental social and moral tasks. But the reasons for these causes have not been sufficiently threatening to comparably mobilize social science, as the fascist seizure of major nations did earlier.

391.I go into Maslow, Assagioli and Dabrowski at greater length in *The Glacier and the Flame.* The brain research, which I touch on in various journal pieces and in *The Sphinx and the Rainbow* and *An Arrow Through Chaos,* I will bring together in a work in progress *The Guidance System of Higher Mind.*

392. See Preface to Maslow's *Toward a Psychology of Being* describing the original lineup for this third force, including post-Freudians such as Karen Horney and Erich Fromm, both the Gestalt therapists and the formal Gestalt psychologists such as Kurt Lewin, personality psychologists such as Gordon Allport, the existential psychologists such as Rollo May, and the Jungian and self-psychologists. Almost all passed into history now, these were the saints and the angels for me as a young psychologist in training.

393. Maslow, *Toward a Psychology of Being*, p. 59.

394. Ibid, p. 153.

395. As a psychologist in training, my own first association with his work came with Maslow and Mittelman's classic text on abnormal psychology. He knew Freud in greater depth than most Freudians and the same for behaviorism. He also knew the history of both natural and social science better than most scholars in this area. He also had a breadth of scholarship in the humanities rare for your standard psychologist. In varying degrees, this scope was also true of Kurt Goldstein, Erich Fromm, Hadley Cantril, Gordon Allport, Gardner Murphy, Carl Rogers, and others associated with or influenced by humanistic psychology's predecessor, the "organismic" theory keying back to Jan Smuts' *Holism and Evolution,* as well as to terms I will further develop in *Darwin for the 21st Century,* as the "holoDarwinian perspective." In short, the rejection of the traditional paradigm by Maslow, Assagioli, Dabrowski, and others noted above, was based on knowledge of this repressive paradigm, as well as on the pioneering vision of the good sense, decency, and practicality of its alternative.

396. See Chapter 18, Depew and Weber, *Darwinism Evolving,* for the seven key inter-relationships in the work of Kaufman, Lewontin, Goodwin, Salthe, Ho, etc. I find this connection quite fascinating: that defense motivation should be the analogue for natural selection, and growth motivation the analogue for self-organizing processes.

397.MacLean, *The Triune Brain in Evolution*; Luria, *The Working Brain.*

398.Ibid.

399.Maslow, *The Further Reaches of Human Nature.*

400.Maslow, *Toward a Psychology of Being*, p. 157.

401.Maslow, *Religions, Values, and Peak Experiences*, p. 63.

402.Maslow, *The Farther Reaches of Human Nature*, p. 289.

403.Ibid, pp. 298-299.

404.Ibid, p. 299.

405.Among Darwin's modern heirs in the science of moral development were Erich Fromm, Jean Piaget, Lawrence Kohlberg, Carol Gilligan, Milton Rokeach, all of whom I write of in *The River and the Star* and *The Glacier and the Flame.*

406.See *The Glacier and the Flame.*

407.Ibid, p. 8.

408.Ibid.

409.For implicate and explicate order, see Bohm, *Wholeness and the Implicate Order.*

410.See Paul Ray, What Might Be the Next Stage in Cultural Evolution? In Loye, *The Evolutionary Outrider.* His basic report, funded by and available from the Institute for Noetic Sciences and the Fetzer Institute, is "The Integral Culture Survey: A Study of the Emergence of Transformational Values in America."

411.For the most devastating picture of the situation of the bypassed and denied peoples of our world that I know of, see Thom Hartmann, *The Prophet's Way* and *The Last Hours of Ancient Sunlight.*

412.See Salthe, *Development and Evolution*, re differences of level and scale. The inadequacy of first half Darwinism is really horribly simple to see, or rather that the horror is in how for so long most of us could fail to see the simple fact of its inadequacy even in terms of the most basic of considerations of methodology for science. Not, for goodness sake, as a matter of blaming, but to help us rapidly get the past behind us and move on together, I will develop this thought in terms of sampling, set, and systems perspectives and methodologies in *Darwin for the 21st Century*.

413. See Introduction and references for specific works.

414. The reader who feels this may be an exaggeration is invited to consider this definition by one of the chief architects of *Origin* level Darwinian theory, Julian Huxley. Here Julian Huxley is contrasting the operation of natural selection with his proposal for the counterpart operation of *psychosocial selection* on the human level. "Though natural selection is an ordering principle, it operates blindly," Huxley observed. It "pushes life onwards from behind." It "brings about improvement automatically, without conscious purpose or any awareness of an aim." Psychosocial selection also "acts as an ordering principle. But it pulls [us] onwards from in front. For it always involves some awareness of an aim, some element of true purpose." In psychosocial evolution "the selective mechanism itself evolves as well as its products. It is a goal-selecting mechanism, and the goals that it selects will change with the picture of the world and of human nature provided by [our] increasing knowledge." (Huxley, *Essays of a Humanist*, p.34). Many "first halfers" do concede the operation of other mechanisms besides natural selection and random variation—but this is incidental to the basic operation as stated here and by Huxley, who was ostracized by many of his peers in biology for daring to so speak out.

415. See Kauffman, *At Home in the Universe*; Wheeler, *At Home in the Universe*; also Laszlo, *The Interconnected Universe* and *The Whispering Pond*.

416. This is not just an arbitrary selection of values. All, which Darwin identifies operating either at the prehuman or human level, or both, have been extensively empirically defined by Rokeach. See Chapter 10 here: also Rokeach, *The Nature of Values*; Loye and Rokeach, "Ideology, Belief Systems, Values, and Attitudes"; or Loye, *The River and the Star* for an account of Rokeach's great cross-cultural study of values within the context of the scientific exploration of morality.

417. 8. The love of beauty, or aesthetic sensitivity, is not commonly thought of as being related to moral sensitivity. Hence, we have the abysmal drive by moralizing rightists to abolish the National Endowment for the Arts. However, the

linking of "the true, the good, and the beautiful" by philosophers is not coincidental. Nor is the fact, as I bring out in *The River and the Star*, that the three were one by one explored by Immanuel Kant in the pivotal *Critique of Reason*, *Critique of Practical Reason*, and *Critique of Judgement*. See Chapter 6 here, "If Music Be the Food of Love," for a touch of Darwin's thought directed toward trying to scientifically root this connection in evolution. See also the book I have found most enjoyable to write, *Darwin in Love*, for more here.

418.Ah ha! says the sociobiologist. Proof positive of both the reciprocal altruism of Trivers and the kin selection of Hamilton. Yes—but follow it from its rooting in the self-transcendence of the sexual instinct (see chapter one here) and Darwin's theory of the moral agent indicates that, by whatever name one chooses to call it, self-transcendence too is involved. Self-transcendence as a value is extensively explored by Maslow in, e.g., *The Further Reaches of Human Nature*.

419.See Loye, *An Arrow Through Chaos, The Knowable Future, The Healing of a Nation*.

420.In *The Glacier and the Flame* and *The River and the Star*, I go much more extensively into the definition of all aspects of morality, including the vast difference for meaning according to whether one is dealing with "dominator" or "partnership" morality. See also Loye, "The Concept of Evil" in *The Encyclopedia of Violence, Peace, and Conflict*.

421.Significantly, a very clear statement of the relation of the moral sense to moral agency (and of emotion and reason to will) was offered by Darwin's theological mentor on the subject, James Mackintosh. The following is a passage in Darwin's copy of Mackintosh's *A General View of the Progress of Ethical Philosophy* that Darwin not only marked, but underlined in regard to the phrases "emotion" and "impell the will." "That the main, if not sole, object of conscience is to govern our voluntary exertions, is manifest. But how could it perform this great function if it did not *impell the will?* and how could it have the latter effect as a mere act of reason, or indeed in any respect otherwise than as it is made up of *emotions*, by which alone its grand aim could in any degree be attained?" (See "Old and Useless Notes," p.412, in Gruber and Barrett, *Darwin on Man*).

422.This seems a fair conclusion if one reads what these four great Asian minds actually had to say about life and how it was to be lived, rather than apply to them the model for western religious mind. See also Loye, *The Glacier and the Flame*.

423. In sizeable portions of *The Descent of Man* as well as in his private notebooks and *Autobiography*, Darwin did considerable more ruminating about the possible existence, nature, and social and psychological function of God than most people realize.

424. See James Lovelock, *Gaia: A New Look at Life on Earth*; Peter Russell, *The Global Brain Awakens: Our Next Evolutionary Step*; Ralph Abraham, *The Web Empowerment Book*.

425. Loye, D. 1998. A Brief History of the General Evolution Research Group. In Loye, D., Ed., *The Evolutionary Outrider: The Impact of the Human Agent on Evolution*.

426. For references, see books listed by above names in References.

REFERENCES

Abraham, R. *Chaos, Gaia, and Eros.* San Francisco: HarperSanFrancisco, 1995.

Abraham, R., Jas, F., and Russell, W. *The Web Empowerment Book.* New York: Springer-Verlag, 1995.

Abraham, F.D., and Gilgen, A.R., Eds. 1995. *Chaos Theory in Psychology.* New York: Praeger, 1995.

Abraham, F.D. "An Historical Holistic Thread in the Dynamical Fabric of Psychology." *World Futures: The Journal of General Evolution* (1997): 49, 1-2, 159-201.

Adler, A. *Understanding Human Nature.* Greenwich, CT: Fawcett,1954.

Allott, R. "Objective Morality." *Journal of Sociological and Biological Structures* 1991. 14 (4): 455-471.

Allott, R. "Evolutionary Aspects of Love and Empathy." *Journal of Sociological and Biological Structures* (1992): 15 (4): 353-370.

Allport, G. *Becoming.* New Haven: Yale University Press, 1955.

American Heritage Dictionary of Science, Robert K. Barnhart, Ed. Boston: Houghton-Mifflin, 1986.

Ardrey, R. *African Genesis.* New York: Atheneum, 1961.

Augros, R., and Stanciu, G. *The New Biology.* Boston: Shambhala Publications, 1987.

Axelrod, R. *The Evolution of Cooperation.* New York: Basic Books, 1984.

Alexander, R. *The Biology of Moral Systems.* New York: Aldine, 1987.

Barash, D. *The Whispering Within.* New York: Harper & Row, 1979.

Barkow, J., and Tooby, J. *The Adapted Mind: Evolutionary Psychology and the Generation of Culture.* New York: Oxford University Press, 1992.

Barnett, S.A., Ed. *A Century of Darwin.* Cambridge, MA: Harvard University Press, 1958.

Bellah, R., Madsen, R., Sullivan, W., Swidler, A., and S. Tipton. *The Good Society.* New York: Knopf, 1991.

Benedict, R. The Synergy Lectures. In Combs, A., Ed. *Cooperation: Beyond the Age of Competition.* Philadelphia: Gordon and Breach, 1992.

Berkowitz, L., R. Corwin, and M. Heironimus. "Film Violence and Subsequent Aggressive Tendencies." *Public Opinion Quarterly* (1963): 27,217-229.

Berne, E. *Games People Play: The Psychology of Human Relationships.* New York: Grove,1964.

The Bible of the World. New York: Viking, 1939.

Bohm, D. *Wholeness and the Implicate Order.* London: Routledge and Kegan Paul, 1980.

Bonner, J.T., and R.M. May. Introduction to Darwin's *The Descent of Man.* Princeton, NJ: Princeton University Press, 1981.

Bowlby, J. *Charles Darwin: A New Life.* New York: Norton, 1991.

Brockman, J. *The Third Culture.* New York: Simon and Schuster, 1996.

Browne, J. *Charles Darwin: A Biography.* Princeton: Princeton University Press, 1997,1995.

Cantril, H. "The Human Design." In Hollander, E.P., and R.G. Hunt, Eds., *Current Perspectives in Social Psychology.* New York: Oxford University Press, 1967.

Capra, F. *The Turning Point.* New York: Simon & Schuster, 1982.

Capra, F. *The Web of Life.* New York: Doubleday Anchor, 1996.

Capra, F. Evolution: The Old View and the New View. In Loye, D., Ed., *The Evolutionary Outrider: The Impact of the Human Agent on Evolution.* Twickenham, England: Adamantine; Westport, CT: Praeger, 1998.

Carroll, J.B. *Language and Thought.* Englewood Cliffs: Prentice-Hall, 1964.

Ceruti, M. *Constraints and Possibilities: The Evolution of Knowledge and the Knowledge of Evolution.* Switzerland: Gordon & Breach, 1995.

Chaisson, E. *Cosmic Dawn: The Origins of Matter and Life.* Boston: Atlantic, Little-Brown, 1981.

Chaisson, E. *The Life Era: Cosmic Selection and Conscious Evolution.* New York: Atlantic Monthly Press, 1987.

Clark, R.W. *The Survival of Charles Darwin.* New York: Random House, 1984.

The New Columbia Encyclopedia, Harris, W.D., and J.S. Levey, Eds. New York: Columbia University Press, 1975.

Combs, A. *The Radiance of Being: Complexity, Chaos, and the Evolution of Consciousness.* St. Paul, MN: Paragon House, 1997.

Combs, A. *The Enchanted Loom: A Course on the Mind and the Brain.* Work in preparation, 1999.

Corning, P. "Holistic Darwinism: 'Synergistic Selection' and the Evolutionary Process." *Journal of Social and Evolutionary Systems* (1997): 20 (4): 363-400.

Csanyi, V. *Evolutionary Systems and Society.* Durham, N.C.: Duke University Press, 1989.

Csikszentmihalyi, M. *The Evolving Self: A Psychology for the Third Millennium.* New York: HarperCollins, 1993.

Dabrowski, K. *Positive Disintegration.* Boston: Little Brown, 1964.

Dart, R. *Adventures with the Missing Link.* New York: Harper & Row, 1959.

Darwin, C. *The Descent of Man.* New York: Appleton and Company, 1879.

Darwin, C. *The Voyage of the Beagle.* New York: P.F. Collier Harvard Classics, 1909.

Darwin, C. *The Origin of Species.* Chicago: Encyclopedia Britannica, Great Books, Vol. 49, 1952.

Darwin, C. *The Descent of Man*. Chicago: Encyclopedia Britannica, Great Books, Vol. 49, 1952.

Darwin, C. *The Expression of the Emotions in Man and Animals*. Chicago: University of Chicago Press, 1965.

Darwin, C. *The Descent of Man*. Princeton: Princeton University Press, 1871/1981.

Darwin, C. *Autobiography*. Edited by Nora Barlow. New York: Norton, 1887/1993.

Dawkins, R. *The Selfish Gene*. New York: Oxford University Press, 1976.

Dawkins, R. *The Blind Watchmaker*. New York: Norton, 1987.

Dawkins, R. *River Out of Eden*. New York: Basic Books, 1995.

Dennett, D. *Darwin's Dangerous Idea*. New York: Simon & Schuster, 1995.

De Waal, F. *Goodnatured*. Cambridge: Harvard University Press, 1996.

Depew, D., and Weber, B. *Darwinism Evolving*. Cambridge, MA: MIT Press, 1996.

Desmond, A., and Moore, J. *Darwin: The Life of a Tormented Evolutionist*. London: Penguin, 1991.

Dobzhansky, T. *Mankind Evolving: The Evolution of the Human Species*. New Haven: Yale University Press, 1987.

Eisler, R. *The Chalice and the Blade: Our History, Our Future*. San Francisco: Harper & Row, 1987.

Eisler, R. *Sacred Pleasure: Sex, Myth, and the Politics of the Body*. San Francisco: HarperSanFrancisco, 1995.

Eisler, R. "Action Research and Human Evolution: David Loye's Lifelong Exploration of Moral

Sensitivity." *World Futures: The Journal of General Evolution* (1997): 49, 1-2, 89-101.

Eisler, R., and Loye, D. *The Partnership Way*. Brandon, VT: Holistic Education Press, 1998.

Eisler, R *Tomorrow's Children: A Blueprint for Education in the 21st Century.* Boulder, CO: Westview Press, 2000.

Eisley, L. *Darwin's Century: Evolution and the Men Who Discovered It.* New York: Doubleday, 1958.

Eisley, L. *Darwin and the Mysterious Mr. X: New Light on the Evolutionists.* New York: Dutton, 1979.

Eldredge, N., and M. Gren. *Interaction: Biological Context of Scientific Systems.* New York: Columbia University Press, 1992.

Elgin, D. *Awakening Earth: Exploring the Evolution of Human Culture and Consciousness.* New York: Morrow, 1993.

Engels, F. *Dialectics of Nature.* New York: International, 1940.

Freeman, W.J. *Psychosurgery: Intelligence, Emotion and Social Behavior following Prefrontal Lobotomy for Mental Disorders.* Springfield, Ill: C.C. Thomas, 1942.

Freud, S. *Introductory Lectures on Psychoanalysis.* New York: Liveright, 1989.

Freud, S. *New Introductory Lectures on Psychoanalysis.* New York: Norton, 1990.

Fromm, E. *Man for Himself: An Inquiry into the Psychology of Ethics.* New York: Holt, Rinehart and Winston, 1947.

Fuster, J. *The Prefrontal Cortex: Anatomy, Physiology, and Neuropsychology of the Frontal Lobes.* Philadelphia: Lippincott-Raven, 1997.

Galtung, J., and Inayatullah, S., Eds. *Macrohistory and Macrohistorians.* Westport, CT: Praeger, 1998.

Gerbner, G., and N. Signorelli. *Violence and Terror in the Media: An Annotated Bibliography.* Westport, CT: Greenwood, 1988.

Gimbutas, M. *The Civilization of the Goddess.* San Francisco: Harper San Francisco, 1991.

Gleick, J. *Chaos: The Making of a New Science.* New York: Penguin, 1988.

Goerner, S. *After the Clockwork Universe.* Edinburgh: Floris Books, 1999.

Golding, W. *Lord of the Flies.* London: Faber, 1954.

Gorney, R., Loye, D., and Steele, G. "Impact on Adult Males of Dramatized Television Entertainment." *American Journal of Psychiatry* (1977): 134 (2), 170-174.

Gould, S.J. *Ever Since Darwin*. New York: Norton, 1980.

Gould, S.J. *Hen's Teeth and Horses' Toes*. New York: Norton, 1983.

Gould, S.J. *Bully for Brontosaurus*. New York: Norton, 1991.

Gould, S.J. *The Panda's Thumb*. New York: Norton, 1992.

Gould, S.J. "Curveball: A Review of 'The Bell Curve.'" *New Yorker* (1994): 70, 39, 139-50.

Gruber, H.E., and Barrett, P.H. *Darwin on Man: A Psychological Study of Scientific Creativity*, together with Darwin's Early and Unpublished Notebooks. New York: Dutton, 1974.

Hager, L.D. *Women in Evolution*. New York: Routledge, 1997.

Halstead, W.C. *Brains and Intelligence: A Quantitative Study of the Frontal Lobes*. Chicago: University of Chicago Press, 1949.

Hamilton, W.D. "The Evolution of Altruistic Behavior." *American Naturalist* (1963): 97:354-56.

Hartmann, T. *The Prophet's Way*. Northfield, VT: Mythical Books, 1997.

Hartmann, T. *The Last Hours of Ancient Sunlight: Waking up to Personal and Global Transformation*. New York: Harmony Books, 1999.

Ho, M.W. Organism and Psyche in a Participatory Universe. In Loye, D., Ed., *The Evolutionary Outrider: The Impact of the Human Agent on Evolution*. Twickenham, England: Adamantine; Westport, CT: Praeger, 1998.

Ho, M.W., and Saunders, P., Eds. *Beyond Neo-Darwinism: Introduction to the New Evolutionary Paradigm*. London: Academic Press, 1984.

Hofstader, R. *Social Darwinism in American Thought*. Boston: Beacon, 1955. Sims, M. *Darwin's Orchestra*. New York: Henry Holt, 1997.

Hosken, F. *The Hosken Report: Genital and Sexual Mutilation of Females*, 4th edition. Lexington, MA: Women's International Network News, 1994.

Hubbard, B.M. *Conscious Evolution*. Novato, CA: New World Library, 1998.

Hume, D. *An Enquiry Concerning the Principles of Morals.* La Salle, IL: Open Court, 1751/1966.

Huxley, T.H. *Evolution and Ethics.* Princeton: Princeton University Press, 1989.

Huxley, J. *Touchstone for Ethics 1893-1943.* New York: Harper, 1947.

Huxley, J. *Essays of a Humanist.* New York: Harper, 1964.

Huxley, J. *Charles Darwin and his World.* New York: Viking, 1965.

Irvine, W. *Apes, Angels, and Victorians: The Story of Darwin.* New York: McGraw-Hill, 1955.

Jantsch, E. *The Self-Organizing Universe.* New York: Pergamon Press, 1980.

Jastrow, R., and Kovey, K. *The Essential Darwin.* New York: Little Brown, 1984.

Jung, C. *Psychological Reflections: A New Anthology of His Writings, 1905-1961*, edited by Jolande Jacobi. Princeton: Princeton University Press, 1970.

Kant, I. *The Critique of Pure Reason.* New York: St. Martin's Press, 1969.

Kant, I. *The Critique of Judgement.* New York: Macmillan, 1970.

Kant, I. *The Critique of Practical Reason.* New York: Macmillan, 1993.

Kaplan, A., and Jennings, B. *Darwin, Marx, and Freud: Their Influence on Moral Theory.* New York: Plenum, 1984.

Kauffman, S.A. *At Home in the Universe.* New York: Oxford University Press, 1996.

Kent, E.W. *The Brains of Men and Machines.* New York: McGraw-Hill, 1981.

Kohler, W. *The Mentality of Apes.* New York: Norton, 1976.

Korten, D. *When Corporations Rule the World.* San Francisco: Berrett-Kohler, 1996.

Korzybski, A. *Science and Sanity.* Institute of General Semantics, 1995.

Kropotkin, P. *Mutual Aid: A Factor of Evolution.* Boston: Porter Sargent, 1950.

Kropotkin, P. *Ethics: Origins and Development.* New York: Dial Press, 1924.

Kung, H., and Kuschel, K.J., Eds. *A Global Ethic: The Declaration of the Parliament of the World's Religions.* London: SCM Press, 1993.

Kung, H., Ed. *Yes to a Global Ethic: Voices from Religion and Politics*. New York: Continuum, 1996.

Kung, H. *A Global Ethic for Global Politics and Economics*. London: SCM Press, 1997.

Laszlo, E., Ed. *The New Evolutionary Paradigm*. Philadelphia: Gordon and Breach, 1991.

Laszlo, E. *The Choice: Oblivion or Evolution*. Los Angeles: Tarcher, 1994.

Laszlo, E. *The Interconnected Universe*. London: World Scientific, 1995.

Laszlo, E. *Evolution: The General Theory*. Cresskill, N.J.: Hampton Press, 1996.

Laszlo, E. *The Whispering Pond*. London: Element Books, 1996.

Lerner, M. *The Politics of Meaning: Restoring Hope and Possibility in an Age of Cynicism*. Reading, MA: Perseus Books, 1997.

Lewin, K. *A Dynamic Theory of Personality*. New York: McGraw-Hill, 1935.

Lewin, K. *Field Theory in Social Science*. New York: Harper and Row, 1951.

Lewin, K. *Resolving Social Conflicts*. New York: Harper and Row, 1948.

Lewontin, R.C., S. Rose and L. Kamin. *Not in Our Genes*. New York: Pantheon, 1984.

Lorenz, E. "Irregularity: A Fundamental Property of the Atmosphere." In *Tellus* (1984): 36A, pp. 98-110.

Lovelock, J. *Gaia: A New Look at Life on Earth*. New York: Oxford University Press, 1987.

Loye, D. *The Healing of a Nation*. New York: Norton, 1971. [ToExcel, 1998, www.toexcel.com].

Loye, D., and Rokeach, M. Ideology, Belief Systems, Values, and Attitudes. In *International Encyclopedia of Neurology, Psychiatry, Psychoanalysis and Psychology*. New York: Van Nostrand, 1976.

Loye, D. *The Leadership Passion: A Psychology of Ideology*. San Francisco, CA.: Jossey-Bass, 1977. [ToExcel, 1999, www.toexcel.com].

Loye, D., Gorney, R., and Steele, G. "Effects of Television: An Experimental Field Study." *Journal of Communications* (1977): 27:3, 206-216.

Loye, D. May. "Television Effects: It's Not All Bad News." *Psychology Today* (1978a).

Loye, D. *The Knowable Future: A Psychology of Forecasting and Prophecy.* New York: Wiley-Interscience, 1978b. [ToExcel, 1999, www.toexcel.com].

Loye, D. *The Sphinx and the Rainbow: Brain, Mind, and Future Vision.* New York: Bantam, 1984. [ToExcel, 1999, www.toexcel.com].

Loye, D., and Eisler, R. "Chaos and Transformation: The Implications of Natural Scientific Nonequilibrium Theory for Social Science and Society." *Behavioral Science* (1987): 32, 1, pp. 53-65.

Loye, D. Chaos and Transformation: Implications of Non-Equilibrium Theory for Social Science and Society. In Laszlo, E., Ed., *The New Evolutionary Paradigm.* New York: Gordon and Breach, 1990.

Loye, D. Moral Sensitivity and the Evolution of Higher Mind. In Laszlo, E., Masuli, I., Artigiani, R., and Csanyi, V., Eds. *The Evolution of Cognitive Maps: New Paradigms for the Twenty-First Century.* Philadelphia: Gordon and Breach, 1993.

Loye, D. How Predictable is the Future: The Conflict Between Traditional Chaos Theory and the Psychology of Prediction, and the Challenge for Chaos Psychology. In Robertson, R., and Combs, A., Eds., *Chaos Theory in Psychology and the Life Sciences.* Mahwah, NJ: Erlebaum, 1995b.

Loye, D. "Scientific Foundations for a Global Ethic at a Time of Evolutionary Crisis." In Montuori, A., Ed., The Dialectic of Evolution: Essays in Honor of David Loye, *World Future: The Journal of General Evolution* (1997): 49, 1-2, pp. 3-17.

Loye, D., Ed. *The Evolutionary Outrider: The Impact of the Human Agent on Evolution.* Twickenham, England: Adamantine; Westport, CT: Praeger, 1998.

Loye, D. Evolutionary Action Theory: A Brief Outline. In Loye, D., Ed., *The Evolutionary Outrider: The Impact of the Human Agent on Evolution.* Twickenham, England: Adamantine; Westport, CT: Praeger, 1998.

Loye, D. A Brief History of the General Evolution Research Group. In Loye, D., Ed., *The Evolutionary Outrider: The Impact of the Human Agent on Evolution.* Twickenham, England: Adamantine; Westport, CT: Praeger, 1998.

Loye, D. The Concept of Evil. *The Encyclopedia of Violence, Peace, and Conflict.* San Diego: Academic Press, 1999.

Loye, D. "Can Science Help Construct a New Global Ethic? The Development and Implications of Moral Transformation Theory." *Zygon* (1999): 34, 3, 221-235.

Loye, D. "Darwin's Lost Theory: The New Grounding for a Scientific Revolution." Paper presented at the 43rd meeting of the International Society for the Systems Sciences, June 27-July 2, 1999, at Asilomar, Pacific Grove, California.

Loye, D. "Darwin's Lost Theory: A New Grounding for the Chaos Revolution." Paper presented at the ninth annual international conference of the Society for Chaos Theory in Psychology and the Life Sciences, July 23-26, 1999, University of California at Berkeley.

Loye, D. The Guidance System of Higher Mind: Implications for Science and Science Education. In Chaisson, E., and Kim, T.C., Eds. *The Thirteenth Labor: Improving Science Education*. Philadelphia: Gordon & Breach, 1999.

Loye, D. *An Arrow Through Chaos: How We See Into the Future*. Rochester, VT: Park Street Press, 2000.

Loye, D. *Making It in the Dream Factory: Creativity, Prediction, and Survival in Hollywood and the Global Marketplace*. Cresskill, NJ: Hampton Press, 2000.

Luria, A. *The Working Brain*. New York: Basic Books, 1973.

Mackintosh, J. *A Dissertation on the Progress of Ethical Philosophy*. Edinburgh: Adam and Charles Black, 1836.

MacLean, P. *The Triune Brain in Evolution: Role in Paleocerebral Functions*. New York: Plenum Press, 1990.

Mallory, J.P. *In Search of the Indo-Europeans: Language, Archaeology, and Myth*. London: Thames and Hudson, 1989.

Margulis, L. Early Life. In Thompson, W.I., Ed., *Gaia: A Way of Knowing*. New York: Lindisferne Press, 1987.

Margulis, L. *Symbiosis in Cell Evolution*. San Francisco: W.W. Freeman, 1993.

Margulis, L., and Sagan, D. *The Mystery Dance: On the Evolution of Human Sexuality*. New York: Summit Books, 1991.

Margulis, L., and Sagan, D. *Origins of Sex: Three Billion Years of Genetic Recombination*. New Haven: Yale University Press, 1986.

Marx, K. *Capital: A Critique of Political Economy*. New York: Penguin, 1992.

Marx, K. *Capital*. Chicago: Charles H. Kerr, 1906.

Maslow, A. *Toward a Psychology of Being*. Princeton, NJ: Van Nostrand, 1968.

Maslow, A. *The Farther Reaches of Human Nature*. New York: Viking, 1971.

Mason, J., and S. McCarthy. *When Elephants Weep: The Emotional Lives of Animals*. New York: Delacourte Press, 1995.

Maturana, H., and Varela, F. *The Tree of Knowledge*. Boston: Shambhala Publications, 1992.

Maturana, H., and Verden-Zoller, V. *The Origins of Humanness in the Biology of Love*. Durham, NC: Duke University Press, 1998.

Maxwell, E. "Self as Phoenix: A Comparison of Assagioli's and Dabrowski's Developmental Theories." *Advanced Development* (1992): Vol. 4, January, 31-48.

Mead, G.H. *George Herbert Mead on Social Psychology*. Edited by Anselm Strauss. Chicago: University of Chicago Press, 1956.

Miller, G.A., Gallanter, A., and Pribram, K.H. *Plans and the Structure of Behavior*. New York: Henry Holt, 1960.

Miller, J.G. *Living Systems*. New York: McGraw-Hill, 1978.

Min Jiayin, Ed. *The Chalice and the Blade in Chinese Culture: Gender Relations and Social Models*. Beijing: China Social Science Publishing House, 1995.

Monod, J. *Chance and Necessity*. New York: Vintage, 1971.

Montagu, A. *Darwin, Competition, and Cooperation*. New York: Henry Schuman, 1952.

Montagu, A. *The Direction of Human Development*. New York: Hawthorn, 1970.

Montagu, A. *The Nature of Human Aggression*. New York: Oxford University Press, 1976.

Montagu, A. *Man's Most Dangerous Myth: The Fallacy of Race*. Walnut Creek, CA: Altamira Press, 1997.

Montuori, A. *Evolutionary Competence: Creating the Future*. New York: John Benjamins, 1990.

Montuori, A. *From Power to Partnership*. San Francisco: HarperSanFrancisco, 1993.

Montuori, A., Ed. "The Dialectic of Evolution: Essays in Honor of David Loye." *World Futures: The Journal of General Evolution* (1997): 49, 1-2, 1-202.

Morbeck, M.E., Galloway, A., and Zihlman, A., Eds. *The Evolving Female: A Life History Perspective*. Princeton: Princeton University Press, 1996,1996.

Morris, D. *The Naked Ape*. New York: McGraw-Hill, 1967.

Nelson, K.C. "Dabrowski's Theory of Positive Disintegration." *Advanced Development* (1989): Vol. 1, January, 1-14.

Ornstein, R. *The Evolution of Consciousness*. Englewood Cliffs: Prentice Hall, 1991.

Perper, T. *Sex Signals: The Biology of Love*. Philadelphia: ISI Press, 1985.

Pope, S.J. *The Evolution of Altruism and the Ordering of Love*. Washington: Georgetown University Press, 1994.

Piaget, J. *The Moral Judgement of the Child*. New York: Free Press, 1965.

Pribram, K. *Brain and Perception*. Hillsdale, NJ: Lawrence Erlebaum Associates, 1991.

Pribram, K. On Brain, Conscious Experience, and Human Agency. In Loye, D., Ed., *The Evolutionary Outrider: The Impact of the Human Agent on Evolution*. Twickenham, England: Adamantine; Westport, CT: Preger, 1998.

Prigogine, I., and Stengers, I. *Order Out of Chaos*. New York: Bantam, 1984.

Prigogine, I., and Stengers, I. *The End of Certainty: Time, Chaos, and the New Laws of Nature*. New York: Free Press, 1997.

Rachels, J. *Created from Animals: The Moral Implications of Darwinism*. New York: Oxford University Press, 1998.

Raphael, D.D. *A Century of Darwin*. Cambridge: Harvard University Press, 1958.

Richards, R. *Darwin and the Emergence of Evolutionary Theories of Mind and Behavior*. Chicago: University of Chicago Press, 1987.

Robertson, R., and Combs, A., Eds. *Chaos Theory in Psychology and the Life Sciences*. Mahwah, NJ: Erlebaum, 1995.

Rokeach, M. *The Nature of Human Values*. New York: Free Press. 1973.

enjoy this book as it seems
helpful also, are you familiar
with The Teaching Company?
4151 Lafayett Center Dr. Suite 100
Chantilly, Virginia 20151·1232
·800·TEACH-12 (1·800·832·2412) I
ave mostly audio tapes from them
it some videos (which I try to look
t when I go someplace I have
ccess to a player) I recommended
them that you could do a course on
ltruism for their company when
ey did a general survey on what
ubjects people were intrested in. You
night want to contact them your-
lves. I have their excellent
ewish Intelectual History, which,
hope when I finally finish
iewing it (its on video) I plan
· donate to the Temple library -
Sometime we might arrange to
ook at it so you can see their
ormat - Best wishes,
naomi silverbee

Hi Sam, hi Pearl—
Thanks for your presentation
the other night. I haven't
finished reading this but I
feel its important for you to
have it— I have another copy
on order so will be able to
resume my read before long.
I'm doing research to develop
a class I will call the History of
Heresy which is, at the moment
all over the board trying to
create an overview of the "dark
side" of western among
civilization—
other things I'm
scattering
my life over still putting one
foot after the other. Hope you
are

Romanes, G. *Darwin and After Darwin*. Chicago: Open Court, 1987.

Russell, P. *The Global Brain Awakens: Our Next Evolutionary Step*. Global Brain, Inc., 1995.

Russell, R.J. *The Lemur's Legacy*. New York: Tarcher/Putnam, 1993.

Salthe, S. *Development and Evolution: Complexity and Change in Biology*. Cambridge, MA: MIT Press, 1996.

Saunders, P. "Evolution Theory as a Creation Myth." *World Futures: The Journal of General Evolution Theory* (1993): 38, 1-3, pp. 89-106.

Schlegel, S. *Wisdom from a Rain Forest*. Athens, GA: University of Georgia Press, 1998.

Sen, A. "More Than 100 Million Women are Missing." *The New York Review* (1990): December 20, pp. 61-66.

Shore, A.N. *Affect Regulation and the Origin of Self: The Neurobiology of Emotional Development*. Hillsdale, N.J.: Erlebaum, 1994.

Smith, A. *The Wealth of Nations*. Middlesex, England: Penguin Books, 1986.

Smith, A. *The Theory of Moral Sentiments*. Oxford: Clarendon Press, 1976.

Smith, J.M. *Theory of Evolution*. New York: Cambridge University Press, 1993.

Smuts, J.C. *Holism and Evolution*. Westport, CT: Greenwood, 1993.

Sober, E., and Wilson, D.S. *Unto Others: The Evolution and Psychology of Unselfish Behavior*. Cambridge, MA: Harvard University Press, 1998.

Sorokin, P. *Sociological Theories of Today*. New York: Harper & Row, 1966.

Soros, G. "The Capitalist Threat." *Atlantic Monthly*, 279, 2, July, 45-55, 1997.

Stent, G.S. *Morality as a Biological Phenomenon: The Presuppositions of Sociobiological Research*. Berkeley, CA: University of California Press, 1978.

Stern, D.N. *The Interpersonal World of the Infant: A View from Psychoanalysis and Developmental Psychology*. New York: Basic Books, 1985.

Stone, I. *The Origin*. New York: Doubleday, 1980.

Swimme, B., and Berry, T. *The Universe Story*. San Francisco: HarperSanFrancisco, 1992.

Tanner, N. *On Becoming Human.* New York: Cambridge University Press, 1981.

Trivers, R. *Social Evolution.* Menlo Park, CA.: Benjamin-Cummings, 1985.

Von Bertalanffy, L. *General System Theory.* New York: George Brazilier, 1976.

Wesson, R. *Beyond Natural Selection.* Cambridge, MA.: The MIT Press, 1991.

West, C. *Race Matters.* Boston: Beacon Press, 1992.

Wheeler, J.A. *At Home in the Universe.* New York: American Institute of Physics, 1996.

White, R.W., Ed. *The Study of Lives.* New York: Atherton, 1965.

White, M., and Gribben, J. *Darwin: A Life in Science.* New York: Dutton, 1996.

Wilson, D.S. and Sober, E. "Reintroducing Group Selection to the Human Behavioral Sciences," *Behavioral and Brain Sciences* (1994): 17, 585-608.

Wilson, E.O. *Sociobiology: The New Synthesis.* Cambridge: Harvard University Press, 1975.

Wilson, E.O. *Human Nature.* Cambridge, MA: Harvard University Press, 1978.

Wilson, E.O. *The Diversity of Life.* Cambridge, MA: Harvard University Press, 1992.

Wilson, J.Q. *The Moral Sense.* New York: Free Press, 1993.

Wright, R. *The Moral Animal.* New York: Random House, 1994.

Yoganada, P. *The Autobiography of a Yogi.* Encinitas, CA: Self-Realization Fellowship, 1997.

About the Author

While pursuing an active career as a scientist over a number of years, David Loye has written many books for a wide range of readers.

A psychologist and systems scientist by training, Dr.Loye is a former member of the Princeton psychology department and UCLA School of Medicine faculties. While at UCLA, he was a professor in the research series and the Director of Research for the Program on Psychosocial Adaptation and the Future of the Neuropsychiatric Institute. Out of increasing concern for the future of our species, he became a co-founder with evolution theorist Ervin Laszlo and other scientists of the multidisciplinary and multinational General Evolution Research Group, formed to help develop a more adequate, humanistic, and action-oriented evolution theory that could be useful in guiding our species through the difficulties it faces in the 21st century. As an offshoot of the same purpose originally, he was also a co-founder of the Society for Chaos Theory in Psychology and the Life Sciences.

Of his many books, *The Healing of a Nation* is a national award-winning book on the psychology, sociology, and history of race relations in America. In *The Leadership Passion* he pioneered in the development of a systems psychology of liberals and conservatives and the dynamics of politics. In *The Knowable Future* he moved on to explore the new field of futures studies and to begin the work of many years in the study of how we predict the future. *The Sphinx and the Rainbow* expanded this venture into brain research and his development of a holographic brain-mind theory for futures prediction. All of these books have been republished and are now again available through iUniverse.com, amazon.com, bn.com, and fatbrain.com.

With Riane Eisler, with whom he co-founded The Center for Partnership Studies, Loye co-authored *The Partnership Way*. He is the editor of *The Evolutionary Outrider*, a book of essays by Ervin Laszlo, Fritjof Capra,Hazel Henderson, Riane Eisler, Loye and others on the human impact on evolution. Currently, besides *Darwin's Lost Theory of Love*, three more new books of his are being published. *An Arrow Through Chaos* applies pioneering work by Loye to show we have a far greater capacity for both predicting and shaping the future than present chaos theory allows. *Making It in the Dream Factory* is a 20 year systems study and hard-hitting critique of the making, marketing, and impact of movies and television programs on the American and global mind. *The Parable of the Three Villages* is a commentary in story form on the major problems our species faces in the 21st century and how to overcome them.

In private life Loye is married to the wellknown cultural historian Riane Eisler, author of *The Chalice and the Blade, Tomorrow's Children*, and—also published by iUniverse—The *Gate*. They live in northern California.

Printed in the United States
913400003B